Sinfree Makoni

Linguistic Ideologies, Sociolinguistic Myths and Discourse Strategies in Africa

Selected papers
Volume 3
Including papers written in collaboration with
Ashraf Abdelhay, Arnetha F. Ball, Janina Brutt-Griffler,
Marika K. Criss, Busi Makoni, Ulrike Meinhof,
Alastair Pennycook, Aaron Rosenberg, Cristine Severo,
Geneva Smitherman and Arthur K. Spears

Edited by David Bade

www.integrationists.com
**International Association for the Integrational Study of
Language and Communication**

This collection ©2020 by Sinfree Makoni.
Acknowledgements:
An integrationist perspective on African philosophy, ©2017 by Sinfree Makoni and Cristine Severo. Originally published in *Critical Humanist Perspectives: The Integrational Turn in Philosophy of Language and Communication.* Taylor and Francis Inc., pp. 63-76.
Deconstructing the discourses about language in language planning in South Africa, ©1995 originally published in *South African Journal of African Languages,* 15:2, 84-88.
Some of the metaphors about language in language planning discourses in South Africa ©1995 originally published in *Per Linguam.* 11(1), 25–34
Colonial linguistics and the invention of language, ©2020 by Sinfree Makoni, Ashraf Abdelhay and Cristine Severo. Originally published in Ashraf Abdelhay, Sinfree B. Makoni and Cristine G. Severo (eds.), *Language Planning and Policy: Ideologies, Ethnicities, and Semiotic Spaces of Power.* Newcastle upon Tyne: Cambridge Scholars, p.211-228.
When God is a inguist: missionary orthographies as a site of social differentiation and the technology of ocation , ©2017 by Ashraf Abdelhay, Busi Makoni and Sinfree Makoni. Originally published in C. Weth & K. Juffermans (editors), *The Tyranny of Writing: Ideologies of the Written Word* (pp. 97–112). London: Bloomsbury Academic.
Toward Black Linguistics, ©2003 by Sinfree Makoni, Geneva Smitherman, Arnetha F. Ball, and Arthur K. Spears. Originally published in Sinfree Makoni, Geneva Smitherman, Arnetha F. Ball and Arthur K. Spears (eds.), *Black Linguistics: Language, Society, and Politics in Africa and the Americas.* (pp. 1-11). London; New York: Routledge.
Regional and international perspectives on language activism, ©2017 by Sinfree Makoni and Marika K. Criss. Originally published in *Multilingua* 36(5), pp.533–540.
An argument for ethno-language studies in Africa, ©2006 by Sinfree Makoni and Ulrike Meinhof. Originally published in Paul Tiyambe Zeleza (Ed.), *The Study of Africa: Volume 1: Disciplinary and Interdisciplinary Encounters* (pp. 117-135). Dakar: CODESRIA.
Conflicting reactions to chi'ixnakax utxiwa: A reflection on the practices and discourses of decolonization, ©2019 Sinfree Makoni. Originally published in *Language, Culture and Society* 13, pp.147-151.

International Association for the Integrational Study of Language and Communication

2015

David Bade, Rita Harris, Charlotte Conrad. *Roy Harris and Integrational Semiology 1956-2015: A bibliography.*

2020

Sinfree Makoni. *Language in Africa.* Selected papers vol. 1
Sinfree Makoni. *African Applied Linguistics.* Selected Papers, vol. 2
David Bade. *Efficiencies and Deficiencies: Essays on Cataloging and Communication in Libraries.*
David Bade. *Integrational Linguistics for Library & Information Science: Linguistics, Philosophy, Rhetoric and Technology*
Sinfree Makoni. *Linguistic Ideologies, Sociolinguistic Myths and Discourse Strategies in Africa.* Selected Papers, Vol. 3
Sinfree Makoni. *Languages and Language Planning in Zimbabwe.* Selected Papers, Vol. 4

In Preparation

Cristine Severo and Sinfree Makoni. *Language in Lusophonia: Perspectives from Bakhtin, Southern Theory and Integrational Linguistics.*
David Bade. *Epistemologies of Rape and Revelation.*
David Bade. *Making Mongolians: Linguistics, Historiography, Fiction*

The International Association for the Integrational Study of Language and Communication

The IAISLC was founded in 1998. It is managed by an international Executive Committee, whose members are:

Adrian Pablé (University of Hong Kong), Secretary
David Bade (University of Chicago, retired)
Charlotte Conrad (Dubai)
Stephen J. Cowley (University of Southern Denmark)
Daniel R. Davis (University of Michigan)
Dorthe Duncker (University of Copenhagen)
Jesper Hermann (University of Copenhagen)
Christopher Hutton (University of Hong Kong)
Peter Jones (Sheffield Hallam University)
Nigel Love (University of Cape Town)
Sinfree Makoni (Penn State University)
Rukmini Bhaya Nair (Indian Institute of Technology)
Jon Orman (Brighton)
Talbot J. Taylor (College of William & Mary)
Michael Toolan (University of Birmingham)

Anyone wishing to join the Association can do so by email apable@hku.hk or by sending their name and address to the Secretary:

Dr Adrian Pablé
School of English
Run Run Shaw Tower
Centennial Campus
The University of Hong Kong
Hong Kong S.A.R

In response to "New Englishes", ©1992. Originally published in *Per Linguam*, 8(1), 2-13.
On speaking multilanguages: Urban lingos and fluid multilingua francas, ©2010 by Sinfree Makoni, Busi Makoni and Alastair Pennycook. Originally published in Paul Cuvelier & Theodorus du Pleiss (Eds.), *Language Planning from Below* (pp. 147-165). Pretoria.
The use of heritage languages: An African perspective, ©2005 by Janina Brutt-Griffler and Sinfree Makoni. Originally published in *Modern Language Journal*, 89(4), pp. 610-612.
The discursive construction of the female body in family planning pamphlets, ©2011 by Sinfree Makoni and Busi Makoni. Originally published in Paul McPherron and Vaidehi Ramanathan (Eds.), *Language, Body, and Health* (pp. 193-220). De Gruyter Mouton.
The wordy worlds of popular music in Eastern and Southern Africa: possible implications for language-in-education policy, ©2010 by Sinfree Makoni, Busi Makoni and Aaron Rosenberg. Originally published: *Journal of Language, Identity & Education* 9(1), pp. 1-16.
Multilingual discourses on wheels and public English in Africa: A case for 'vague linguistique', ©2009 by Busi Makoni and Sinfree Makoni. Originally published in In J. Maybin & J. Swann (Eds), *The Routledge Companion to English Language Studies* (pp.258-270). Routledge.

In addition to thanking the co-authors of the papers collected in this and the preceding two volumes, the author and editor would like to offer our thanks to those who assisted us in obtaining library materials during this time of world wide troubles: Atoma Batoma, Esmeralda M. Kale, Shoshanah Seidman, Pat Williams and Sun Yingyuan.

Contents

Editor's Introduction..9
I. An integrationist perspective on African philosophy
(with Cristine Severo)..13
II. African oral tradition, parrhesia and integrationism
(with Cristine Severo)..35
III. Deconstructing the discourses about language in language
planning in South Africa..53
IV. Some of the metaphors about language in language
planning discourses in South Africa..67
V. Colonial linguistics and the invention of language
(with Cristine G. Severo and Ashraf Abdelhay)..................................83
VI. When God is a linguist: missionary orthographies as a site
of social differentiation and the technology of location
(with Ashraf Abdelhay and Busi Makoni)...109
VII. Toward Black Linguistics (with Geneva Smitherman, Arnetha F.
Ball, and Arthur K. Spears)..135
VIII. Regional and international perspectives on language
activism (with Marika K.Criss)...157
IX. An argument for ethno-language studies in Africa
(with Ulrike Meinhof)...163
X. Conflicting reactions to chi'ixnakax utxiwa: A reflection on
the practices and discourses of decolonization.................................193
XI. In response to "new Englishes"..201
XII. On speaking multilanguages: urban lingos and fluid multi-
lingua francas (with Busi Makoni and Alastair Pennycook)............221
XIII. The use of heritage languages: an African perspective
(with Janina Brutt-Griffler)...255
XIV. The discursive construction of the female body in family
planning pamphlets (with Busi Makoni)..263
XV. The wordy worlds of popular music in eastern and
southern Africa: possible implications for language-in-
education policy (with Busi Makoni and Aaron Rosenberg)............297
XVI. Multilingual discourses on wheels and public English in
Africa: a case for 'vague linguistique' (with Busi Makoni)..............327

On the importance of paying attention,
or,
How experience combats ideology, myth and the historical weight of the beliefs and presuppositions of scientists

a short introduction
by the Editor

According to recent opinion "all basic scientific training emphasises the need to change your mind based on new findings. This is what separates us from zealots."[1] Unfortunately, as Max Planck famously noted, the progress of science through time is more directly related to the death of famous scientists than to the weight of evidence or the force of argument. There has been a great deal of commentary responding to "Planck's Principle" leading one commentator to remark "Knowledge accumulation — the process by which new research builds upon prior research — is central to scientific progress, but the way this process works is not well understood."[2] Perhaps this process "is not well understood" for the simple reason that, as popular science writer Brian Resnick noted, "Science may be a noble discipline based

---

[1] Adrian Barnett, quoted by Dalmeet Singh Chawla in "Science really does advance one funeral at a time, study suggests" published in *Chemistry World* (a publication of the Royal Society of Chemistry), 12 September 2019. https://www.chemistryworld.com/news/science-really-does-advance-one-funeral-at-a-time-study-suggests/3010961.article

[2] Jay Fitzgerald, "Does science advance one funeral at a time?", *NBER Digest* (Cambridge: National Bureau of Economic Research, March 2016, pp.3-4)

on cold logic and rational observation; but humans are animals fueled by emotion and bias."[3]

Indeed, once we admit that humans are "fueled by emotion and bias", any belief that science is simply logic and observation must be set aside as an obstacle to any scientific progress. And this, we should understand, is not reactionary 'anti-science' but a necessary conclusion drawn from paying attention to the most obvious facts about human beings and the life of science as a social project. That some phenomena attract a scientist's attention, that some question presents itself to her, that a particular problem is identified and its solution sought—none of these matters are products of 'cold logic and rational observation'. In their paper "Multilingual discourses on wheels and public English in Africa" Sinfree and Busi remind us of Fasold's observation that 'for every research report that indicates that mother tongue education is effective there is another one that indicates that it is not'.[4] To suppose that science is simply method is to misunderstand science from beginning to end, for it always begins somewhere, and usually with an end already in mind.

Decolonial theory is founded upon the recognition that the colonial system oriented, and to that extent determined, the science that it produced and supported. To examine colonial ideology and the myths upon which it was (is) founded is the primary and necessary task for any science that would not reproduce those ideologies and myths. That task is fraught with difficulties as it requires putting into question precisely that science which our civilization regards as the sole path to knowledge. The science we have inherited, the science we are taught from the time we enter school, the only language of science that we know and have at our disposal, is the science and the language

---

[3] Brian Resnick, "Study: Elite scientists can hold back science" *Vox*, 15 December 2015 https://www.vox.com/science-and-health/2015/12/15/10219330/elite-scientists-hold-back-progress

[4] Quoted from Fasold, R. (1984) *The Sociolinguistics of Society*, Oxford: Basil Blackwell Ltd., p.312.

that underwrote colonialism. It is that science which began with the assertion that "the end of knowledge is power" (Hobbes) and ended up believing "the end of power is knowledge", i.e. technoscience as described by Hottois[5]: whatever enables us to dominate and control the world in which we wish to act, that is knowledge. Anything else is simply not knowledge.

The papers collected in this volume have a triple focus: linguistic ideologies, the social-linguistic myths upon which they are based, and real-world social-linguistic practices, attention to which reveals the misfit between myth, ideology and reality. And as Sinfree argues, even those whose intentions are specifically to overturn colonial ideologies are often reinforcing and solidifying those linguistic myths upon which colonial ideologies were/are based. It is not just reactionary colonialist ideologues who maintain colonial structures and their underlying myths, but often also anti-colonial activists.

To stake out his position, sometimes seemingly on the wrong side of the issue for mother tongue advocates, language rights activists, and bilingual education promoters, Sinfree has recourse to nothing other than the linguistic situation we find all around us. What is the language being created in abundance on the streets, on Facebook, in vocal music and other arts, public signs and in any situation where the overriding concern is to communicate and to be understood? In paying attention to the language he finds all around him, Sinfree brings *everyone* into the debates about our and their language. The vibrant, changing, unfixed and creative linguistic world in which we live must not be denied in favour of a textbook presentation of a theoretical fiction, a linguistic ideology, a socio-linguistic myth.

Twelve of the sixteen papers that follow were written in collaboration with one or more coauthors. This volume is

---

[5] Gilbert Hottois, *Généalogies philosophique, politique et imaginaire de la technoscience,* Paris: Vrin, 2014. The phrase "the end of power is knowledge" is my own and not taken from Hottois, though he may well have written that somewhere.

therefore a tribute not only to Sinfree's explorations but to all those who have ventured with Sinfree into the real world of men and women making language together, in Africa, to meet their needs, as best they can, in a world that cannot remain the same and should not be held hostage by theory, ideology or myth. By simply paying attention, science can indeed progress without having to bury someone.

Instead of an obituary, this volume is a celebration of decolonizing linguistics, of Sinfree and his partners in ... crime? However you judge it, here is a flagrant assault on that science which proceeds from the belief that "the end of knowledge is power" as well as from that which believes that "the end of power is knowledge".

David Bade
Rachel's Farm
21 July 2020

I

An integrationist perspective on African philosophy
(with Cristine G. Severo)

Introduction
There is a substantial body of research into integrationism in Western contexts, taking into account the impact of several issues such as writing, history, semiotics and economics. Even though integrationism has developed considerably and made substantial contributions to language scholarship, most of the research has largely been situated in Western contexts. From an African perspective, it can unfortunately be construed as Eurocentric. In this chapter, we contribute to a development of the concept of 'integration' in non-Western contexts by analyzing *Ubuntu* (Tschaeege 2013), African secular humanism, from an integrationist perspective. We carry out the analysis by focusing on the following important dimensions of *Ubuntu*, African humanism: independence and interdependence, individual, person and human rights.

Writing, transition, world and humanism
Historically, the term *Ubuntu* has its origins in the Niger/Congo family language group. Through a process of morphological and phonological reduction, the term was subsequently framed as *Ubuntu*. According to Gade (2013) the term *Ubuntu* was first

cited in European writing on Africa in 1850; however, it had been used in speech in African communities before 1850. Gade (2013) explores a historical development of written discourses of *Ubuntu*. Writing as a semiotic modality narrowed, stabilised and created an illusion of stability of the meanings of *Ubuntu* in writing. The semiotic modality of writing reinforced by Structuralism created *Ubuntu* as an object abstracted from its speakers and hearers.

Ubuntu can be found in Zunda varieties of Nguni languages, Zulu, Xhosa, Ndebele spoken largely in southern Africa and in the Tekela varieties, Sotho-Tswana. Linguistically, *Ubu* is an abstract prefix that means 'possessing the qualities of being human'. *Ntu* is a root which means a person. *Ubuntu,* in both Nguni varieties Zunda and Tekela, means *umuntu nga-muntu ngabantu* and *mutho ke mutho Ka batho babag*, meaning 'I am what I am because of who we all are'. *Ubuntu*, as a form of secular humanism, is also found in other parts of Southern Africa in Zimbabwe, notably among the Shona in Zimbabwe. The equivalent of *Ubuntu* in Shona is *hunhu*. *Hunhu* is also interpreted as good manners. *Hunhu* and *Ubuntu,* although closely related, are different because *hunhu* refers to manners, but the primary meaning of *Ubuntu* is being human. The notion of what it means to be human varies between different languages and communities and sociopolitical contexts.

The term *Ubuntu* was popularised in southern Africa in the 1980s and 1990s, a period related to the transition from white rule in southern Africa in Zimbabwe. The term was used by the African nationalist Stanlake Samukange and subsequently by Desmond Tutu (a former Anglican Arch Bishop of Cape Town), who defined it (*Ubuntu*) as 'amnesty and love', a view reinforced by Tutu's involvement in the Truth and Reconciliation Commission (TRC), which was held in South Africa after the end of apartheid. It also appears in the Epilogue of the South African Constitution (Act 200 of 1993) as the following:

'There is a need for understanding but not vengeance, reparations but not retaliation, *Ubuntu* but not victimization'.

While it is feasible to establish the meaning of *Ubuntu* from a Structuralist perspective, it is difficult to do so in integrational linguistics because many factors have to be taken into account in the analysis, which include but are not restricted to type of genre, narrative contexts, agency, feelings of responsibility, misunderstanding, conflict and individual social trajectory. It is necessary to include a speaker's individual trajectory because no two or more people experience language in an identical way (Pablé & Hutton 2015: 41), and consequently, individuals may have different understandings of *Ubuntu* and by extension humanism. Another important feature relevant to an analysis of *Ubuntu* (African secular humanism) are laypeople's experiences of language. Using laypeoples' experiences of language as an analytical category legitimates ordinary people's expertise therefore challenging professional linguists' sole authority over language. The notion that the language expertise of lay-people is as important as that of professional linguists is liberating in African humanism, particularly in societies that are highly stratified along class, race, caste and so on. A justification of ordinary people's expertise is well articulated by Orman and Pablé when they write: 'There are no impenetrable semiological truths hidden from lay thinking which the academic linguist can somehow bring to the fore' (2015: 5).

Language typologies

The use of lay people's experiences as an important site of analysis complicates because of the different names and meanings speakers of African languages assign to their speech practices. While linguists may use names such as Shona, Ndebele or Xhosa, laypeople may define what they speak as 'human language', and conversely, speakers whose languages differ from their own are categorised as not speaking a human language. They may refer to what other people speak pejoratively as chirping of birds, for example, typically South Africans refer to people who speak a language different from their own as *ikwerekwere* ('they do not speak a human language; they sound like birds'). The critical issue is that the sociolinguistic world of some indigenous communities revolves around African indigenous peoples. From their perspective, they are the center of their universe. Thus, questioning the linguistic use of Western categories such as minority languages, when applied to African sociolinguistics, is relevant because one cannot be on a periphery of a world in which they are at the center of their universe. Such an aspect has an impact on African humanism. Humanism is therefore a social and contextualised process.

Ubuntu, pan-Africanism and naming of languages

Some scholars regard *Ubuntu* as a pan-African concept with variants found in different languages and regions across Africa. The concept *Ubuntu* is found in other African languages and is not restricted to southern Africa. The term is *umundu* in Kikuyu, *umuntu* in Kimeru, *bumuntu* in KiSukuma and KiHaya both spoken in Tanzania and Kenya, *vumuntu* in ShiTsonga and ShiTswa of Mozambique. In Mozambique, linguistic variations of *Ubuntu* are *muthu* in Chubo, *bvantu* in Ndau and *mundhu* in XiSena. In Angola, similar terms include *munu* and *giuntu* in Kikongo and *omanu* in Umbundu, and in Congo, the equivalent of *Ubuntu* is *muntu* in Tshiluba. GiKwese is used in the Congo and Angola. The last examples show that the concept of *Ubuntu* is not restricted to South Africa and Zimbabwe but is also found in ex-Portuguese countries. Whether the list of morphological variants of *Ubuntu* cited by Kamwangamalu (1999) and Chaua (2014) correspond with that of *Ubuntu* in southern Africa remains an open question because *Ubuntu* has a number of closely related but distinct meanings, so it is not clear which meaning Kamwangamalu and Chaua had in mind. When trying to establish ways in which humanism is expressed in different languages, it is important to bear in mind that in some cases, the same language has many names, which complicates the issue because at times, it is not clear whether the comparison that is being made about *Ubuntu* is from the same language with different names. For example, the following are the names for Anni, a language used in Togo, and Benin in west Africa: *Basila, Bassilia, Basela* and *Ounji~Ounji Winji-Wingi.*

The idea of 'one language, one name, one expression' of *Ubuntu* reflects a monolingual approach, a situation that is radically different in multilingual contexts when a language may have many different names and many different languages may have the same name.

From an integrationist approach in colonial and post-colonial Africa, lay naming is important because the lay naming is therefore a challenge to colonial naming. Colonial naming of languages in Africa, particularly in the colonial era, tended to be pejorative. When names are assigned to language, the assumption is that there is an object called *language*. In integrationism, names in Africa are not only second-order macrosocial abstractions or metalinguistic categories but political creations as well, and in integrationism second-order concepts are mostly considered from a philosophical perspective.

Ubuntu, law and jurisprudence

The South African Interim Constitution of 1993 set the tone and atmosphere for South African sociopolitical transformation in post-apartheid South Africa. The constitution aimed to create a historic bridge between the past of a deeply divided society characterised by strife, conflict and untold suffering and injustice, seeking to promote a peaceful coexistence, a need for reparation and not retaliation. In addition, the constitution recognised the need for *Ubuntu*, although attaching great importance to *Ubuntu*, in the Interim Constitution, the term is not explicitly defined, opening the constitution to a critique that *Ubuntu* in jurisprudence is not helpful because the term is vague. Despite the vagueness of the term, the court used *Ubuntu* as a background to a critique of the loss of respect of human life and inherent dignity as apparent in *Ubuntu* (*S v Makwanyane and Another*, 1995: 227). The Constitutional Court in South Africa adopted the approach that the range of constitutional values contained in the Constitution does not constitute a *numerus clausus* and that other values such as *Ubuntu* can be elevated to that status (Tshoose 2009).

The underpinning juridical principle of *Ubuntu* is that life should be taken from a communal perspective in which justice is ensured by supernatural forces. In this sense, justice is seen as "the restoration of equilibrium [...] as a continually lived experience" (Ramose 2001: 4). Laws are committed to the concrete and immediate life of people. It is not about abstract values (as in the Western model) but embodied values in a contextualised and dynamic life. Because of such dynamism, the concept of law does not exist *a priori* in an abstract way but is shaped according to local and negotiated needs of equilibrium. Such a perspective destabilises the Western concept of language rights because rights are not abstract and universal categories but should be considered in relation to a communitarian and shared everyday life.

Ubuntu, the individual and personhood

Ubuntu is a philosophical view, a form of African humanism, a world perspective and ideology that captures kindness and virtue in an individual and the moral and ethical obligation an individual has towards other individuals. *Ubuntu* and moral commitment is 'not an innate instinct but a learnt tradition ... morals do not always operate as explicit rules, but may manifest themselves, as do true instincts, as vague distillations to, or distate for, certain kinds of action. Often they tell us how to choose among, or to avoid, inborn instinctual drives' (Hayek 1988: 13) In *Ubuntu,* assistance to other people is regarded as a reflection of a moral commitment, a type of social behavior. Social behavior acceptable to *Ubuntu,* like other behaviors, can be construed as a type of activity, which can be defined thus:

Crucially, human behavior cannot (or should not) be understood as a product made of joint contributions from independently and analyzable kinds of activity ('linguistic', 'cognitive', and 'practical' ones): rather human activity has a different character, with words, actions and thoughts being all mixed up together in some way, precisely as an 'integrated continuum'. (Pablé & Hutton 2015: 116)

The following are the *Pro tanto* moral principles that are unacceptable by and large to African humanism:

1 To kill innocent people for money
2 To deceive people at least when not done in self defense
3 To steal or take from rightful owner
4 To violate trust or to discriminate on the basis of race when distributing and allocating opportunities to individuals
5 The moral judgement regards it as immoral to make decisions that accentuate divisions instead of seeking consensus.
6 To make retribution a foundational and central aim of criminal justice as opposed to reconciliation; to create wealth on competitive basis as opposed to a cooperative one

The notion of an individual, however, in *Ubuntu* is different from that in Western philosophy. Western philosophy tends to construe an individual in an *atomistic* manner. In African philosophy and humanism, individuals are influenced by powerful central normative principles, and an individual is composed of two aspects – one is visible and the other invisible. The duality is apparent in how an individual is framed. Second, an individual is both a medium and center of his or her own universe. In *Ubuntu* in some African contexts, individuals defined by communities they belong to and the communities that shape them. In

Ubuntu, both the individual and community rights have to be upheld in order to realise issues about 'social justice' (Piller 2016) or more specifically in sociolinguistics, human rights.

Ubuntu, language and morality: 'the story of the fat man'

Ubuntu has been linked to discussions about morality, but there is no connection that has been proposed between language and morality over and above either the meanings and translations of *Ubuntu* or the implications of integrationism on *Ubuntu*. There is a relatively large number of Africans who are bilingual and a sizeable literature on Ubuntu. However, there is very little research that has explored whether Africans will make different moral judgments when a sensitive question is posed in a first as opposed to a second language. The 'story of the fat man' is used in a famous experiment to investigate the type of judgements that people make and whether there is any variation in the judgments when the question is posed in a first or a second language (Edmonds 2013). The results seem to suggest that people make different judgments depending on whether the issue is presented in a first as opposed to a second language. When the dilemma is presented in a first language, the subjects make judgments that take into account moral issues, but when presented in a second language or any other language that is not the mother tongue, they make utilitarian judgements. Extrapolating from the results of the 'story of the fat man', it appears Africans are likely to make decisions and judgments that are morally sensitive aligned to *Ubuntu* when using a first language as opposed to a second language. *Ubuntu* is therefore likely to occur when speaking in a first language as opposed to a second language.

Ubuntu and intersubjectivity and interdependence

Ubuntu is a relational philosophy. In *Ubuntu*, when drawing upon relational philosophy, an individual cannot be separated from the context she is situated in. *Ubuntu* from a relational perspective highlights the importance of a subjective and healthy emotional experience that avoids Cartesian dual distinctions between mind and the body. *Ubuntu* reinforces appropriate social relationships, in which communication is an integral part of social relationships. The use of what may be deemed as inappropriate communication may have an adverse effect on social harmony. In some cases, designs to retain social harmony are apparent in the enforcement of regimented social language. An excellent example is the use of *hlonipha*. *Hlonipha* is a language variety and genre that ideally is used as a marker of respect when women are interacting with either their fathers-in-law or mothers-in-law. An individual who does not use appropriate *hlonipha* when interacting with her in-laws is defined as lacking *Ubuntu*. In such cases, *Ubuntu* has a linguistic dimension. In integrationism, the use or lack thereof using *hlonipha* is an activity, a type of discourse. *Hlonipha*, like other forms of communication, when viewed from an integrationist perspective demands continuous creative monitoring, even the most trivial act requires monitoring. In such contexts, as Rossi-Landi argues, drawing attention to language and *hlonipha* is best treated as a form and type of work.

> I purposely speak of work rather than activity because words and messages, which are products, constitute the concrete social reality from which we must begin. (Rossi-Landi 1983: 36).

Ubuntu and personhood

Communities are based upon communication; personhood is only feasible via communication. There is no human society or community in which there is no communication. In African humanism, communication is therefore a precondition for being human. The issue in African humanism is not whether communication is necessary for personhood to take place but the nature of the communication. Because of the dynamic nature of African communication, a conduit metaphor in which language is encoded on one end and decoded at another will be inadequate because communication in African contexts is energetic, flowery, replete with aphorisms and morals about humanism. In such contexts, the communication has to be constructed as open-ended and the form it will take unpredictable in advance. African humanism is therefore articulated in creative ways. Even though common themes run though African humanism, each communicative humanistic event is unique and in a manner consistent with integrationism.

Communication understood from an integrationist perspective considers that "language is not an autonomous mode of communication and languages are not autonomous systems of signs" (Harris 1987: 136). Along with this perspective, in *Ubuntu*, we must take into account not only the local dynamics of meaning construction and negotiation but also what or who is there to be communicated with and the message to be communicated. Communicating is not about a system of signs that can be mechanically or pragmatically decoded and categorised; rather, it is about being human as a necessary response to the other, in which subjects are in front of the other, facing the other. The political implication of such a perspective is that politics and ethics are closely tied. Thus, language—along with other semiotic elements—is in the service of creating a communitarian way of being in the world. In this sense, *Ubuntu* is in line with Arendt's (1958: 4) concept of politics: 'Men in the plural, that is, men in so far as they live and move and act in this world, can experience meaningfulness only because they can talk with and make sense to each other and to themselves'. Talking does not mean a process of encoding and decoding verbal messages through separable episodes of speech acts but covers a broader and more complex meaning-making process.

Although *Ubuntu* can be labelled as philosophy, it is not about a metaphysical and abstract set of principles and ideas constructed by reasoning and expressed through written form. *Ubuntu* exists in relation to principles constructed and shared in ordinary and daily life. Human experience that underlines African humanism is built of several local practices, which include different ways of constructing relationships through language and communication. Examples are the use of proverbs, songs, narratives, tales, myth, poetry, aphorisms and several other oral discursive practices. Therefore, *Ubuntism* as African philosophy has its roots inscribed in popular and oral practices (Castiano 2010). One of the strongest contributions of such flexible roots of *Ubuntu* is that it remains as a relative open philosophical space that allows critical thinking in relation to contextualised and communitarian human condition (Tschaeege 2013).

The communication model that forms the basis of interdependence in *Ubuntu* is different from a telementation perspective that is implied when labels of *Ubuntu* are identified as discrete. The idea of *Ubuntu* categories is a reflection of segregationalism in which language is separated from its users and speakers, which undercuts humanism. A telementation model cannot be reconciled with a communication relevant to *Ubuntu*. The communication model (Pablé & Hutton 2015: 115–116) pertinent to *Ubuntu* from an integrationist perspective is based on at least five types of integration:

1 Interpersonal integration
2 Environmental integration
3 Transmodal integration
4 Temporal integration
5 Conjunctive integration

Two types of people may be defined as possessing *Ubuntu*. Whereas the weak version regards anyone who is part of the *Homo sapiens* as persons, the stronger one restricts personhood to Blacks who meet the moral, social and ethical obligations necessary in *Ubuntu*.

Ubuntu, language rights and integrationism

Ubuntu involves the co-occurrence among the following elements in Zulu (Venter 2004): *unzimba* (body), *umoya* (breath), *umphefumela* (spirit), *amandla* (energy), *inhliziyo* (heart), *umqond* (head), *ulwimi* (language) and *Ubuntu* (humanness). From this perspective, personhood, language and being human are strongly connected. This means languages cannot be taken as individual and autonomous unities that can be counted and named but as embodied realities whose meanings exist only in relation to being human. *Ubuntu* and integrationism can be approximated in relation to the way languages are understood from a broader and complex perspective because for integrationism, 'Language as social interaction involves not just vocal behavior but many kinds of behavior' (Harris 1987: 141). This means that languages must be understood in relation to discursive and semiotic practices that bring together body, soul, reason, emotion and morality. *Ubuntu* and integrationism when applied in colonial and postcolonial Africa share a communitarian and thus politicised concept of language built on the idea that language practices only make sense when radically contextualised into specific modes of being in the world. Language policy studies may benefit from *Ubuntu* and integrationism towards a broader concept of public sphere in which action and discourse only make sense from the perspective of plurality and coexistence (Arendt 1958).

Discourses on language rights are part of human rights ideology of universalism. In this perspective, a common concept of human being crosses different times and spaces. Such abstraction is typical of Eurocentric thinking that was 'imposed as globally hegemonic in the same course as the expansion of European colonial dominance over the world' (Quijano 2000: 542). The language rights framework inherits such universal tendencies of human rights discourses to define and classify different experiences from a common view. For language rights discourses, languages are taken from segregationalism (Harris

1987) that considers languages as countable and nameable units. Such a perspective cannot apprehend the linguistic complexities of plurilingual societies where linguistic boundaries are fuzzy, language identity is dynamic and moving, communicative practices extrapolate the idea of language as unit, and language is sensitive to intra- and intergroup power relations (Makoni 2011).

The roots of human and language rights discourses are attached to the early modern European culture and politics. Enlightenment and liberalism contributed to the emergence of human rights as a universal category. The world wars in the twentieth century reflected the formal creation of the Universal Declaration of Human Rights in 1948. The Universal Declaration of Linguistic Rights dates to 1996, used particularly when referring to the trope of 'endangered languages'. The trope of 'language endangerment' is politically tricky because it reinforces a biological concept of language based on the ideas of language development, evolution, language competition, language loss and language extinction. From the point of view of integrationism, languages are not natural species but cultural and contextualised practices (Makoni 2011). Even though language rights were officially recognised only in the 1990s, the roots of such discourses can be traced back to the emergence of both modernity and capitalism, which were only possible because of colonization. Thus, by contextualizing human language rights, it is possible to identity a complex set of power relations that involved the ideas of race, racism and exploitation that deeply affected Africa, America and Asia for more than four centuries. This way, we argue that the language rights discourse must go through deep epistemological and political revisions; otherwise, it runs the risk of reproducing colonial ideologies that deprive Africans of their human condition: 'Colonization was predicated on the idea that the African was not a full and complete human being' (Ramose 2001).

Ubuntu, capitalism and resistance

Although *Ubuntu* is a powerful framework to criticise capitalism and individualism, it has also been used for utilitarian purposes 'in service of ideologies, such as corporate South African capitalism' (Venter 2004: 150). The same occurs with other philosophies, such as the indigenous Latin American ones that have been appropriated to justify a commodified vision about environment, life and tourism. Such appropriation of discourses of diversity and resistance by capitalism was classified as functional interculturality (Walsh 2009), and focused on liberal politics of inclusion and tolerance supported by global capitalism, without problematizing the deep roots of power relations that helped to frame modern institutions and knowledge. Examples are the discourses of UNESCO, the United Nations, human rights, language rights and cultural heritage, among many others. A critical perspective requires a deep revision of colonial structural power relations that include the ideas of race and racism. Critical thinking problematises capitalism and its capacity to transform everything into something capable of being consumed, including culture, people, beliefs and languages. Even though capitalism may be seen as 'indestructible' (Žižek 2007), several 'politics of resistance' reveal possibilities for local resistance. A perspective that recognises the fatal victory of capitalism would include as possible forms of resistance the bombardment of 'those in power with strategically well-selected, precise, finite demands' (Žižek 2007: para. 17).

More radical politics of resistance against capitalism would be in line with the politics of decolonization, which include a critical and historical attitude towards capitalism. It is about deconstructing colonial power relations on several levels: economic, political, cultural, epistemic and subjective (Quijano 2000; Walsh 2009). One example of decolonization in Latin America is the official recognition by the Constitution of Ecuador of *sumak kawsay* (*bem viver*, "good living"), a principle of strong coexistence between human beings and nature in line with Andean and Indigenous worldviews. In an African context, *Ubuntu* can also be considered an example of a 'politics of resistance' in relation to several aspects: (1) economic, by proposing communitarian values that problematise the commodification of people and culture; such a perspective prioritises the group survival to the detriment of the individual necessity; (2) political, by recognizing the evolving nature of power relations in search of the restoration of equilibrium; (3) cultural, by recognizing the importance of local and ordinary practices and knowledge; (4) epistemic, by proposing critical thinking about human beings, ethics and morality; and (5) subjective, by recognizing otherness as central to self-constitution. Although the aim of this chapter is not to itemise the several ways *Ubuntu* may work as a critique of capitalism, it is relevant to consider such a political dimension.

Ubuntu in Africa and diaspora

Considering that Africa is not a preexisting and homogeneous reality but an invention, we may consider that *Ubuntu* plays a central role in defining Africa as an idea (Mbembe 2015). Several meanings and histories helped to construct different narratives about Africa from different perspectives. Colonial narratives have been powerful in the construction of negative stereotypes that steal Africans' humanity, as the ideas of racism and the practice of slavery. In the colonial era, race was used as a category that created hierarchies and legitimated power relations and exploitation by the use of violence: 'Domination is the requisite for exploitation, and race is the most effective instrument for domination that, associated with exploitation, serves as the universal classifier in the current global model of power' (Quijano 2000: 572). The colonial history of Africa implies the recognition of strong and intense processes of forced diaspora through the slavery system. This means that for four centuries, Africans from different parts of Africa were sent to several places, mainly America. Colonialism seeks to deprive the colonised of their *Ubuntu* and paradoxically has the likelihood of depriving the colonisers of chances of either retaining or securing their humanity.

In the context of the colonial diaspora, Brazil was the destiny of most Africans between the sixteenth and nineteenth centuries, representing nearly 4 million people against 0.4 million taken to the United States. The origin of Africans is varied, although a large proportion were taken from current regions of Angola and Côte d'Ivoire. Angola became the central target in the trade of slaves when, between 1701 and 1810, 1.285.900 Africans were brought to Brazil (Brazilian Institute of Geography and Statistics[1]). African people taken to Brazil were grouped into two major ethnicities: Sudanese, coming from West Africa, and the Bantus, coming from equatorial and tropical Africa. Among these groups, the Bantu presence was significant in the linguistic and discursive formation of Brazil, with strong influence of Kikongo, Kimbundu and Umbundu in Brazilian Portuguese (Castro 2001; Mendonça 2012 [1935]). We understand, however, that such ethnic classifications can be complicated because they do not represent the complexity of the local situation.

Currently, more than half of the Brazilian population is made up of Afro-Brazilians, according to the category of 'self-identification'. Brazil has inherited several African practices, languages, cultures, customs and variations of *Ubuntu*; African communication styles; and the African languages, which reflect the Africanity of Brazilian social practices, even in the spoken Portuguese of Brazil. Our focus, however, is to identify the *Ubuntu*'s footprints in the Afro-Brazilian worldview. We believe one powerful connection between the African diaspora in Brazil and *Ubuntu* is the idea of *Quilombo*. The concept of Quilombo has historically evolved since power relations pro-

---

[1] Brazilian Institute of Geography and Statistics. Available at http://brasil500anos.ibge.gov.br/territorio-brasileiro-e-povoamento/negros Other statistical information can be found at www.slavevoyages.org.

duce new political configurations: 'the various meanings of quilombo, including its appearance in Angola during Portuguese colonization, reinforce the organizational sense and struggle for autonomy that are reconfirmed and highlighted in current struggles for territory' (Leite 2015: 1226).

We argue that this kind of organizational sense has philosophical connections with *Ubuntu*. To better justify such an argument, we present Abdias do Nascimento's Manifesto in defense of Afro-Brazilian memory. Nascimento (1914–2011) was an Afro-Brazilian scholar, artist and activist who strongly defended Afro-Brazilian civil rights. His Manifesto, called *QUILOMBISMO: An Afro-Brazilian Political Alternative* (1980), was an effort to include Afro-Brazilians into a larger project of reconstructing Africans' memories in diaspora. Quilombism was initially related to a communitarian form of resistance against slavery in Brazil. Later on, several other meanings were attributed to *Quilombism*, turning it into a robust project of shared existence, as pointed out by Nascimento (1980: 160):

> Black people have a collective project: the erection of a society founded on justice, equality and respect for all human beings [. . .] We have no interest in proposing an adaptation or reformation of the models of capitalist class society [. . .] An operative conceptual tool must be developed, then, within the guidelines of the immediate needs of the Black Brazilian people.

Quilombos were designed as specific modes of experience, in which the main principles of *Ubuntu* would be presented: a radical communitarian perspective together with values that reinforced collective experiences rather than individual ones. This idea of living together was strongly reinforced by the Manifesto, aiming at an economic egalitarianism. The philosophical nature of Quilombism, including a concept of the subject with political implications, can be exemplified by the following quote:

> Quilombismo is a scientific historical philosophy whose pivotal focal point is the human being, as actor and subject (not merely as passive object, as in the Western scientific tradition), within a worldview and a conception of life in which science constitutes one among many other paths of knowledge. (Nascimento 1980: 162)

In diasporic contexts, African experience must take into account the different ways Africanity was resignified in dialogue with several historical experiences. Quilombos do not exist only in Brazil. Several Latin American countries, such as Colombia and Haiti, have shared similar experiences in relation to a more solidary, shared and communitarian perspective of human beings and of life. Quilombo is currently seen as an economic, political, juridical, social, cultural and subjective mode of existence better defined as 'a system of social organization and a right' (Leite 2015: 1226) rather than a racial category. A post-utopian conception on Quilombo focuses on the idea of Quilombo as a human right, deconstructing color and race as criteria of exclusion (Leite 2015). Quilombo integrates this large African *Ubuntu* humanism that extrapolates geopolitical boundaries.

Conclusion
In this chapter, we explored the theoretical and practical potentialities of the African concept *Ubuntu*, considered as a mode of existence shared in the daily life. Even though the origins of Ubuntism may be strongly connected to South Africa, it extrapolates this context and covers different regions and languages in Africa and abroad. Examples are the concept of Quilombo in Brazil (Nascimento 1980) and the idea of Black theology in the United States (Castiano 2010). *Ubuntu* works as a philosophical humanistic orientation whose roots are based on

popular practices, including a vast amount of knowledge shared through orality as proverbs, tales, narratives and stories. Being together and sharing the public space through a dialogic relationship define the political facet of *Ubuntu*. Such an aspect is deeply embedded in an otherness-oriented ethical behavior, which means that 'I' exist only in relation to 'us'. The linguistic implication of such a perspective is that language cannot be reduced to an abstract, countable, nameable and separable unity. Language is a complex set of elements that only make sense together, including emotion, reason, body and verbal expression, among others. Integrationism is a strong theoretical approach that can be approximated to *Ubuntu* by considering the complexity of language practices considered from contextual and historical perspectives. Despite the capitalistic use of *Ubuntu* to justify renewed forms of control by reinforcing the idea of authenticity, we argue that *Ubuntu* works as a powerful political and ethical framework that helps us to think about different possibilities of being together in public and shared space. Such an aspect, however, does not mean that power relations do not exist, but they make sense in a social dynamics that work towards restoring equilibrium. *Ubuntu*'s strength is rooted in its evolving nature because it is based on experience rather than on abstract principles. This creates an opened space for reflection that at the same time reinforces the discourses of tradition and allows space for utopia and creativity. Such openness reflects the way sharing life and being together are continually molding and remolding the subjects.

References
Arendt, Hannah (1958). *The Human Condition*. Chicago:
    University of Chicago Press.
Castiano, José P. (2010). *Referenciais da filosofia africana:
    em busca da intersubjetivação*. Maputo: Ndira.
Castro, Yeda Pessoa (2001). *Falares Africanos na Bahia*.

Rio de Janeiro: Topbooks Editora e Distribuidora de Livros Ltda.

Chaua, Roberto (2014). "Sobre África: questões, tradições e Ubuntu" *Revista Teias* 15(35): 38–53. Retrieved 29 May from www.periodicos.proped.pro.br/index.php/revistateias/article/download/1631/1214.

Edmonds, David (2013). *Would You Kill the Fat Man? The Trolley Problem and What Your Answer Tells about What Is Right or Wrong*. Princeton: Princeton University Press.

Gade, Christian B.N. (2013). "What is Ubuntu? Different interpretations among South Africans of African descent" *South African Journal of Philosophy* 31(3): 487–497.

Harris, Roy (1987). "Language as social interaction: Integrationalism versus segregationalism" *Language Sciences Sciences* 9(2): 131–143.

Hayek, F. August (1988). *The Fatal Conceit: The Errors of Socialism*. Edited by W. W. Bartley, III. Chicago: University of Chicago Press.

Kamwangamalu, Nkonko M. (1999). "Ubuntu in South Africa: A sociolinguistic perspective to a pan-African concept" *Critical Arts: South-North Cultural and Media Studies* 13(2): 24–41.

Leite, Ilka Boaventura (2015). "The Brazilian quilombo: 'Race', community and land in space and time" *The Journal of Peasant Studies* 42(6): 1225–1240.

Makoni, Sinfree (2011). "Language and human rights discourses in Africa: Lessons from the African experience" *Journal of Multicultural Discourses* 7(1): 1–20.

Makwanyane, S. v. & An-other (1995). Constitutional Court of the Republic of South Africa. Retrieved 25 May from https://h2o.law.harvard.edu/collages/12436.

Mbembe, Achille (2015). *Crítica da Razão Negra*. Lisboa: Antígona.

Mendonça, Renato (2012 [1935]). *A influência africana do Português no Brasil*. Brasília: FUNAG.
Nascimento, Abdias do (1980). "Quilombismo: An Afro-Brazilian political alternative" *Journal of Black Studies* 11(2): 141–178.
Orman, Jon & Pablé, Adrian (2015). "Polylanguaging, integrational linguistics and contemporary sociolinguistic theory: A commentary on Ritzau" *International Journal of Bilingual Education and Bilingualism* 19(5): 592–602.
Pablé, Adrian & Hutton, Christopher (2015). *Signs, Meaning and Experience: Integrational Approaches to Linguistics and Semiotics*. Boston/Berlin: Mouton De Gruyter.
Piller, Ingrid (2016). *Linguistic Diversity and Social Justice*. New York: Oxford University Press.
Quijano, Aníbal (2000). "Coloniality of power, eurocentrism, and Latin America" *Nepantla: Views from South* 1(3): 533–580.
Ramose, Mogobe B. (2001). "An African perspective on justice and race" *Forum for Intercultural Philosophy*, 3. Retrieved 29 May from http://them.polylog.org/3/frm-en.htm.
Rossi-Landi, Ferruccio (1983). *Language as Work and Trade: A Semiotic Homology for Linguistics and Economics*. South Hadley, MA: Bergin & Garvey, 1983.
Tschaeege, Mark (2013). "The humanistic Ethic of Ubuntu: Understanding moral obligation" *The American Humanistic Association* 21(2): 47–61.
Tshoose, Clarence (2009). "The emerging role of the Constitutional value of ubuntu for informal social security in South Africa" *The African Journal of Legal Studies* 3(1): 12–19.
Venter, Elza (2004). "The notion of Ubuntu and Com-

munialism in African educational discourse. *Studies in Philosophy and Education* 23(2): 149–160.

Walsh, Catherine (2009). "Interculturalidade e (des) colonialidade: Perspectivas críticas e políticas" *Proceedings of XII Seminar ARIC*, Florianópolis/SC, Brazil.

Žižek, Slavoj (2007). "Resistance is surrender" *London Review of Books* 29(22). Accessed 9 July 2020 at: https://www.lrb.co.uk/the-paper/v29/n22/slavoj-zizek/resistance-is-surrender

II

African oral tradition, parrhesia and integrationism
(with Cristine G. Severo)

In this chapter we discuss the relation between orality – oral tradition – and writing as frameworks to define languages based on Harris (2000; 1998; 2009) and on the concept of oral tradition in African Studies.

By bringing together such concepts we aim at problematizing the centrality of a European perspective that considers writing as an espistemological and political template to conceptualize language practices. Even though Harris has not focused his attention on oral practices, we argue his theoretical reflections on the language myth, writing, the lay-oriented perspective and the integrational semiotic perspective may help us expand our understanding on the role played by oral tradition in a development of a productive concept of language consistent with African narratives.

Also, our focus is not on the several concepts of literacies that have been discussed in the so called "New Literacy Studies" (Street 1995); rather, our objetive is to discuss the political and ethical importance of understanding the concept of oral tradition from a semiotic and lay-oriented perspective consistent with Integrational Linguistics. We argue that such a perspective recognizes the political and epistemological role played by African narratives and oral practices in defining "true" discourses about Africa and Africans. We discuss the concept of truth from the Foucauldian perspective of parrhesia. Drawing on these aspects, we address the two related questions: Is it possible to orally produce an authentic African discourse? If so, what are the socio-historical and cultural conditions that legitimizes oral traditions authentically African?

Concerning the Eurocentric orientation underpinning the concept of writing, Harris (2000: viii) has pointed out the historical relation between alphabetic writing and speech in the European tradition:

> The traditional wisdom is based on certain assumptions about the relationship between speech and writing. Throughout the Western tradition, original contributions to analytic reflection on those assumptions have been few and far between.
>
> Throughout the European tradition there is a tendency to conceptualize sounds in terms of letters. Greek and Roman authors so frequently refer to sounds as 'letters' that one might be forgiven for supposing that they failed to distinguish between the phonetic phenomena and the marks on the page. (Harris 2000: 99)

Such a tradition has not only created a symbolic hierarchy between writing and speech, but has defined alphabetic writing as a universal template broadly used in the colonial era to define local language practices. We do not deny that the massive emergence of written practices based on alphabetic template has produced changes in language practices. Rather, we believe such changes have less to do with any idea of cognitive progress or technological revolution than with the way people experience language. We may say that "the 'literate revolution' in Western thinking seems to have been first and foremost a revolution in the way people thought about their own linguistic experience" (Harris 2009: 147). Such a perspective is radically committed to the lay-oriented conception of language adopted by us here.

Our aim in this chapter is to discuss the colonial inventions of indigenous languages which has resulted in a paradoxical situation in which languages are in search of people (see the following for discussion of the topic (Irvine 1993; Makoni 1998; Makoni and Pennycook 2006; Makoni and Meinhof 2004; Makoni 2015; Abdelhay et al 2014; Abdelhay et al 2020; Pennycook and Makoni 2020). The scholarship on the invention of indigenous languages provides a unique interpretation of what Harris refers to as the language myth (Harris 1998), in which there is a fixed relationship between language forms and functions, and that ideas are automatically transferred between speakers in communication, that dialects are uniform and codifiable entities. Instead, we argue "'languages' have to be seen not as fixed codes given in advance of communication, but as constructs we derive by generalization from our communicational experience" (Harris 1998: 48). Languages from our perspectives are products of interaction and do not precede discourse. In this chapter we focus on how African oral tradition plays an impotant role in redefining not only African local languages, but also what counts as Africa and its history. Integrationism helps us expand our perspective of language by avoiding a dichotomous view: "Where integrational semiology differs from other semiologies is in not restricting the linguistic sign either to speech or to writing" (Harris 1998: 19).

We intend to argue that African oral tradition constitutes a challenge to segregationalism in linguistics (Harris 1998) because of the complex connection between language practice, history, tradition, memory and subjectivity. By seriously considering the role played by the performer in African oral tradition, we assume that "Language is an activity which would be meaningless unless the language-users also engaged in other forms of social interaction" (Harris 1998: 6). By focusing on African concepts of language we priorize the role played by language users in defining not only what counts as language but also the narratives that should be deployed to legitimize what constitutes and can be defined as African and African histories.

Evidently, the use of oral speech is oriented by conditions that regulate its production, circulation and reception. We do not focus here on the conditions for the production of specific African oral practices. Instead, what matters is the way oral tradition in African universes can be used to index specific social and linguistic experiences. Drawing on the concept of "order of discourse" (Foucault 1981) we argue that African oral practices are embedded in historical, cultural and social conventions that regulate the functioning of such discourses. Oral tradition is deeply connected to the ideas of memory, time, space, body and rhythm, which demand a complex semiological perspective of analysis. This is because "Human beings do not inhabit a communicational space which is compartmentalized into language and non-language, but an integrated space where all signs are interconnected" (Harris 1998: 2). The instrinsic relationship between subjectivity and language in oral tradition has been pointed out by Hampaté Bâ (1981: 168): "Based on initiation and experience, oral tradition engages man in his total being, and therefore we can say it has served to create a particular type of man, to sculpt the African soul."

This chapter is divided into two sections: first we explore the relationship between African orality and the educational and revolutionary discourses; after that we then proceed to discuss the relationship between the African performer and a sense of history.

1 African oral tradition as discoursive practice: the revolutionary and the educational

We consider oral tradition from the perspective of Africanists who have been engaged in the academic effort to reconstruct the "official" history of Africa based on the eight volumes of the *History of Africa* (UNESCO). According to one of its main editors, Ki-Zerbo (1981: viii), this project takes Africans' perspectives as central to define the truth (Foucault 2001) about Africa: "In exercising their right to take the historical initiative, Africans themselves have felt a deep-seated need to re-establish the historical authenticity of their societies on solid foundations."

The performer in oral traditions is given a status of truth-teller who inscribes singular meanings through a specific way of narrating, with effects on the narrator himself. In this respect, it is less about the object of the speech and more about the rules that define the speaker as the one who announces the truth, a kind of *parrhesiastes* (Foucault 2001: 17): "the *parrhesiastes* primarily chooses a specific relationship to himself: he prefers himself as a truth-teller rather than as a living being who is false to himself." In the context of African oral tradition, a special role is attributed to the so called masters, those who have the knowledge and the power to narrate. Drawing on the Bambara culture, in Mali, the *doma* or *soma* is the one who is knowledgeable and can promote healing, as well as the intellectual and moral life of the informants:

> One and the same old man [the doma] will be learned not only in plant science (the good or bad properties of every plant) but in earth sciences (the agricultural or medicinal properties of the different kinds of soil), and water sciences, and astronomy, cosmogony, psychology, and so on. What is involved is a *science of life* in which knowledges can always be turned to practical use (Hampaté Bâ 1981: 173).

That is a way of constituting true-knowledge deeply connected to a given way of enunciating that knowledge, by specific subjects. This modality of narration has an impact on the interlocutor, be it healing, moral or intellectual training. The narrated knowledge produces political effects on modes of social organization, and has an impact on the narrator's ethics as well. Orality is construed here not only as the use of verbal language, but it integrates a set of elements that help to build and produce a given oral speech, which includes the use of musical instruments, fine arts and music: "As a matter of fact, music is so much a part of oral tradition that some stories can only be told in song" (Ki-Zerbo 1981: II).

In mapping the Africanists' meanings of oral tradition we turn to the writings of Franz Fanon, who was strongly engaged in the struggle for Algeria's independence from French domination. It is a discourse strongly allied with broader movements of political and cultural emancipation of African peoples, parallel to the the process of constituting a national identity as a form of resistance against historical processes of constituting the so-called colonized subjects. Franz Fanon represents a group of intellectuals who aimed at endorsing a renewed idea of "Africanity" in search for autonomy and an authoral voice. We consider Fanon's discourse as an example of a revolutionary parresiastic modality that works as a critique of the colonial reality. According to Foucault (2011: 30), "Revolutionary discourse plays the role of parrhesiastic discourse when it takes the form of a critique of existing society". The search for a proper and courageous voice is illustrated in the excerpt below, representing the entry of the colonized subject in the discursive order of the "human", understood as the one who can and must speak:

> General de Gaulle speaks of "the yellow multitudes" and Francois Mauriac of the black, brown, and yellow masses which soon will be unleashed. The native knows all this, and laughs to himself every time he spots an allu-

sion to the animal world in the other's words. For he knows that he is not an animal; and it is precisely at the moment he realizes his humanity that he begins to sharpen the weapons with which he will secure its victory. (Fanon 1968: 43)

African orality is strongly related to the movement of African liberation, in search of autonomy and an African voice that resonates their own memory and, at the same time, builds new narratives about what counts as Africanity. It was not by chance that "the traditionalists were brushed aside if not actually proceeded against by the colonial power, which needless to say sought to uproot local traditions in order to implant its own ideas" (Hampaté Bâ 1981: 174). We recognize that this revolutionary discursive practice was not restricted to African liberation movements, but echoed in other contexts, such as those of African diaspora, like in Brazil. In this context, the term "African-Brazilian" helped to resignify the idea of being Brazilian.

Critical concepts of oral tradition also include the writings of Joseph Ki-Zerbo and Hampaté Bâ, African activists and co-organizers of the "General History of Africa" collection, edited by UNESCO, an eight-volume project organized by 39 scholars, of which 2/3 are Africans. This collection was built in the course of 20 years (1962-1982). The symbolic founding landmark of this work was the *1st International Congress of Africanists* that occured in Ghana, 1962. The importance of this collection is that it seeks to present "African" voices that inscribe a local vision in the regime of contemporary knowledge about Africa. The volume production process was neither homogeneous nor linear, but was affected by at least two delicate moments surrounding the construction of the 'African vision' (Barbosa 2012): a controversial one, between 1975-1978, in defense of an "African perspective"; and a pragmatic one, between 1978-1982, in defense of a more "tolerant" enviroment in face of the dominant position on the "African perspective". Such tension, however, did not erase the editors' commitment to inscribe the point of view of African authors in the collection.

In Brazil, this collection is available on the Ministry of Education's website, which signals an educational interest in the discourses on Africa: "The objective of the initiative is to fill a gap in the Brazilian formation regarding the legacy of the continent for its own national identity"[1] (MEC). On the other hand, African education can be understood from a "traditional" perspective as a non-schooling practice, in which older parents and family members are responsible for the first moral lessons, through oral transmission: "They are the ones who give the first lessons in life, not only through experience but through the medium of stories, fables, legends, maxims, adages, and so on. Proverbs are missives bequeathed to posterity by the ancestors." (Hampaté Bâ 1981: 179).

We underline the role played by western schooling in helping to shape a concept of prestigious language based on a written template: "Furthermore, our modern concept of literacy is essentially the product of a certain educational tradition, which already incorporates certain attitudes towards the written word, its function, and its social value" (Harris 1998: 230). That has a strong effect on the way oral tradition has been ressignified by literate practices, mainly in the African context. The power of prestigious indexalities ascribed to literacy can be inversely noticed by the negative terms and images used to describe literacy rates in Africa as being equivalent to poor cognitive ability, poverty and diseases (Abdelhay et al. 2014).

We flag up that African languages do not need to be systematized to be taught (Makoni and Meinhof, 2004). In terms of oral tradition we have to deal with both orders related to languages (Harris 1998): while the first order concerns the contextualized production of unique utterances, the second order

---

[1] "O objetivo da iniciativa é preencher uma lacuna na formação brasileira a respeito do legado do continente para a própria identidade nacional."

represents the institutionalized and stabilized languages that emerge from a metalinguistic process applied over the first order reality. We propose that an African perspective has also to do with creating new modes of narrating the first order oral practices.

Provided that education regulates the way discourses function in a given society (Foucault 2001), we should consider the idea of traditional African education as strongly influencing the way knowledge circulates and is appropriated, producing modes of subjectivation affected by the way people learn and teach:

> Traditional education, especially when it concerns knowledge associated with an initiation, is linked with experience and integrated into life. That is why the researcher, European or African, who wants to get close to African religious facts condemns himself to remaining on the outer edge of the subject unless he consents to live the initiation that corresponds to them and accept its rules, which presupposes at the very least a *knowledge of the language*. For there are things that are not to be explained but are experienced and lived (Hampaté Bâ 1981: 178).

African oral practices, together with the "African languages", are constitutive of what counts as education, in opposition to a universalist and institutional perspective, such as UNESCO's that takes language as a cognitive, neutral and apolitical element (Santos 2017). Furthermore, it should be noted that the African *parrhesiastes* is not a teacher since he/she is not restricted to the domain of technique and expertise; his/her way of producing knowledge is different, which also differs from the role of the prophet and the sage (Foucault 2014), as we explain in the next section.

2 On oral practice: the utterer, the transmission process and the concept of history

For Ki-Zerbo (1969, p. 114), oral tradition can be defined in the following terms:

> the collection of all the types of witness transmitted verbally by people through their own past. There are then two ideas necessary, and sufficient: spoken witness and transmission. Insults in your own home are not oral tradition, because you would not want to repeat them. It is the passing on of a spoken message in a temporal sequence that constitutes tradition.

Oral tradition, for Ki-Zerbo, is defined by a particular oral practice transmitted across generations that carries some relevant meaning, usually linked to the moral sphere. Such transmission works as an "oral testimony", being validated by the group. The relation between oral practice and writing can be illustrated by the following: "Where writing does not exist, man is bound to the word he utters. He is committed by it. He is his word and his word bears witness to what he is" (Hampaté Bâ, 1981, p. 167). This relationship between the spoken word and the embodied word inscribes a mode of subjectification in which the enunciator necessarily speaks in the first person: his body operates as the signature of his saying that is transmitted through the testimony.

The intrinsic relationship between what is said and the subject who enunciates characterizes the parrhesiastic discourse: "Parrhesia, then, is linked to courage in the face of danger: it demands the courage to speak the truth in spite of some danger" (Foucault 2001: 16). And what risk does the African *parrhesiastes* take? The one who lies runs the risk of dissociating himself from the group with which he lives and from himself: "In traditional Africa the man who breaks his word kills his civil, religious and occult person. He cuts himself off from himself and from society. Better for him to die than to go on living, both for himself and for his family." (Hampaté Bâ 1981: 172). If the true-word is the link of the present with a given African ancestry, which legitimizes the veracity of the oral discourse, the lie would operate as a breach of that transmission link, that is of the rules that underlie the true narration.

This is why "transmission" is a central discursive procedure that legitimates the truth of the oral practice. The lie would invalidate the parrhesiastic speech itself, breaking its effect of truth and authority: "The reason for the ban on lying is that if an officiant lied he would vitiate ritual acts. He would no longer fulfil all the ritual conditions necessary for performing the sacred act " (Hampaté Bâ 1981: 174-175). It is worth considering that this parrhesiastic role is attributed to *doma*, in the Bambara culture, different from the uncompromised oral practices of the griots who are troubadours, storytellers or popular animators. Such a relation between truth-telling (parrhesia) and African oral tradition may lead us "[...] to think about lying in our own society and to question the assumptions of our tradition about the nature and uses of language, and in particular of truth-telling" (Morris 1998: 320).

The African enunciator-narrator, on the one hand, would play a role similar to that of the prophet, who does not speak in his name, but operates as a kind of mediator, who "speaks for another voice; his mouth serves as intermediary for a voice which speaks from elsewhere" (Foucault 2011: 15). His/her speech is often not evident, in the form of parables, narratives and songs that carry some moral message destinated to effect the interlocutor. On the other hand, unlike the prophet, the African narrator-parrhesiastic is implicated in his speech, because his conduct is judged by his interlocutors as proof of the truth of his speech.

In historiographical terms, this true-saying of African oral practice is sometimes questioned by the academic field of Oral History that tends to assess the narrator's subjectivity marks would blur the boundary between fiction and fact. We argue that one of the parrhesiastic effects of African orality for the disciplinary field of historiography is to question the very definition of what counts as history and truth: "In appreciating narratives of cultural history, in particular, we need to rethink the all-too-easy lines we draw between truth and lying" (Okpewho, 2003, p. 228). The risk, in this case, is the impossibility of validation, by the historian, of African oral tradition as being capable of telling the truth of Africa, hence the tensions that occurred in the process of production of the volumes of African history (UNESCO).

In the context of literary discourses, the testimonial narrative has been aesthetically recognized as a form of report of post-war survivors, whether in Europe, Latin America or Africa. As a discursive genre, "The testimony, as we know, carries a marked political connotation by allowing the use of the word by those who are traditionally excluded" (Reis, 2007, p. 79). That is about the construction of another memory – pervaded by the experience of historically invisible and silenced witnesses –, which aligned fragments passed on orally between generations. In building this memory, "one cannot make a valid history of the African peoples without the oral tradition" (Ki-Zerbo, 1969, p. 123). The testimonies, therefore, have been used as central discursive elements in the reconstruction of another history about Africa, one that highlights the voices historically silenced. In this regard, Hrbek argues in favour of the reconstruction of South African history (1981, p. 124) from the perspective of 'African voices':

> the struggle now going on in South Africa in every field of human activity necessitates also a new approach to the sources; particular attention must be paid to the written evidence of the hard struggle of the Africans for their rights. Only research based on all the evidence and

material will allow the writing of a truthful history of South Africa.

In the oral tradition, the relationship with the past intensifies, since it is a central element in the validation of this discourse: "In a society without writing the sense and the meaning of the past weigh much more heavily" (Ki-Zerbo 1969: 117). There is no a-temporal language practice, which does not mean that all societies define and experience time the same way. For an integrationist perspective, the individual's temporal experience is instrisic to any language phenomena:

> Whatever activities are integrated in the course of human communication are always integrated into a temporal framework of some kind. Communication does not somehow lie outside the time-track of other events but is cotemporal with them. This cotemporality is not the theoretical fiction of Saussurean 'synchrony' but the cotemporality of human experience, in which there is always a past and a (possible) future. A past and a future are implicit in every semiological phenomenon (Harris 2000: 163)

The discursive reference to a mythical past is central to the definition of what counts as oral tradition in African context. This means we must seriously consider that "The thing traditional Africa holds dearest is its ancestral heritage" (Hampaté Bâ 1981: 174). There is an intrinsic relationship between language and a sense of temporality which makes transmission an important language practice in oral tradition. The process of oral transmission enhances the possibilities of reinterpretations and reappropriations, in a rhytmic movement between repetition and novelty, past and present.

The relationship between speech and rhythm (temporal and spatial) in the African perspective can be exemplified through a myth of West African origin:"If speech is strength, that is because it creates a bond of coming-and-going (*yaa-iparta*, in Fulfulde) which generates movement and rhythm and therefore life and action." (Hampaté Bâ 1981: 170), symbolized by the work of the weaver's feet. In this mythological context, speech is represented by the power of creation and destruction, hence its relationship with mystical and religious ritual. Speech occupies a crucial role in African mythical representation, by helping to orient modes of subjectification. Religion, moral education and language are strongly connected in oral tradition through ritualist practices. This means "It must be borne in mind that in a general way all African traditions postulate a *religious vision of the world"* (Hampaté Bâ 1981: 171) that mixes a ritual movement between the visible and the invisible: "the terms 'speaking' and 'listening' refer to realities far more vast than those we usually attribute to them" (Hampaté Bâ 2010: 171). There is, therefore, a certain way of chanting (and hearing) this African truth.

In short, it can be said that African oral tradition carries a certain concept language, in which orality – testimonial speech, singing, proverbs, narratives, rituals – plays a central role in the contitution of Africans' subjectivity and in the production of the truth about Africa. In other words, "every African is to some extent a storyteller" (Hampaté Bâ, 1981, p. 199-200). Such definition matters if we consider an Integrationist lay-oriented perspective of language that recognizes individual's experience of language as constitutive of what counts as language: "Integrationism is lay-oriented, in that it puts individual experience at the centre of its theoretical concerns. It rejects the annexation by academic linguists of intellectual authority over the domain of language [...]" (Hutton & Pablé, 2011, p. 478).

Concluding remarks
In this chapter we explored the idea of African orality as a discoursive and parrhesiastic modality whose political effects work

as a critique of colonial epistemic, political and ethical domination. What is at stake is the discursive use of African languages which means considering African languages as products of African discourses, such as oral practices. In this sense we propose that language policy and planning must consider the political modalities of saying, as the African oral speech, considered as a parrhesiastic speech. Integrationism may help us expand the concept of language by allowing us to seriously consider the perspective of the lay individual about what counts as language practices. African voice therefore is a discursive construction that regulates ways of using language. Therefore, the idea of orality and oral tradition transcends the notion of languages as a decodifiable phonological entity. African discourse implies something more, as previously signaled by Fanon (1986: 18-19):

> To speak means to be in a position to use a certain syntax, to greasp the morphology of this or that language, but it means above all to assume a culture, to support the weight of a civilization.

References

Abdelhay, A.; Asfaha, Y. & Juffermans, K. (2014). "African literacies: ideologies, scripts, education" Chapter 1 in A. Abdelhay, Y. Asfaha & K. Juffermans. *African Literacies: Ideologies, Scripts, Education* (pp. 1-62). Cambridge: Cambridge Scholars Publishing.

Barbosa, M . (2012) "A construção da perspectiva africana: uma história do projeto História Geral da Africa (Unesco)" *Revista Brasileira de História* 32(64), 211-230.

Fanon, F. (1963). *The Wretched of the Earth*. New York: Grove Press.

Fanon, F. (1986). *Black Skin, White Masks*. London: Pluto Press.

Foucault, M. (1981). "The order of discourse" In *Untying the*

Text: A Post–Structuralist Reader, ed. Robert Young (pp. 48–78). London: Routledge and Kegan Paul.

Foucault, M. (2001). *Fearless Speech*. Los Angeles: Semiotext(e).

Foucault, M. (2011). *The Courage of the Truth (The Government of Self and Others II) Lectures at the Collège De France 1983–1984*. Translated by Graham Burchell. New York: Palgrave Macmillan.

Hampaté Bâ, A (1981). "The living tradition" In J. Ki-Zerbo (Ed.), *General History of Africa I: Methodology and African Pre History* (pp. 166-205). Berkeley: UNESCO, University of California Press.

Harris, R. (ed.) (1998). *Integrational Linguistics: A First Reader*. Oxford, UK: Elsevier Science.

Harris, R. (2000). *Rethinking Writing*. New York, NY: Continuum.

Harris, R. (2009). *Rationality and the Literate Mind*. New York, NY: Routledge.

Hrbek, I. (1981) "Written sources from the fifteenth century onwards" In J. Ki-Zerbo (Ed.), *General History of Africa I: Methodology and African Pre History* (pp. 114-141). Berkeley: UNESCO, University of California Press.

Hutton, C., & Pable, A. (2011). "Editorial" *Language Sciences*, 33, 475–479.

Irvine, J. (1993). "Mastering African languages: the politics of linguistics in nineteenth-century Senegal" *Social Analysis: The International Journal of Social and Cultural Practice*, 33, 27-46.

Ki-Zerbo, J. (1981). "General Introduction" In J. Ki-Zerbo (Ed.), *General History of Africa I: Methodology and African Pre History* (pp. 1-24). Berkeley: UNESCO, University of California Press.

Ki-Zerbo, J. (1969). "The Oral Tradition as a Source of African History" *Diogenis,* 17(67), 110-124.

Makoni, S. (1998). "In the beginning was the missionaries' word: The European invention of African languages: The case of Shona in Zimbabwe" In K. Prah (Ed.), *Between extinction and distinction: The harmonization and standardization of African languages* (pp. 157–165). Johannesburg, South Africa: Witwatersrand University Press.

Makoni, S., & Severo, C. G. (2017). "An integrationist perspective on African philosophy. In A. Pablé (Ed.), *Critical Humanist Perspectives: The Integrational Turn in Philosophy of Language and Communication* (pp. 63–76). London, UK: Routledge.

Makoni, S., Severo, C. G., & Abdelhay, A. (2020). "Colonial linguistics and the invention of language" In A. Abdelhay, S. B. Makoni, & C. G. Severo (Eds.), *Language Planning and Policy Ideologies, Ethnicities, and Semiotic Spaces of Power* (pp. 211–228). Newcastle upon Tyne, UK: Cambridge Scholars.

Makoni, Sinfree, and Meinhof, Ulrike (2004). "Western Perspectives in Applied Linguistics in Africa" *AILA Review* 17: 77-104. doi:10.1075/aila.17.09mak

Makoni, S., & Pennycook, A. (2006). *Disinventing and Reconstituting Languages.* Clevedon: Multilingual Matters.

Morris, M. (1998). "What Problems? On Learning to Translate" In R. Harris (ed.), *Integrational Linguistics: A First Reader* (pp. 313-323). Oxford, UK: Elsevier Science.

Okpewho, I. (2003) "Oral Tradition: Do Storytellers Lie?" *Journal of Folklore Research*, 40(3), 215-232.

Reis, L. (2007) "Testemunho como construção da memória" *Cadernos de Letras da UFF*, Dossiê: Letras e Direitos Humanos, 33, 77-86.

Santos, M. (2017). "A oferta do letramento e a garantia de

futuros sociais: análise das políticas de letramento da UNESCO e de suas ideologias linguísticas" *Trabalhos em Linguística Aplicada.*, 56(2), 641-667.

Pennycook, A. & Makoni, Sinfree (2020). *Innovations and Challenges in Applied Linguistics from the Global South.* London: Routledge.

Severo, C. & Makoni, S. (2015). *Políticas Linguísticas Brasil-África.* Florianópolis, Brazil: Insular.

Street, Brian V. (1995). *Social Literacies: Critical Approaches to Literacy in Development, Ethnography and Education.* London: Longman.

III

Deconstructing the discourses about language in language planning in South Africa

Abstract
There has been a considerable amount of interest in language policy in a multilingual South Africa. A large number of different professions, educationists, sociologists, political activists and linguists have contributed, in various ways, to the debate. In spite of the input of linguists to the debate, there has been very little analysis about the language component of the language policy debate. The aim of this article is to attempt to rectify the situation by critically deconstructing the various discourses about language and demonstrating the implications of such discourses on policy implementation.

Preamble
Debates about language policy have always been extremely controversial in the past and there is no reason to expect that the situation is going to be different in the future. In the past the controversies hinged on the various policy options which could be pursued by a post-apartheid government. After the recent announcement of the eleven language policy and its entrenchment in the transitional constitution the debates are now focused on the implementability of the policies. Because language imple-

mentation requires a long-term perspective, the construct of sustainability will soon enter the discourse. The language policy debates attract participants from a wide range of disciplines,

- linguists
- sociologists
- political students
- educationists,

because language policy issues are at the crossroads of the arts, social sciences and education.

All these disciplines regard changes in language policy as crucial because changes in language policy are likely to have more far reaching effects than changes in any part of the curriculum.

King expresses it aptly when he writes:

> Decisions about language innovation require very long time horizons, and a much greater feel for the interaction of language in school and language in society than would be the case for a shift in Maths or Science. After all school science, geography or history content can be readily forgotten whereas the medium will continue to play an important role in access to the job market and to further education. (1986: 40)

Shifting the direction of the debate

Although the recent announcement of the eleven language policy and its entrenchment in the constitution has intensified rather than subdued debates on issues about language policy, my main aim is to take the debate in a different direction by arguing that although linguists have been at pains to either support or challenge the desirability or implementability of specific policies, there is one crucial aspect which has been conspicuous by its absence. There has not been any concerted effort to deconstruct the notions of language underlying the policy debates. I see the key contribution of this article as a way of opening up debates about the language component in the policy debates; a component of the debate which has been surprisingly missing given the contribution of linguists to the evolving debate.

This article will seek to explore five main ways in which the concept of language has been implicated in debates on language policy. The following are the various ways in which the constuct of language has been investigated:

1. Language as discrete categories (boundaries phenomena)
2. The commodification of language
3. Conventions of map making as geographic location
4. The language for specific purposes issue as functional location
5. Language as an interpenetreable phenomena (the frontiers phenomenon).

The announcement that South Africa will officially, at a national level, have eleven official languages, was welcomed as an improvement on the past situation in which only two languages, English and Afrikaans, were officially recognized.

The main purpose of my article is to explore the concept of language implicated in announcements of that type.

The announcement of the eleven official languages and subsequent entrenchment in the constitution has the effects of conflating language and standardization by aligning itself with those codes which, for one reason or another, had already been standardized. Such an announcement has the effects of creating the impression that the complex relationship between language and dialect has been 'fixed'. Experience from other parts of Africa has demonstrated that such fixing cannot easily be achieved.

Bamgbose (1994) cites an interesting example which supports the dynamic nature of the relationship between languages and dialects. Using examples drawn from Ghana, he shows that differences in dialects between Twi and Fante which were magnified in the immediate post-independence period (Ghana got its independence from Britain in 1957), to the status of separate languages are now being considerably down-played, consequently the number of languages which Ghana has 37 years after independence is in decline.

> The converse also does apply. The Efik-Ibibio dialect cluster in Nigeria has for years been accepted as practically one language with Efik as the literary form of the language. The position is now being reversed and Ibibio is more and more being emphasised as a separate language. This trend is likely to be intensified with the creation of a new state Alwa-Iboru in 1987 in which the Ibibio form the dominant group. (Bamgbose, 1994: 34)

The upshot of the argument is that there is *nothing magical in the number of languages* which a country officially recognizes, because whether speech forms are recognized as separate languages or dialects of the same, language does change across time with the Ghanaian example illustrating a situation in which differences between speech forms are downplayed, whereas the Nigerian experience demonstrates a process in which the differences are magnified.

Announcements about language which emerge from a top-down perspective about language are in conflict with those prioritizing local practices in language. I return to this point later in the article.

Languages as discrete entities: the boundaries phenomenon
Closely aligned to the idea that the speech forms are either separate languages or dialects of the same language is the metaphor of languages as discrete categories. Fardon & Furniss (1994: 3) aptly decribe such a way of thinking about language as

a boundaries phenomenon. It is a boundaries phenomena because speech forms are seen as falling into mutually exclusive categories called languages. The boundaries way of thinking about language is characteristic of a top-down approach to language (starting from the assumption of diverse languages). The discourse of boundaries is also typical of language planning discourses which seek to "address (language) problems posed in terms of national, international, continental and intercontinental relations" (Fardon & Furniss, 1994: 3).

Paradoxically, in Africa and indeed even more so in South Africa, the boundaries conceptualization of language is also typical of colonialist and neo-apartheid discourses about language. Le Page & Tabouret-Keller (1982) citing a Bantu linguist argue that "the existence of separate labelled (African) languages is a British innovation expedited by the work of Clement Doke and other like-minded linguists". It is linguists who decided to elevate Hurutse at the expense of other dialects in forming standard Tswana. They sought to divide the Sotho in the north from their cousins in the south using language as a dividing instrument.

The division of African speech forms into different languages is reinforced by state, legal and educational pressures. In South Africa when African children enter school they have a mother tongue designated to them even though the language may be as alien to them as English (Street, 1993: 35). The essence of the point Street is making, is that the language forms most African children encounter during their primary socialization are so radically different from the ones they encounter when they are supposed to be receiving instruction through their mother tongue, that I would argue that African children are not receiving the benefit of mother-tongue instruction, but of *step-tongue instruction.* One way in which the drift between the language of primary socialization and the step-tongue instruction is created, is through a process of restandardization. The restandardization would mean that the speech forms used as media of instruction would more closely resemble those used in the local communities in which the children live. In order for this to happen, it may be necessary to free ourselves from thinking about language solely in terms of discrete categories. The multicultural lobby being 'fixated' by the problems of African children in English classrooms (The Model C Hypnosis) overlooks a much more serious problem in the African classroom in which African children are receiving step-tongue instruction; so much for the arguments that it is beneficial, if not revolutionary for children to learn through their mother tongue.

Commodification of language
There is also the discourse of acquisitional planning which tends to discuss language in the metaphor of a commodity. The commodification of language manifests itself most clearly in the domain of second and foreign language learning and teaching (Coulmas, 1992). Fairclough describes the commodification of language as the

> process whereby social domains and institutions, whose concern is not producing commodities in the narrow economic sense of goods for sale come nevertheless to be organised and conceptualised in terms of commodity production, distribution and consumption. (1992: 206)

The commodification of language reflects the extent to which the discursive practices about language have come to be dominated—to use Fairclough's term, colonized—by the world of economics. The impact of the process of commodification can be felt in two ways, language learners are constructed as clients or customers, who may in the South African context opt to buy one or more of the eleven language commodities. The commodification of language creates an image of the eleven languages as being in competition rather than in a complementary relationship with one another. The idea of the eleven languages as being in competition with one another is one of the consequences of the commodification of language, because the eleven commodities are in market terms competing for the same clientele or customers. If the eleven languages are seen as commodities in open competition with one another, the competition is unfortunately not *an equal one*. For example, if all the eleven officially recognized South African languages were to function as media of instruction (pushing aside the mother-tongue debate), materials would have to be provided in each of the individual languages.

> Provision of these materials is very expensive and requires a high degree of expertise. Hard economic realities mean that governments rely heavily on commercial publishers. Unfortunately, because "economies of scale" dictate that publishers invest in instructional materials for languages with relatively large numbers of speakers, it means that languages with relatively few speakers such as Pedi and Venda may not receive fair treatment (Makoni, 1993: 17)

Central to the commodification of language is the notion of the market value of a language. In this type of discourse the idea that language is a commodity is seen as justifiable because acquiring a second/foreign language is costly both to the individual and society. In the South African context, knowledge of an African language may be seen as economically exploitable (see the increasing number of advertisements in South African newspapers in which knowledge of an African language is a prerequisite for employment). The number of such advertisements can only increase as the market value of African languages increases.

In the Western Cape, if the educational system cannot successfully meet the demands for Xhosa as a second/foreign language, the niche for the private entrepreneur will expand.

Demands for Xhosa as a second/foreign language are likely to lead to more people wanting to learn it. This has what Coulmas aptly calls a snowball effect because the more people learn a language, the more useful it becomes, and the more useful it becomes, the more people want to learn it. In the South African context another argument may also have to be used— opportunities for learning African languages were formerly so few and unsatisfactory that the desire has accumulated. Both teachers and learners are benefitting by arrears. The number of people learning a language as a second/foreign language is however not a perfect criterion of the value of the language in a community. For instance, there is a considerably large number of students learning Latin at the University of the Western Cape. Hopefully, this does not necessarily reflect the value of Latin in the community at that university. It reflects curriculum decisions in which Latin was made a prerequisite for courses which at this stage are popular, hence the large number of Latin students; a sure case of intellectual misinvestment.

The metaphor of language as a commodity has some in built self-contradiction. On the one hand, language is commodified through monolingual dictionaries and grammar books which objectify and reify the vocabulary of a language, thus turning it into a potential material possession (Coulmas, 1992: 71), but on the other hand, language is an intangible commodity. When a student pays to learn a language the language teacher does not diminish his stock by teaching the student as would have been the case with most tangible commodities.

Linguistic atlas
Another discursive practice whose conventions influence our way of thinking about language is the linguistic map. The map shows how speakers of different languages are geographically distributed and language consequently becomes *objectified spatially*. All the discourses about language have their own assumptions, including the discourses of the linguistic map,

hence the danger of responding to the discourse of the map as though it were 'an unmediated reality'. Because of the way the maps are constructed there is always a part of the story which is not captured. The key issue is whether that which is included is more important than that which convention demands should be left out.

For example, the reader of a language map has to appeal to other sociolinguistic processes in order to understand why particular speech forms are regarded as an instance of a language and not a dialect and *vice versa*. Such an interaction of ethnic and linguistic considerations are not easily captured on a linguistic map. The main strength of a language map is to identify the language, and to list the number of speakers, but alas even the methods used to determine the language an individual speaks are not beyond doubt!

Language maps will also be hard pressed to represent any area in terms of more than one salient language. Thus, for instance, in some maps a large part of the Western Cape is presented in terms of Afrikaans only, when in the urban areas there clearly are a large number of different languages spoken in addition to Afrikaans. The discourse of the language map is prone to perpetuate a myth of monolingualism when announcement of the eleven official language policy is aimed at conjuring up an image of multilingualism at both an individual and a state level.

Language and sectoral usage

Another new type of discourse about language is beginning to emerge in the talk about a Pan South African language board. The key aspect in the discourse is the notion of Language for Specific Purposes in which languages are allocated specific functions. Whereas the map distributes language *geographically*, the language for specific purposes distributes them *functionally*. The language for specific purposes is comparable to the issue about the geographical distribution of language captured on a map. In both cases the analyst or in this case the discourse is trying to 'locate' a language or a variety of language, the difference, however, lies in the fact that the 'location' is being carried out geographically in the case of the map, while it is being carried out functionally in the case of Language for Specific Purposes. Admittedly, the location in the case of Language for Specific Purposes is operating at a much more metaphoric and abstract level than that which is taking place geographically.

The idea of languages for Specific Purposes is often construed to mean that certain languages are appropriate for certain levels. *Whereas the linguistic map divides people geographically, the division of languages for Specific Purposes takes place sectorally.* But perhaps such a distinction is inevitable because as Whitley (1974) insists it might always be necessary to make choices at different levels, and that even within a single institution e.g. the educational system or legal system, it may not be prudent to opt for a unilingual solution

> and it is always necessary to be aware of differential function and of the presence of variable domains within uniform will ... Efficiency is not necessarily achieved by uniformity, rather by sympathetic understanding of complex demands and dynamic uncertainty (Davies, 1986: 8)

Language frontiers
The last discourse about language which I would like to talk about, is the one which emerges from a microethnographic approach and associated with the work of Gumperz (1971) and Le Page & Tabouret-Keller (1989) whereas other discourses have discussed language as discrete categories, which are more or less given. The microethnographic approach would argue that such views about language do not accurately reflect the sociolinguistic situation prevailing on the ground. The main thrust of ethnographic approaches is on local practice.

Thus for Le Page the language or languages an individual uses cannot be determined by either her geographical location or sectoral placement but by the identity which she seeks to project at any individual moment. *Language for Le Page is therefore not a reifed object but an act of identity.* Thus, for example in my family there are people who linguistically I thought spoke different languages. The claim they are now making that they are speaking the same language can only make sense, if I argue that the desire to interact, to mutually identify, to reach out on both sides has led to a considerable degree of mutual intelligibility—what more effective way to demonstrate that than by claiming that you are speaking the same language. The situation which I am describing is not restricted to a small household in an uncelebrated part of Cape Town.

Le Page & Tabouret-Keller cite similar evidence concerning the problematic nature of assigning words to a particular language, in their case either Spanish or a Creole. They aptly comment:

> Linguists would do well to listen to the debate taking place within evolutionary genetics; especially at a time when to understand these problems is to contribute to the solution of grave problems. We would want to see linguists chary of talking about a language, in any monosystemic sense as biologists are by now of talking about a human race (Le Page & Tabouret-Keller, 1982: 181)

The main point which the microethnographic perspective makes is that languages and language boundaries are permeable and therefore language should be seen as interpenetreable hence the frontiers metaphor. Within this type of discourse the analyst feels that it is prudent to talk of language repertoires or as Fardon & Furniss (1994) prefer to put it workable portfolios.

The notion of language repertoires has implications on the dynamics of social interaction. Frequency of interaction could lead to speakers becoming more like one another both in their repertoire, and in the repertoire they draw upon and the social marking which they attach to each selection from their repertoire.

Although the frontiers metaphor is sensitive to local practice, it is difficult to see of what immediate relevance such complex information could be to the language policy operator, who is likely to 'abandon' her implementation because of the complexity of the information she is presented with, such feelings of despair would be unnecessary.

Because the frontiers metaphor is sensitive to local language practices, the information which it provides could be invaluable to any bottom-up approach to language implementation, since detailed anthropological descriptions provide insights into true community language usage. I, however, am not arguing for a bottom-up strategy to language implementation only because

> in reality what is required for a policy to be implementable is a mixture of top-down and bottom-up strategies. With local initiatives exerting upward pressures on national policies and national policies imposing downward pressure - so that local initiatives can reflect national policies (Makoni, 1993: 19)

Conclusion

In this article, I have tried to deconstruct the various ways in which the concept of language is used. I have argued that the announcement of an eleven language policy is intellectually oriented towards a view of language as made up of discrete categories; the boundaries phenomena. The boundaries phenomena is converted into commodified language in the discourse of acquisitional planning. The Language for Specific Purposes issue is like the map concerned with objectified language. The location is carried out geographically, thanks to the linguistic map sectorally in the language for specific purposes discourse. The microethnographic approach with its emphasis on local practice is in potential tension with the topdown view of language boundaries, but any successful implementation requires a combination of bottom-up and topdown strategies.

References

Bamgbose, A. (1994). 'Pride and prejudice in multilingualism and development'. In Fardon R. & Furniss, G. (Eds.). *African Languages, Development and the State.* London: Routledge Press.

Coulrnas, F. (1992). *Language and the economy.* Oxford: Blackwell.

Davies, A. (Ed.). (1986). *Language in Education in Africa.* Seminar Proceedings at the Centre of African Studies. Edinburgh: University of Edinburgh.

Fardon, R. & Furniss, G. (Eds.). (1994). *African Languages, Development and the State.* London: Routledge Press.

FaircLough, N. (1992). *Discourse and Social Change.* Cambridge: Polity Press.

Laitin, D. (1992). *Language Repetoires and State Construction in Africa.* Cambridge: Cambridge University Press.

LePage, R.B. & Tabouret-Keller, A. (1985). *Acts of identity.* Cambridge: Cambridge University Press.

Makoni, S. (1993). 'The futility of being held captive by language policy issues in South African applied linguistics', *Per linguam,* Vol. 9, No.2.

Routh, H. V. 1941. *The Diffusion of English Culture Outside England.* Cambridge: Cambridge University Press.

Whitley, W. (Ed.). (1914). *Language in Kenya.* Oxford: Oxford University Press.

IV

Some of the metaphors about language in language planning discourses in South Africa: boundaries, frontiers and commodification

Since April 1994, when eleven languages (instead of two) were given official recognition, language planning debates have focused on implementabilty rather than policy options. This paper explores three of the metaphors which influence language planning discourses in South Africa: the boundaries metaphor, the frontiers metaphor and the commodity metaphor, and the effect they have on the way language is constructed The discussion centres on the tensions between a "bounded" view of language and a frontier view of language. Aspects such as frequency of usage and the distribution of languages would be significant in language planning discourses based on a frontier view of language, whereas the number of mother tongue speakers would be significant in a "bounded" view of language. Finally, the paper stresses that commerce influences discourses about language.

Introduction
This paper seeks to examine critically some of the assumptions about language in language planning discourses in South Africa. It does so by analysing various metaphors current in the debate. The following are the three main ways in which the construction of language has been metaphorised in discourses about language:

i) language as a discrete category (the boundaries phenomena)
ii) language as an interpenetrable phenomenon (the frontiers metaphor)
iii) language as a commodifiable entity.

Contextualising the paper
Language planning policy can be loosely interpreted as an organised approach to language problems, typically at the national level. This normally involves discussions about which languages to be accorded official recognition, or the role which some of the languages could play in education. In South Africa, the debates also involve the amount of air time some languages should be accorded on radio and TV. This does not preclude debates at a local level. Arguments about language planning policies at a national level are guided by metaphors about language which are different from those influencing the conceptualisation of language from local perspectives.

In the apartheid era, debates about the various language planning policy options which a future government in a post-apartheid era could adopt were often extremely volatile because language policy was interpreted by all the protagonists as a vehicle through which different political ideologies could be articulated. Since the announcement in April 1994 by the new democratic government that South Africa would officially recognise eleven languages, the debate has shifted from a discussion of policy options to the implementability of the policy. Because language implementation requires a long-term perspective, the discourse on language policy will soon begin to address issues about sustainability as well.

In the apartheid era, Afrikaans and English were the only two officially recognised languages in South Africa. In addition to the above two, nine other languages have been granted official status. The following table (Ridge 1994) lists the number of languages officially recognised in South Africa and the estimated number of speakers of each language. The table accounts for 98% of an estimated total population of approximately 40 million. The remaining 2 % is made up of community languages (also referred to as heritage languages) such as Hebrew, Gujarati, etc. that have not been granted official recognition. Besides heritage languages, another notable language which has not been granted official recognition is Fanakalo, a South African pidgin spoken mainly in the mines.

Zulu	21.95%	8.8 million
Xhosa	17.03%	6.8 million
Afrikaans	15.03%	6.0 million
Northern Sotho	9.64%	3.8 million
English	9.01%	3.6 million
Tswana	8.59%	3.4 million
Southern Sotho	6.73%	2.7 million
Tsonga	4.35%	1.8 million
Swati	2.57%	1.0 million
Venda	2.22%	0.9 million
Ndebele	1.55%	0.6 million

The announcement that South Africa would officially recognise eleven languages and the entrenchment of language rights in the transitional Constitution were welcomed as improvements on a past situation in which only English and Afrikaans were recognised and there were no language rights entrenched in the Constitution.

Languages as discrete entities: the boundaries metaphor and Occam's Razor principle

According to Fardon and Furniss (1994),

> [i]n the process of interaction between state and citizens particular speech forms get converted by the state into languages; they become reified as social facts which are mutually exclusive.

The creation of mutually exclusive speech forms gives rise to a way of thinking about language which can be neatly captured by the boundaries metaphor. The boundaries metaphor is based on the assumption that speech forms fall into separate boxes in spite of the fact that one can walk from the southernmost tip of South Africa to the northernmost point without being able to identify a specific point where one language ends and another begins.

> The imposition of determinate linguistic boundaries on speech forms is typical of a top-down approach to language (starting from the assumption of the existence of diverse languages). The discourse of boundaries is also typical of language planning approaches which address language problems in terms of national, international, continental and intercontinental relations (Fardon and Furniss 1994: 3)

Paradoxically, in Africa and indeed even more so in South Africa, the boundaries conceptualisation of language which creates insiders and outsiders is also typical of colonialist and neo-apartheid discourses on language. Le Page and Tabournet-Keller (1982), citing a Bantu linguist, argue that the "existence of separate labelled (African) languages is a British innovation expedited by the work of Clement Doke and other like-minded linguists" with a dualist orientation to issues about language. It is linguists who decided to elevate Hurutse at the expense of other dialects in forming standard Tswana. They sought to divide the Sotho in the North from their cousins in the South using language as a dividing instrument. The point I am trying to make here is that in some situations the 'bounded' notion of language violates Occam's Razor principle because it results in a creation of more 'languages' than would be necessary.

The 'boxing' of African speech forms into different languages is reinforced by state, legal and educational pressures. In South Africa when children enter school, they have a mother tongue assigned to them even though the language may be as alien to them as English (Street 1993: 35). The essence of the point Street is making is that the speech forms most African children encounter during their primary socialisation are so radically different from the ones they encounter at school, even in situations in which they are supposed to be receiving instruction through their mother tongue, that I would like to argue that they are receiving the benefit of step-tongue (see Gupta 1994) and not mother tongue instruction. One way in which the drift between the language of primary socialisation and the language in step-tongue instruction could be restrained is through a process of restandardisation. The restandardisation would mean that the speech forms used as media of instruction would begin to resemble more closely those used in local communities in which the children live. This would require a liberation from the 'boxing' of speech forms.

One of the sociolinguistic consequences of a top-down perspective about language is its reification arising from a separation of language from its users, as is demonstrated by the entrenchment of language rights in the constitution as opposed to the rights of the language users. One also seriously doubts the extent to which the language rights of all the speakers of the eleven official languages can be said to be honoured, if the Constitution in which those rights are entrenched, is available in English and Afrikaans only.

The entrenchment of these eleven languages in the South African Constitution has had the effect of conflating language and standardisation: all eleven are codes which for one reason or other have already been standardised. Such an announcement creates the impression that the complex relationship between language and dialect has been fixed. Experience from other parts of Africa has demonstrated that such fixing cannot be easily achieved. Bamgbose (1994) cites an interesting example which supports the dynamic nature of the relationship between languages and dialects. Using examples drawn from Ghana, he shows that the differences in dialects between Twi and Fante which were magnified in the immediate post-independent period (Ghana obtained its independence from Britain in 1957) to the status of separate languages are now being considerably downplayed, concomitantly reducing the number of languages which Ghana has 37 years after independence.

The converse also applies. The Efik-lbibio dialect cluster in Nigeria has been accepted for years as one language, for all practical purposes, with Efik as the literary form of the language. The position is now being reversed and lbibio is more and more being emphasised as a separate language. The trend is likely to be intensified with the creation of a new state in 1997 in which the lbibio form the dominant group (Bamgbose 1994: 34).

The upshot of the argument is that the number of languages which a country officially recognises is not ultimately significant, because speech forms may change their status as separate languages to dialects of the same language (or vice versa) over the course of time. The Ghana example illustrates a situation in which differences between boundaries are downplayed, whereas in Nigeria the differences are magnified.

The list and the map as discursive conventions in the boundaries metaphor
The list and the linguistic atlas are the two main ways in which the boundaries metaphor is presented.

The list
After the speech forms have been converted into discrete boxes, a demographic process is then set in motion. In the demographic process the number of speakers of each of the boxes is counted. A list is then presented reflecting the number of mother tongue speakers of each of the various languages. Implicit in the listing strategy is a view of the relative strength of each language partially dependent upon the number of mother tongue speakers of that particular language. There are two main limitations to the listing strategy. One of the limitations is peculiar to South Africa and another is more universal. The demographic data for users of African languages in South Africa is notoriously unreliable. The data on the number of speakers were gleaned from aerial photographs in 1980 rather than the result of comprehensive surveys. The listing strategy also fails to take into account that simply enumerating mother tongue speakers of each box (language) may not be adequate. As Derive and Derive (1986: 45) remind us, frequency of usage of the languages may be just as important as the number of speakers; if not even more important.

The linguistic atlas
Another discursive practice whose conventions for the representation of language are influenced by the boundaries metaphor is the linguistic atlas. The map shows how speakers of different languages are geographically distributed and consequently language becomes **objectified spatially**. Because the map 'orders' language in a two-dimensional space, the reader has to appeal to other sociolinguistic processes in order to understand why certain speech forms are regarded as an instance of a language and not a dialect and vice versa. Furthermore, language maps are hard pressed to represent any area in terms of more than one salient language. Thus, for instance in some maps a large part of the Western Cape is represented in terms of Afrikaans only, while in the urban areas there are clearly a large number of other

languages spoken in addition to Afrikaans. The discourse of the language map tends to perpetuate a myth of monolingualism when multilingualism might be the norm.

Discourse of the Pan South African Language Board

Another group whose principles of talking about language are closely related to those of the linguistic atlas is the Pan South African Board. The linguistic map distributes languages geographically, but the Pan South African board distributes them functionally according to the role and purposes the languages are to play in the various sectors. In other words, the discourse conventions of the linguistic map are concerned with geographic location, while the Pan South African Language Board concerns itself with sectoral location.

In spite of the importance attached to functional location by the Pan South African Language Board, the Board does not officially recognise the role played by Fanakalo in South African mines, nor is it likely to do so. In my view, a recognition of the importance of Fanakalo would have rehabilitated its image and begun the process of dispensing with the apartheid and colonialist baggage the language carries. This would create the possibility of raising its status and consequently setting in motion a series of processes which would subsequently lead to its elaboration and standardisation. Unfortunately, the Pan South African Board is too bureaucratic in its thinking to adopt such a revolutionary policy. As Latin (1992) suggests, it would take a populist government keen on gaining and consolidating political capital to recognise speech forms such as Fanakalo since they are held in painful disregard by bureaucrats and in some cases even by those who speak them.

Perhaps the distinction between a geographical and sectoral division of languages is inevitable because as Whitley (1974) insists it might always be necessary to make choices at different levels, even within a single institution, e.g. the educational or legal system. It may not be prudent to opt for a unilingual solution because "it is always necessary to be aware of differential function and of the presence of variable domains ... Efficiency is not necessarily always achieved by uniformity, rather by sympathetic understanding of complex demands and dynamic uncertainty" (Davies 1986: 8). Thus, for instance, English and Afrikaans may have a similar distribution in South Africa since they are both used as media of instruction in tertiary education. The differences may, however, be of scope and extent, since English has a much wider distribution than Afrikaans.

Language frontiers
Another type of metaphoric description of language which is radically different from the boundaries metaphor and the listing and linguistic atlas conventions, which are associated with the boundaries metaphor, is the frontiers metaphor. The frontiers metaphor is strongly influenced by microethnographic research, particularly the work of Gumperz 1971; Le Page and Tabouret-Keller 1989, etc. Microethnographic approaches prioritise local-level language practices, arguing that discourses which discuss language as discrete and more or less given misrepresent the sociolinguistic situation on the ground. Thus, for Le Page the language or languages an individual uses cannot be determined by her geographical location, but by the identity which she seeks to project at any individual moment.

Giddens (1991) uses the phrase "the reflexive project of the self" to deny the existence of a fixed identity and, by extension, a fixed bounded language. Within a perspective which places emphasis on local practices, identity is interactionally accomplished and since individuals engage in different communicative acts, their identity is consequently a variable one.

In terms of a microethnographic perspective, language and language boundaries are permeable and therefore language should be seen as interpenetrable hence the appropriacy of the frontiers metaphor. Research within the frontiers metaphor tradition emphasises how, in spite of the large number of languages cited within the boundaries tradition, it is rare to find any extended conversations within a single language. "Conversations drift into and out of particular languages as the subject and register seem to require" (Fardon and Furniss 1994: 14), making it difficult in some cases to determine in which language the conversation occurred because the languages are in a state of semi-permanent mixture. Language is therefore construed to be a multilayered and interconnected chain offering a range of options in terms of registers and styles, depending on how the user seeks to align herself to her changing circumstances.

This permanent mixture is creating conditions which favour the creolisation of African speech forms. It is interesting that the creolisation of African languages is occurring without the languages having gone through a precreole stage. This situation challenges the view that a creole necessarily has to have its origins in a pidgin. However, the situation of a creole without a preceding pidgin is not unique to South Africa; it has also been reported in Reunion. Baker and Corne (1982) demonstrate that a creole was established in Reunion without a pidgin emerging, because of the presence of a large proportion of white French native speakers.

Because the frontiers metaphor is sensitive to local language practices, the information it provides would be invaluable in addressing the "step-tongue syndrome" because it provides insight into true community usage.

The commodification of language

The third and last type of metaphor which I would like to explore in relation to language is the one which has its origins in the world of commerce, i.e. the commodification metaphor. The discourse of acquisitional planning discusses language in terms of a commodity. The commodification of language manifests itself most clearly in the domain of second and foreign language learning and teaching (Coulmas 1992). Fairclough (1992: 206) succinctly describes the commodification of language as the "process whereby social domains and institutions, whose concern is not producing commodities in the narrow economic sense of goods for sale, come nevertheless to be organised and conceptualised in terms of commodity production, distribution and consumption." The commodification of language has been taken to its most extreme extent by the British Council in its promotion of English language. The Director General of the British Council, John Hanson CBE, describes teaching as an industry in the 1992/3 British Council annual report:

> The global spread of the English language is fundamental to Britain's trade, culture and development. English Language Teaching (ELT) is therefore one of the main pillars of the Council's overseas operations. It is closely integrated with other elements of our work, particularly the promotion of British arts and education, and is a significant element of Britain's aid programme in many Third World countries. It also brings major earnings to British publishers and suppliers of E.L.T. materials.

The commodification of English is unlike the commodification of African languages in South Africa. Whereas the commodification of English is promoted by a British institution manned largely by the British, the commodification of African languages is a European project seeking to promote African languages by making knowledge of an African language a strong recommendation for a job.

The commodification reflects the extent to which discursive practices about language have come to be dominated by the world of economics. The impact of the process of commodification is felt in two ways. First, language learners are constructed as clients or customers who may opt to buy one or more of the eleven commodities. The commodification of language conjures up a sociolinguistic situation in which languages are in competition and not in a complementary relationship with each other.

Second, if the eleven languages in South Africa are seen as commodities in competition with one another, the competition is unfortunately not an equal one. For example, if all the eleven official languages as constructed in the boundaries metaphor were to function as media of instruction (pushing aside the step-tongue phenomenon), materials would have to be provided in each of the individual languages. Provision of these materials is very expensive and requires a high degree of expertise. Hard economic realities mean that governments have to rely heavily on commercial publishers. "Unfortunately, because economies of scale dictate that publishers invest in instructional materials for languages with relatively large numbers of speakers, it means that languages with relatively few speakers may not receive fair treatment" (Makoni, 1993: 17). This may perpetuate a situation inherited from the apartheid era in which some languages are accorded fewer resources than others, a form of linguistic racism which Phillipson aptly (if emotively) describes as 'lingualism'.

Central to the commodification of language is the notion of the market value of language. In this type of discourse the idea that language is a commodity is seen as justifiable because acquiring a second foreign language is costly both to the individual and society. In the South African context, as pointed out earlier, knowledge of an African language is seen as economically exploitable because it is linked to provision of jobs, as the following advertisement illustrates:

> SABC Radio News has three vacancies for experienced reporters in its Johannesburg news office.
>
> Two of the posts will go to Sesotho-speaking reporters, although an ability to speak several South African lang-

uages will in all cases be an advantage. We are looking for energetic people with drive and enthusiasm, lively curiosity and a good news sense. Applicants must be prepared to work odd hours. A driver's licence and typing skills are essential. Radio experience, a good broadcasting voice and computer literacy could all be advantageous.

In the Western Cape, if the educational system cannot successfully meet the demands for African languages, a niche would be created for the private entrepreneur. Demands for African languages are likely to lead to more people wanting to learn them. This has, what Coulmas calls, a "snowball" effect because the more people learn a particular language, the more useful it becomes; and the more useful it becomes, the more people want to learn it. In the South African context another argument may also have to be used: as opportunities for learning particular languages were formerly so few and so unsatisfactory, the desire has accumulated. Both teachers and learners are benefiting from arrears. The number of people learning a language is, however, not a perfect criterion of the value of that language to a community. For instance, there are a large number of students learning Latin at the University of the Western Cape because it is a preequisite for legal training.

The metaphor of a language also has some in-built self contradiction. On the one hand, language is commodified through dictionaries and grammar books which objectify and reify the vocabulary of a language by turning it into potential material resources. On the other hand, language is an intangible commodity. When a student pays to learn a language, the teacher does not diminish his resources by teaching .

Marketing South African languages - Marketing a new South Africa

There are some interesting parallels between the way African languages are being marketed and the way English is being marketed in the former Eastern European countries. In the former Eastern European countries, English is being marketed as the language which facilitates democracy, free markets, etc. In South Africa, African languages are being marketed as the languages which facilitate integration into a new democratic South Africa. In both cases learning either English or an African language is projected as a symbolic acceptance of a new era. The languages are being marketed not for some "undefined communicative purposes", but because they are a reflection of specific ideological positions (Phillipson and Skutnabb-Kangas 1994).

Conclusion
In this paper, I have tried to explore three different ways of talking about language, arguing that the manner in which language is constructed depends on the manner in which we talk about it. I have also argued that there is tension between a "bounded" conception of language and one which places emphasis on local practices (the frontiers metaphor). I have concluded the paper by demonstrating how the discourses about language are not only influenced by state apparatus, but by the world of commerce as well.

Bibliography
Baker, P. and Corne, C. (1982). *Isle De France Creole.*
    Ann Arbor: Karoma.
Bamgbose, A. (1994). "Pride and prejudice in multilingualism and development" In R. Fardon and G. Furniss (Eds): *African Languages, Development and the State.* London: Routledge, pp.33-44.
Coulmas, F. (1992). *Language and the Economy.* Oxford: Blackwell.
Davies, A. (Ed). (1986). *Language in Education in Africa.*
    `Seminar Proceedings at the Centre of African Studies, University of Edinburgh.* Edinburgh: Centre of African Studies, University of Edinburgh.

Derive, J. and M.J. Derive (1992). "Francophonie et practique linguistique en Cote d'Ivoire" In Ngalasso, N.M. and A. Ricard (Eds). *Des langues et des états,* Paris: Katthala. (Politique Africaine, 23)

Fardon, R and G. Furniss (Eds). (1994). *African Languages, Development and the State.* London: Routledge.

Fairclough, N. (1992). *Discourse and Social Change.* Cambridge: Polity Press.

Giddens, A. (1991). *Modernity and Self-Identity: Self and Society in the Late Modern Age*, Cambridge: Polity.

Gupta, A.F. (1994). *The Step-Tongue. Children's English in Singapore.* Clevedon: Multilingual Matters.

Hanson, J. (1993). "The British Council is committed to action" In *The British Council Annual Report and Accounts, 1992/93.*

Laitin, D. (1992). *Language Repertoires and State Construction in Africa.* Cambridge: Cambridge University Press.

Le Page, R.B. and A. Taboiret-Keller (1985). *Acts of Identity.* Cambridge: Cambridg University Press.

Makoni, S. (1993). "The futility of being held captive by language policy issues in South African applied linguistics" *Per Linguam*, 12: 12-21.

Phillipson, R. (1992). *Linguistic Imperialism.* Cambridge: Cambridge Univeristy Press.

Phillipson, R. and T. Skutnabb-Kangas (1994). "English, panacea or pandemic" *Sociolinguistica. Special issue on English Only.*

Routh, H.V. (1941). *The Diffusion of English Culture Outside England.* Cambridge: Cambridge University Press.

Whitley, W. (Ed.). (1974). *Language in Kenya.* Oxford: Oxford University Press.

V

Colonial linguistics and the invention of language
(with Cristine G. Severo[1] and Ashraf Abdelhay)

1. Introduction

The aim of this chapter is to contribute to the large and profitable debate about how language practice and policy have been historically shaped by local contexts. Our focus here is on colonial linguistics in the context of Africa. We problematise the historical and political processes of language invention in the colonial contexts. This means that we do not assume languages as natural or a prior reality but, rather, as a product of social practice. We consider colonial linguistics as a contemporary approach that has revisited colonial narratives on the political role played by language in colonising processes. This means taking into account not only the Age of Discovery, but also the current reconfigured and redesigned colonial and colonising power relations. We interrogate the way that scholarship on language policy has traditionally faced the relationship between colonisation and language.

---

[1] Cristine Severo would like to acknowledge the financial support of the Brazilian National Council for Scientific and Technological Development.

Even though language policy is seen as a modern discipline that arose along with reflections on the relationship between language, 'developing' nations and the emergence of new independent nations in Africa during the 1960s and 1970s, we consider that issues that entail coloniality and language are not sufficiently addressed. Examples include the generic, homogeneous and top-down use of the term 'colonial' to cover complex, ambivalent and heterogeneous colonised and ex-colonised realities through the use of broad categories, such as 'colonial policy', 'colonial expansion', 'post-colonial indigenous language', 'colonial language', 'colonial area', 'colonial power' and 'colonial world', among others, to cover local contexts.

Colonial linguistics is an interpretive perspective that inspects the role that linguistics plays in the construction of specific cultural stereotypes for non-Western individuals and societies. As a programme, colonial linguistics endorses a critical attitude that intends to deconstruct the taken-for-grantedness of language: the concept of 'language' is not treated as a given but, rather, as a problem to be understood through historical and critical enquiries (Warnke and Stoltz 2013: 471). Further, language practice is intimately linked with other wider socio-political phenomena and forces. Although the mainstream (formalised) theory of language reduces language to the 'informative function' of communicating abstract propositions and ideas (language as a 'neutral' means of communication), colonial linguistics focuses on the ideological (or indexical) functions that language use is socially oriented to serve. It tries to understand how cultural politics is conducted through the terrain of language, including how language is used as a proxy to articulate 'extra-linguistic' concerns in settings shaped by unequal power relations, such as colonial contexts (Abdelhay and Makoni 2018; Abdelhay, Eljak, Mugaddam and Makoni 2016; Suleiman 2013).

Colonial linguistics endorses a conflict perspective to understand how macro-scale structures of domination are discursively enacted, appropriated and transformed at the microscale of social interaction. It focuses on the semiotic strategies of identity construction in its all-observable dimensions (Irvine and Gal 2000). Further, colonial linguistics views the canonical formulation of 'language' (as a self-contained entity with a name, e.g. English, French, German) as a political invention, a product of and a resource for the construction of projects of belonging. Generally speaking, the very idea of 'discrete' and 'countable' languages is a modernist construction by orthographic literacy and standardisation procedures to achieve specific socio-economic ends. It is in this sense that language and literacy are instruments of social control and inequality because they are elements of the machinery of modern governmentality (Blommaert and Rampton 2011). Collins (2006: 251) argued, "Orthographies (systems of inscription) are never neutral phenomena. They are instead often the object of sharp controversy over the best (i.e. the most authentic or scientific) way to represent a given language."

The effect of the European colonial text-artefactualisation of local communicative styles (turning languages into 'portable things') is profound: it has created an artificial (mis)representation of socially layered multilingual geographies (Blommaert 2008; Errington 2008; Irvine and Gal 2000; Makoni and Pennycook 2007; Said 1978). Modernist ideologies of language also have led to the emergence of 'discourses of language endangerment' (Duchêne and Heller 2007) and 'language anxiety' (Abdelhay and Makoni 2018). The moment that we try to look at Africa from a non-enumerating ideology, we may have a different epistemological version of reality.

The (colonial) monoglot ideology of language (Silverstein 1996) also has shaped the way that we view Africa through school literacy. In this ideology, Africa and illiteracy are synonyms. This observation should not in any way imply that Africa lacked any pre-colonial literacy traditions; on the contrary, there had always been 'indigenous' literacy practices in Africa (see

Abdelhay, Juffermans and Asfahan 2014). The word 'indigeneity', however, should not invariably be taken to mean 'non-Western' because in some African contexts, such as Sudan, Eurocentric discourses on identity and language operated precisely through what was promoted as 'local' (Abdelhay et al. 2016). As part of this complex of resources, writing is no longer considered a secondary mirror of speech but, rather, a discursive action with serious effects. The task here, then, is to understand how writing as a technology is exploited by colonial missionary linguists to create social semiotic boundaries that, through institutional acts of regimentation, are naturalised and thus converted into 'natural facts'.

As we show in our analytic commentary on the (post-colonial) context of Sudan, the result of the colonial language-planning practices is that script choices are ideological because they implicate issues that are not necessarily purely 'linguistic' (or 'informative'). The observation that the language–theology link is a product of a particular ideological enterprise of language is a case in point. Consequently, (post)colonial debates about orthography and script that are, in principle, debates about socio-political concerns articulated on the terrain of language have some roots in colonial language (educational) policies and practices. Colonial language-planning practices left a socio-linguistic infrastructure that is largely incorporated and integrated into the post-colonial systems of civil service and education in Africa (Bassiouney 2009).

In other words, in contexts of struggle, linguistic choices are converted into metadiscursive statements about spatial and cultural identities. As we see in the case of Sudan, an effect of the colonial missionary regime of language is that Latin script is readily and indexically correlated with Christianity and Western rationalism, while Arabic script is associated with Islam and Eastern traditionalism (Abdelhay, B. Makoni, S. Makoni and Mugaddam 2011). One of the consequences of these observations is that terms such as 'vernacular', 'local language', 'indigenous language' and 'mother tongue' are not part of the 'natural order of things' but, rather, are part of the 'colonial order of things'. Methodologically, to understand the discourses on/about language in Africa, we need to inspect the 'natural history' (Silverstein and Urban 1996) of these discourses by integrating them into the wider socio-political universes within which they were constructed and through which they were naturalised.

In light of the above discussion, we organise our chapter into two sections. First, we consider British colonisation and its effects on Sudan's linguistic contexts. Second, we consider Portuguese colonisation and the Brazilian linguistic contexts. We aim at problematising the concept of language in both colonial contexts, pointing out the political and ideological linguistic frameworks that underlie local language policy and planning.

In general terms, we conclude that the outcomes of a comparative perspective of colonial policies in Sudan and Brazil are the following: (i) while Sudan can be considered a highly divided country, a mosaic of constructed tribal units, Brazil has been invented as a fairly monolingual country; (ii) such realities are aligned to different colonial histories – while Sudan has gone through a process of independence from British politics, Brazil gained its independence at the beginning of the 19th century from Portuguese colonisation; (iii) British and Portuguese colonisations operated differently in terms of language policy; (iv) South America's process of decolonisation should be seen in relation to several independence struggles that occurred in America in the 19th century, while Sudan's independence should be seen in relation to a broader African movement in the 20th century; and (v) while slavery played a key role in Brazilian colonisation, linking Brazil and Africa in specific ways, in Sudan the invention of tribes and indigenous languages integrated a racial and colonial politics.

2. The British colonial linguistics and the villagisation of identities in Sudan

Sudan, like the rest of the nation states in Africa, was formed through various historical forces. One such force is the British colonial system of governance (nominally known as the Anglo-Egyptian rule or Condominium 1898–1956). In this section, we focus on the key British colonial linguistic practices in Sudan, paying special attention to the goal-oriented policies of inventing self-contained villagised and indigenous ethnolinguistic identities. The aim is to show how linguistics was implicated in the colonial production of racially enclosed tribal units in Sudan.

Post-independent language policies were deeply shaped by the British colonial discourses on language and subjectivity (Abdelhay et al. 2016; Sharkey 2008). The systematic British colonial division of the space that 'enregistered' (Agha 2007) specific forms of language with specific places was re-enacted through the very same post-colonial liberating policies that sought to undo this colonial regime of discursive governance. Through the brutal implementation of divide-and-rule policies, such as the 'Southern Policy' (officially declared in a 1930 memorandum), the British colonial system restructured the already-existing cultural geography into the 'South' and the 'North' as socio-political indices of polarised identities, with the 'indigenous' ethnolinguistic identities as the unmarked reference in southern Sudan. The following excerpt embodies the key goal of the colonial Southern Policy:

> The policy of the Government in the Southern Sudan is to build up a series of self-contained racial or tribal units with structure and organisation based, to whatever extent the requirements of equity and good government permit, upon *indigenous* customs, traditional usage, and beliefs … Apart from the fact that the restriction of Arabic is an essential feature of the general scheme it must not be forgotten that Arabic, being neither the language of the gov-

erning nor the governed, will progressively deteriorate. The type of Arabic at present spoken provides signal proof of this. It cannot be used as a means of communication on anything but the most simple matters, and only if it were first unlearned and then relearned in a less crude form and adopted as the language of instruction in the schools could it fulfill the growing requirements of the future. The local vernaculars and English, on the other hand, will in every case be the language of one of the two parties conversing and one party will therefore always be improving the other. (1930 Memorandum on Southern Policy, as cited in Abdel-Rahim 1965: 20–23, emphasis ours)

Before commenting on how the above policy was implemented, we should note that another British colonial policy in Sudan with the same goal (to construct anti-Arab-Islamic indigenous ethnolinguistic identities) is known as the 'Nuba Policy' and was embedded in a 1931 memorandum formulated by A. J. Gillan (then-Governor of Kordofan and later Civil Secretary) (for a detailed discussion, see Abdelhay 2010). The memorandum was titled 'Some Aspects of Nuba Administration'. The goal of this colonial policy was literally the invention of a 'Nuba race' as a self-contained entity. The following excerpt embodies this key goal of the colonial Nuba Policy:

> How many reasonably well informed outsiders are there who realise that there is no 'Nuba' tribe or race, but an as yet unknown number of entirely different stocks, of different cultures, religions and stages of civilisation, speaking perhaps as many as ten entirely different languages and some fifty dialects more or less mutually unintelligible? It is these factors that in broad outline constitute half the 'Nuba Problem' in as far as it concerns native administration and indigenous culture, the other

half being their contiguity with the Arab. If we were dealing with one solid and separate pagan race there might still be a problem, but its solution would be comparatively simple and would not be urgent. We should only have to isolate it within a metaphorical wall and deal with it at our convenience. (Gillan 1931: 6)

What is worth noting here is that, as the above excerpt indicates, there was no 'Nuba tribe or race' in the way imagined by the British colonial system, and, thus, the task was to invent it, using the Western binary system of metaphorical imagination (urban versus tribal identities). Before the colonial policy intervention, there were cross-cultural interactions among the individuals and the groups in the area, and, thus, the boundaries were intersectionally fluid and dynamic. The above Nuba Policy was designed precisely to tribalise identities (anchoring identities to places), using the strategy of villagisation. The result would be, we contend, a colonially created version of multilingualism (urban Arabic-speaking Muslims versus tribal/indigenous pagan /Christian Nubas). The romanticising strategy of villagisation is formulated by Gillan (1931: 28) in the following terms:

Instead of an enlarged town the present plan is to institute a Nuba village, or series of villages, within easy distance of the town, where the Nuba, whether permanently or temporarily, can live as far as possible under tribal conditions ... I am convinced that villagisation rather than urbanisation is the policy to adopt.

Most important, the colonial education system was partly responsible for the implementation of this Nuba Policy of villagisation. In a 'Memorandum on Educational Policy in the Nuba Pagan Area', the Secretary for Education and Health, J. G. Matthew (cited in Gillan 1931: vi), stated more generally: "The wish of the Government is that Nubas should develop on their own lines and be assisted to build up self-contained racial or tribal units." The missionaries' educational practices also played a significant role in the implementation of the colonial Southern Policy. One powerful strategy here was the organisation of colonial conferences, such as the Rejaf Language Conference of 1928, which intended to create 'language groups' in Southern Sudan. Through processes of codification, the linguistic resources in the southern part were developed and formalised by the Christian missionaries into clearly demarcated 'proper languages'. Again, this effected an official image of linguistic pluralism or multilingualism as naturally demarcated homogeneities. The use of the language-planning instruments did not aim solely to improve communicative efficiency but, most importantly, to articulate by proxy extra-linguistic concerns embedded in the larger socio-political project of the colonial government (to divide the space along ethnic and theological lines).

The colonial regime of language systematically correlated Arabic with Islam, and, in effect, Arabic became indexically 'the' carrier of a dangerous discourse. The task orientation of the colonial Southern Policy in its discursive dimension was, thus, to stamp out Arabic from the southern region. A similar policy of cultural control was exercised in the North, where artificial tribal boundaries were constructed, and the tribal chiefs were allocated state powers, such as the collection of taxes. The product of these colonial policies was that the 'South' and the 'North' have become physically and ideologically self-contained social spaces, and the identities anchored to these spaces have become, in effect, particularly through postcolonial practices of social reproduction, part of the 'natural order of things'.

A few years before independence, however, the colonial regime changed its separatist policy and decided to reunite the now-perceived two antagonistic parts. The ideological seeds of one of the longest civil conflicts in Africa, however, had already been firmly planted, and the colonial discourse on 'villagised' and 'indigenous' languages and identities was later (re)appropriated in post-colonial policies and peace agreements.

Following independence, the central governments in the North tried to implement a monoglot ideology of normalisation to reverse the effects of the separatist colonial policies. Arabicisation and Islamisation of the South were the key features of this monoglot scheme, and the state's brutal violence was readily employed to silence the southern resistance (see Nyombe 1997). The north–south relations erupted into a fully-fledged armed conflict that was eventually ended by the Comprehensive Peace Agreement 2005–2011 (CPA 2005), which is also famously known as the Naivasha Peace Agreement (as it is signed in Naivasha in Kenya). It is this peace accord that recognised the right of the Southerners to self-determination through a referendum. Most significantly, it deploys the epithet 'indigenous languages', which is intertextual with the British colonial discourse sketched above. The CPA contained a significant language policy that is known as Naivasha language policy (Abdelhay et al. 2011). This language policy stipulates (CPA 2005: 26–27):

(1) All the indigenous languages are national languages which shall be respected, developed and promoted;
(2) The Arabic language is the widely spoken national language in the Sudan;
(3) Arabic, as a major language at the national level, and English shall be the official working languages of National Government business and languages of instruction for higher education;
(4) In addition to Arabic and English, the legislature of any sub-national level of government may adopt any other national language(s) as additional official working language(s) at its level; and
(5) The use of either language [Arabic or English] at any level of government or education shall not be discriminated against.

Notwithstanding the colonial cultural and political production of 'tribalised/villagised' identities in Sudan, it would be grossly misleading to imply that southern elites or resistance leaders bought into this colonial discourse on language and identity. For example, the late southern leader John Garang's post-colonial project of the 'New Sudan' was intended to dismantle these colonially inherited boundaries, which were blindly embraced as the basis of their cultural politics by a significant number of post-colonial governments:

> The history of the Sudanese people from time immemorial has been the struggle of the masses of the people against internal and external oppression. The oppressor has time and again employed various policies and methods of destroying or weakening the just struggle of our people, including the most notorious policy of 'divide and rule'. To this end the oppressor has divided the Sudanese people into Northerners and Southerners; Westerners and Easterners, Halfawin and the so-called Awlad et Balad who have hitherto wielded political power in Khartoum; while in the South, people have been politicized along tribal lines resulting in such ridiculous slogans as 'Dinka Unity', 'Great Equatoria', 'Bari Speakers', 'Luo Unity' and so forth. The oppressor has also divided us into Muslims and Christians, and into Arabs and Africans. (Garang 1992: 19)

The first step taken by Garang (1992) toward (relative) emancipation from the domination of this (post)colonial discourse was to recognise that these 'homogenised identities' are a product of the historical order of things: we are a product of history and not nature.

3. African-Brazilian Portuguese as a political invention

In this chapter, we avoid reproducing the ideological concepts of languages as compartmentalised, fragmented, labelled and hierarchical units; rather, we assume the conception of language as a political and historical invention (Errington 2008; Irvine 2008; Makoni & Pennycook 2007; Phillipson 1992; Severo & Makoni 2015). Such a political and critical perspective aims at problematising both colonial and modern linguistics' 'politics of truth' (Foucault 1977) by resisting the 'compartmentalisation principle' (Harris 1984), which includes avoiding the reproduction of certain concepts of language, such as the mother language, second language, foreign language and language proficiency, among others. Such concepts are reinforced by ideological ideas, such as the commoditisation of languages, which feed the economic industry of language teaching and testing (Duchêne and Heller 2011), language as natural national flags (Rajagopalan 2013) and the belief in a direct two-way relationship between language and identity (Severo and Makoni 2015).

We recognise that the process of Africanisation of Western languages, by inventing such categories as African-American English or African-Brazilian Portuguese, are ideologically and discursively constituted and, therefore, should be submitted to ongoing review and critical inquiries. We argue that a cross-Atlantic invention of African languages does not necessarily have to correspond with either historical or contemporary descriptions of African languages. (Makoni and Pennycook 2005: 152).

Brazil is a former Portuguese colony and a member of the Community of Portuguese Speaking Countries (CPLP), along with Cape Verde, Mozambique, Angola, East Timor and others. The Portuguese empire created interconnectedness among different geopolitical contexts, mainly Brazil and African countries. These associations were facilitated by a colonial landscape shaped, to a large extent, by language, religion and the military. The relationship between Brazil and Africa can be analysed from the following perspectives: (i) the politics of slavery in the colonial era, between the 16th and 19th centuries; (ii) the religious invention of 'Christian-lects' by Jesuits (Severo and

Makoni 2015); and (iii) the modern and nationalistic politics that invented Brazilian Portuguese as different from European Portuguese, mainly from the 19th century onwards. Such aspects, which are discussed below, contributed to the invention of African-Brazilian Portuguese.

The politics of slavery was a defining feature of Portuguese colonial practice: "Portugal was the first European nation to initiate slavery in Africa, and was the last to abolish it" (Lobban 1995: 25). By way of example, the current estimate of the historical presence of Africans in Brazil is that, between 1550 and 1855, four million enslaved Africans were brought in from different regions, such as Guinea and Costa de Mina in the 16th century, and Congo and Angola in the 17th and 18th centuries. Brazil became the largest destination, outside Africa, of Africans in the colonial era. Linguists classify populations brought to Brazil into two large 'ethnolinguistic groups': the Sudanese from West Africa, and the Bantu from equatorial and tropical Africa.

When comparing Catholic missionary work in Brazil with that in African countries, some important differences can be noticed. In Brazil, the relationship established between the Jesuits and the so-called indigenous people and the African people was different, as the Church condemned indigenous slavery but validated, for economic reasons, African enslavement: "African slavery was approved for reasons of subsistence of the mission"[2] (Hoornaert, Azzi, Der Grijp and Brod 1983: 259). The enslaved African people under control of the missionaries were called 'dos Santos' (Saints), a surname that became common in Brazil, although a few Jesuits, such as Luís do Grã, disapproved of African slavery (Sá 2007). We notice a colonial hierarchical system that classified indigenous groups as different from Africans in Brazil. Whereas the former were capable of being 'civilised' and 'Christianised', the latter had their 'enslaved

---

[2] *"a escravidão africana foi aprovada por motivos de subsistência da missão."*

condition' justified by the rhetorical construction of slavery as a consequence of original sin.

Such rhetoric, together with other elements, helped to construct an image of black African people as coin-men:

> The noun 'Black' is the name given to the product resulting from the process by which people of African cultures are transformed into living minerals ... the plantation in the New World is the place of its smelting, and Europe, the place of its conversion into currency.[3] (Mbembe 2014: 78)

Christianity and slavery were deeply connected, as only enslaved Africans who had become Christians could be sold and only Christians could acquire them: "The Church in Angola derived much of its income by instructing and baptizing the enslaved" (Isichei 1995: 71). Antonio Vieira, a famous Jesuit in Brazil in the 17th century, gave several sermons that justified African slavery of black people:

> Christ naked, and you naked; Christ starving, and you hungry; Christ completely mistreated, and you as well. The irons, the prisons, the lashes, the wounds, the offensive names - all these elements make part of your imitation, which, if accompanied by patience, will also bring the merit of the martyrdom. (Vieira 1958: 261–262).[4]

---

[3] *"O substantivo 'Negro' é depois o nome que se dá ao produto resultante do processo pelo qual as pessoas de origem africana são transformadas em mineral vivo ... a plantação no Novo Mundo é o lugar de sua fundição, e a Europa, o lugar de sua conversão em moeda."*

[4] *"Cristo despido, e vós despidos; Cristo sem comer, e vós faminhos; Cristo em tudo maltratado, e vós maltratados em tudo. Os ferros, as prisões, os açoites, as chagas, os nomes afrontosos, de tudo isso se compõe a vossa imitação, que, se for acompanhada de paciência, também terá merecimento de martírio."*

The extent to which the Portuguese religion contributed to the invention of languages can be exemplified by the first Bible translation to Portuguese in Africa and the first book written in a Bantu language by a Portuguese priest in Brazil in 1642 (Spencer 1974). In addition, "By 1957 there were probably between 8,000 and 10,000 missionaries, Catholic and Protestant, in Sub-Sahara Africa ... Perhaps fifty to sixty percent of missionaries in Africa can claim some competence in an African language" (Welmers 1974: 192–193). The contact between Christian missionaries and the so-called indigenous and African peoples in colonial Brazil and Africa produced the emergence of 'Christian-lects' (Severo and Makoni 2015), a set of linguistic discourses and instruments that were used as a mechanism of domination by framing people and languages in specific ways, inventing and naming local languages, inventing ethnolinguistic categories that overlapped ethnicity and language using literacy as a framework to define what counts as language, and translating several Christian discourses to 'local' languages that, in turn, helped to frame the 'local' in specific ways (Irvine and Gal 2000; Makoni and Pennycook 2007; Phillipson 1992). Currently, missionaries' interest in languages is evident in the description, analysis, writing and teaching of languages, as we can notice in the intense work of Bible translation to 'local' languages by the Summer Institute of Linguistics.

The contemporary linguistic discourse reinforces African-Brazilian Portuguese as a fragmentary conception of language in which pieces of languages, such as lexicon, syntax and prosodic elements, shape a shredded language. African-Brazilian Portuguese, from a linguistic perspective, would be the result of an 'irregular process of acquisition' of Portuguese by Africans (Lucchesi, Baxter and Ribeiro 2009). We problematise the framework of 'languages in contact', as it reproduces the Eurocentric concept of compartmentalised languages. We argue that the Creolist perspective, widely used as a framework to explain the colonial languages, is not neutral but, rather, produces ideological effects on the way that 'local' languages have been framed since the colonial era. Curiously, linguist Hugo Schuchardt (1842–1927) used Portuguese colonial contact with 'local languages' to frame the Creolist perspective.

The creation of modern Brazil started in the mid-19th century, when independence from Portugal took place. Several Brazilian intellectuals, who had studied in Portugal, helped to create the idea of a Brazilian nation. Nation and nationalism are discursively invented, as stated by Said (1989: 221): "Nationalism, resurgent or new, fastens on narratives for structuring, assimilating, or excluding one or another version of history." In Brazil, nationalism constructed specific discourses on the role played by African languages and discourses by bringing together several elements, such as the ideas of Brazilianness, Afro-Brazilianness, regionalism, oral culture, popular culture, rurality and illiteracy. We argue that the historical invention of African-Brazilian Portuguese is related to how discourses on Africa and African people were politically shaped in Brazil, reinforcing and naturalising the asymmetrical and racist as well as excluding power relations in Brazilian society. Some examples of power relations include:

(i) the idea of Brazil being a racial democracy as a result of *Lusotropicalism*, an ideological explication given by the Brazilian sociologist Gilberto Freire (1933) for Brazilian identity formation that would have included the harmonic fusion/miscegenation of the Portuguese and Africans originating the *Mestizo*; in linguistic terms, 'African-Brazilian Portuguese' would reproduce the ideological perspective of fusion and miscegenation, erasing important power relations that involve different symbolic worlds;

(ii) the emergence of dialectology as a way of framing Brazilian linguistic diversity in the 19th century by accommodating linguistic and discursive diversity into a national discourse. Language difference would be labelled as 'linguistic regionalism'. Such discourse submitted African languages and discourses to regional interpretation that worked under a national umbrella (Severo 2015). Dialectology helped to regionalise languages by overlapping geography and language. It is not by chance that dialectology was at the service of legitimation and delimitation of national boundaries: "The 19th century saw the triumph of the nation-state, on the one hand, and the establishment of the dialect geography, on the other" (Auer 2002: 4);

(iii) the construction of a framework that considers African linguistic influences in Brazilian Portuguese from the perspective of 'popular tradition'. Several intellectuals, inscribed into the Modernist Brazilian Movement, proposed the influence of African rhythm, beat, dance and prosody into Brazilian music and orality. Mario de Andrade, a famous Brazilian Modernist (1891–1945), proposed that Brazilian music "comes from strange sources: the Amerindian in small percentage; the African in a much larger percentage; the Portuguese in vast percentage"[5] (Andrade 1928: 7). The idea of a miscegenated cultural and racial society would reverberate into a miscegenated musical expression. In 1932, anthropologist and psychiatrist Nina Rodrigues published the book *Os Africanos no Brasil* (Africans in Brazil) in which he describes the structural linguistic influence of African languages, Yoruba and Bantu, on Brazilian Portuguese. Rodrigues also mentions the African rhythm of these languages and uses a linguistic perspective that divides languages into pieces and codifies them into a script model, reinforcing the 'politics of orthography' (Irvine 2008). We argue that 'popular culture' and 'folklore' are discursive and political constructions that must be contextualised socio-historically (Canclini 2008; Hall 1996). In general, the concept of popular culture, on the one hand, is linked to political projects that seek to assimilate the 'people' within discourses of government and control and, on the other hand, is taken as a sign of ideological struggles and tensions; and

---

[5] *"provém de fontes estranhas: a ameríndia em porcentagem pequena; a africana em porcentagem bem maior; a portuguesa em porcentagem vasta."*

(iv) the modern Brazilian linguistics that has operated with two broad and polarised categories to define Portuguese language in Brazil: popular Portuguese (Vernacular Portuguese, which includes African-Brazilian Portuguese) and Standard Portuguese. This apparently dichotomous view has sometimes been represented by a more fluid one, in which, at one end, there is rural African-Brazilian Portuguese and, at the other end, urban Standard Portuguese. Between these two extremes are rural dialects and non-standard urban speeches (Petter and Oliveira 2011). The categories of rurality and urbanity, instead of regionalism, become central to the definition of what counts as African-Brazilian Portuguese in contemporary discourses. An example of the complicated relationship between rurality and orality versus urbanity and literacy is the political role that literacy plays in reinforcing colonial categories. The Brazilian census of 2010 shows that the highest rate of illiteracy is located in north-east Brazil, especially in rural areas, where a heterogeneous group of people live and which includes *quilombolas*, field workers, farmers, extractivists, landless fishermen and people of the forest; among these groups, the elderly, black and 'indigenous' women stand out with the lowest literacy rates (Peres 2011).

We argue that the ideology of literacy helps to ratify a negative social representation of local people as well as validates differentiation between urban and rural. If, for example, we consider *quilombola* communities, which were constituted as a result of political struggles of former enslaved African people in Brazil to legitimise lands and gain the freedom to exercise their practices, values and beliefs (Leite 2000), the illiteracy rate helps to label communicative practices as discredited, especially in the face of a state whose administrative machinery is based on writing. Writing is effectively a 'technology of power' (Foucault 1977). In addition, the invention of African-Brazilian Portuguese as a rural and isolated variety of Portuguese helps to reinforce the complicated myth of authenticity, a political discourse invented and reinforced by intellectuals and political agents, as what is considered authentic may vary if we consider the local perspective (Makoni and Meinhof 2004).

Finally, by understanding the complex way that African experiences were historically and politically framed by several official and institutional discourses in Brazil, we may problematise power relations inscribed into miscegenated and creolised discourses. We agree with Hall (1996: 225) that: "The ways in which black people, black experiences, were positioned and subjected in the dominant regimes of representation were the effects of a critical exercise of cultural power and normalisation". In this sense, we claim for a critical perspective of language that allows us to destabilise the 'limits of the right to govern' (Foucault 1977).

4. Final remarks

The aim of this chapter was to highlight the political and social importance of a critical perspective toward the relationship between colonial experience and language policy by showing how language in colonised contexts works as an arena of ideological and material struggles, such as in the cases of Sudan and Brazil. In both cases, language viewed as a self-enclosed system of communication is a historical invention that helped to shape power relations through a politics of division, classification, hierarchisation and differentiation. There are points of convergence and difference between the Portuguese and the British colonial systems in Brazil and Sudan, respectively. In both cases, language is cued with a monoglot function to create local ethnic identities to achieve extra-linguistic ends. For example, both the Portuguese and the British systems of colonial control constructed 'local' ethnolinguistic identities through the processes of Africanisation and villagisation in contrast to the Western forms of identity (in Brazil) and Arabic language and Islam (in Sudan).

Again, in both cases, the colonial regimes used 'language' as a geopolitical discursive strategy of 'divide into blocks and rule'. Brazilian Portuguese was created as distinct from Portuguese proper and it was converted into a diacritic of a particular Africanised identity. A similar observation obtains in the case of Sudan where the British colonial policy was intended to invent a 'pure' Nuba race or uncontaminated southern identities (pure and uncontaminated by the effects of Islam and Arabic). In both cases, ideas of north, south, literacy, urbanity, rurality and tribalism are political ideas that, under the linguistic umbrella of Arabic, English or African-Brazilian Portuguese, helped to reinforce power relations, social asymmetry and social injustice.

However, there are points of difference between the two forms of colonial systems of domination. In the case of Brazil, the whole state was imagined as a single, homogeneous and stable socio-linguistic space, whereas in Sudan, the objective was to produce multiple homogeneities (tribal units). Unlike the British colonial practice in Sudan, slavery was the defining motive and feature of the Portuguese colonial rule. In an increasing context of global relations and intercultural encounters, we claim that the field of language policy and, importantly, its researchers should be sensitive to such issues, helping to avoid reproducing colonial ideologies and practices.

References

Abdelhay, A. (2010). "The politics of writing tribal identities in the Sudan: the case of the colonial Nuba Policy" *Journal of Multilingual and Multicultural Development* 31(2): 201–213.

Abdelhay, A., N. Eljak, A. R. Mugaddam and S. Makoni (2016). "The cultural politics of language in Sudan: against the racializing logic of language rights. *Journal of Multilingual and Multicultural Development* 38(4): 346–359.

Abdelhay, A., K. Juffermans and Y. Asfahan (2014). "African literacies: ideologies, scripts, education. In K. Juffermans, Y. Asfahan and A. Abdelhay (eds.), *African*

Literacy Ideologies, Scripts and Education (pp.1–62). Newcastle Upon Tyne: Cambridge Scholars Publishing.

Abdelhay, A. and S. Makoni (2018). "Arabic is under threat: language anxiety as a discourse on identity and conflict" In Y. Mendel and A. Al Najjar (eds.), *Language, Politics and Society in the Middle East: Essays in Honour of Yasir Suleiman*. Edinburgh: Edinburgh University Press.

Abdelhay, A., B. Makoni, S. Makoni and A. Mugaddam (2011). "The sociolinguistics of nationalism in the Sudan: the Arabicisation of politics and the politicisation of Arabic" *Current Issues in Language Planning* 12(4): 457–501.

Abdel-Rahim, M. (1965). *Fourteen Documents on the Problem of the Southern Sudan*. Khartoum, Sudan: Ministry of Foreign Affairs.

Agha, A. (2007). *Language and Social Relations*. Cambridge, UK: Cambridge University Press.

Andrade, M. (1928). *Ensaio Sobre a Música Brasileira*. Retrieved from http://www.ufrgs.br/cdrom/mandrade/ mandrade.pdf.

Auer, P. (2002). "The construction of linguistic borders and the linguistic construction of borders" In M. Filpulla, J. Klemola, M. Palander and E. Penttila (eds.), *Dialects Across Borders: Selected Papers from the 11th International Conference on Methods in Dialectology* (Methods XI) (pp. 3–30). Amsterdam: John Benjamins Publishing.

Bassiouney, R. (2009). *Arabic Sociolinguistics: Topics in Diglossia, Gender, Identity, and Politics*. Washington, DC: Georgetown University Press.

Blommaert, J. (2008). "Artefactual ideologies and the textual production of African languages" *Language & Communication* 28: 291–307.

Blommaert, J. and B. Rampton (2011). "Language and Super-diversity" *Diversities* 13(2): 1–21.

Canclini, N. (2008). "A encenação do popular" In N. Canclini, *Culturas Hibridas*. São Paulo: EDUSP.

Collins, J. (2006). "Literacy practices in sociocultural perspective" In K. Brown (ed.), *Encyclopaedia of Language and Linguistics* (pp. 246–255). Amsterdam: Elsevier.

Comprehensive Peace Agreement (CPA) between the Government of the Republic of Sudan and the Sudan's People's Liberation Movement/Sudan People's Liberation Army (2005). Retrieved from https://www.usip.org/sites/default/files/file/resources/collections/peace_agreements/power_sharing_05262004.pdf.

Duchêne, A. and M. Heller (eds.) (2007). *Discourses of Endangerment: Ideology and Interest in the Defence of Languages*. New York: Continuum.

Duchêne, A. and M. Heller (eds.) (2011). *Language in Late Capitalism: Pride and Profit*. New York: Routledge.

Errington, J. E. (2008). *Linguistics in a Colonial World: A Story of Language, Meaning, and Power*. Oxford: Blackwell.

Foucault, M. (1977). *A História da Sexualidade I: A Vontade de Saber* (13th edition). Rio de Janeiro: Graal.

Freire, G. (1933). *Casa-grande & Senzala: Formação da Família Brasileira Sob o Regime da Economia Patriarcal* (48th edition). São Paulo: Global.

Garang, J. (1992). *The Call for Democracy in Sudan* (2nd edition), edited by M. Khalid. London: Kegan Paul Int.

Gillan, J. A. (1931). *Some Aspects of Nuba Administration*. Sudan Government Memorandum No. 1.

Hall, S. (1996). Cultural Identity and Diaspora. In P. Mongia (ed.), *Contemporary Postcolonial Theory: A Reader* (pp. 222–237). London: Arnold.

Harris, R. (1984). "The Semiology of Textualisation" *Language Sciences* 6(2): 271–286.

Hoornaert, E., R. Azzi, K. Der Grijp and B. Brod (1983). *História da Igreja no Brasil: Ensaio e Interpretação a Partir do Povo* (3rd edition).BPetrópolis, Brazil: Edições Paulina.

Irvine, J. T. (2008). "Subjected Words: African Linguistics and

the colonial encounter" *Language & Communication* 28: 323–343.
Irvine, J. T. and S. Gal (2000). "Language ideology and linguistic differentiation" In P. V. Kroskrity (ed.), *Regimes of Language: Ideologies, Polities and Identities* (pp. 35–84). Santa Fe, NM: Advanced School Press.
Isichei, E. (1995). *A History of Christianity in Africa.* Lawrenceville, NJ: Africa World Press.
Leite, I. B. (2000). "Os Quilombos no Brasil: questões conceituais e normativas. *Etnográfica* IV(2): 333–335.
Lobban, R. (1995). *Cape Verde: Crioulo Colony to Independent Nation.* Boulder, CO: Westview.
Lucchesi, D., A. Baxter and I. Ribeiro (2009). *O Português Afro-Brasileiro.* Salvador, Portugal: EDUFBA.
Makoni, S. and U. Meinhof (2004). "Western perspectives in Applied Linguistics in Africa" *AILA Review* 17: 77–105.
Makoni, S. and A. Pennycook (2005). "Disinventing and (re)constituting languages" *Critical Inquiry in Language Studies: An International Journal* 2(3): 137–156.
Makoni, S. and A. Pennycook (eds.) (2007). *Disinventing and Reconstituting Languages.* Bristol: Multilingual Matters.
Mbembe, A. (2014). *Crítica da Razão Negra.* Lisbon: Antígona.
Nyombe, B. G. V. (1997). "Survival or extinction: the fate of the local languages of the southern Sudan" *International Journal of the Sociology of Language* 125: 99–130.
Peres, M. A. de C. (2011). "Velhice e analfabetismo, uma relação paradoxal: a exclusão educacional em contextos rurais da Região Nordeste" *Sociedade e Estado* 26(3): 631–661.
Petter, M. and M. S. Oliveira (2011). "Novas luzes sobre a descrição do Português Afro-Brasileiro" *Anais do Simpósio Mundial de Língua Portuguesa*, SIMELP. Macau: Universidade de Macau.
Phillipson, R. (1992). *Linguistic Imperialism.* Oxford: Oxford University Press.

Rajagopalan, K. (2013). "Política linguística: do que é que se trata, afinal?" In C. Nicolaides, K. Aparecido da Silva and R. Tilio (eds.), *Política e Políticas Linguísticas* (pp. 19–42). São Paulo: Pontes.

Rodrigues, R. Nina (1932). *Os Africanos no Brasil.* Brasília: Ed. da Universidade de Brasília.

Sá, I. dos G. (2007). "Ecclesiastical structures and religious action" In F. Bethencourt and D. R. Curto (eds.), *Portuguese Oceanis Expandio, 1400–1800* (pp. 255–282). New York: Cambridge.

Said, E. (1978). *Orientalism*. London: Routledge and Kegan Paul.

Said, E. (1989). "Representing the colonized: anthropology's interlocutors" *Critical Inquiry* 15, 2: 205–225.

Severo, C. G. (2015). "Língua Portuguesa como invenção histórica: Brasilidade, Africanidade e poder em tela" *Working Papers em Linguística* (Online) 16: 35–61.

Severo, C. G. and S. Makoni (2015). *Políticas Linguísticas Brasil-África: Por Uma Perspectiva Crítica*. Florianópolis, Brazil: Insular.

Sharkey, H. (2008). "Arab identity and ideology in Sudan: the politics of language, ethnicity, and race" *African Affairs* 107(426): 21–43.

Silverstein, M. (1996). "Monoglot "standard" in America: standardisation and metaphors of linguistic hegemony" In D. Brenneis and R. Macauley (eds.), *The Matrix of Language: Contemporary Linguistic Anthropology* (pp. 284–306). Boulder, CO: Westview Press.

Silverstein, M. and G. Urban (eds.) (1996). *Natural Histories of Discourse*. Chicago: University of Chicago Press.

Spencer, J. W. (1974). "Colonial language policies in Sub-Saharan Africa" In J. Fishman (ed.), *Advances in Language Planning* (pp. 163–176). The Hague: Mouton.

Suleiman, Y. (2013). *Arabic in the Fray: Language Ideology*

and Cultural Politics. Edinburgh: Edinburgh University Press.
Vieira, A. (1958). *Sermões*. São Paulo: Editora das Américas.
Warnke, I. H. and T. Stoltz (2013). "(Post-)Colonial Linguistics, or: What is the colonial in dominated colonial discourses? *Zeitschrift fur Semiotik* 35(3–4): 471–495.
Welmers, W. E. (1974). "Christian missions and language policies in Africa" In J. Fishman (ed.), *Advances in Language Planning* (pp. 191–204). The Hague: Mouton.

VI

When God is a linguist: missionary orthographies as a site of social differentiation and the technology of location
(with Ashraf Abdelhay and Busi Makoni)

1 Introduction

Research on colonial contexts has shown that choosing or developing writing systems for local vernaculars is an area of conflict between missionaries, on the one hand, and government officials and professional linguists, on the other. Although all writing conventions are part of sociocultural systems, it should be understood that writing is not merely a secondary reflection of speech. Rather, it is a symbolic resource with unique affordances for the construction of languages and projects of self-identification and, in some contexts, leads towards a 'tyranny of experts' (Easterly 2013 ; see Chapters 8, 12 and 10 of this book for discussions of other language-making processes[1]). Notably, in conflict-ridden contexts, language and script choices are metadiscursive statements about spatial and cultural identities, as evident, for example, in pre-2011 Sudan, where indexical

---

[1] The reference here is to the work in which this paper was first published: C. Weth & K. Juffermans (editors), *The Tyranny of Writing: Ideologies of the Written Word*. London: Bloomsbury Academic, 2017.

associations between a particular space/theology and language/ script (e.g. Muslim North vs. Christian South) are a product of the colonial missionary regimes of language (Abdelhay , Abu-Manga and Miller 2015 ; Abdelhay , Makoni and Makoni 2010). Just as script choices are statements of cultural identities, so, too, are orthographic choices, with their own cultural ramifications. Distinctions in orthographies project differentiated identities; hence, what constitutes the linguistic 'local' may vary, and consensus may be difficult to achieve about what is authentically local across social dimensions, such as ethnicity, gender and age.

Scripts are different instantiations of writing systems; for example, the Greek, Roman and Cyrillic alphabets, which stem from a common source, are distinct from orthographies, which use the same script in different ways. Scripts and orthographies share the two basic functions of spoken language: the instrumental and the symbolic. The former refers to the use of writing to convey propositional content, while the latter manipulates the resources of writing systems as a proxy for articulating sociopolitical considerations, such as the construction of social and political categories of identification (Suleiman 2013). In language-planning terms, corpus-planning measures, for instance, address the instrumental function by providing the necessary resources (e.g. orthographies, dictionaries, style guides) to improve communicative efficiency in a society. However, in contexts of sociopolitical domination and transformation, these linguistic resources cumulatively acquire a cultural load as markers of social distinction (Edwards 2009 ; Suleiman 2013).

As we see in the debates over script in British colonial Sudan, script choice is not a neutral corpus-planning endeavour but, rather, is deeply associated with theological and political issues to the extent that script choices are often oriented towards the production of binary, socially fragmented spaces of identification (e.g. North vs. South, Muslim vs. Christian, Arab vs. African). In contrast, status-planning decisions (e.g. selecting a national language) address the symbolic dimension of language. As such, both aspects of language planning are sociopolitically driven because they are goal-oriented (thus prescriptive) and are conducted in a historical context already structured through indexical relations of power and social conflict. In short, in colonial and postcolonial contexts, ideological debates about language and script choice are part and parcel of doing politics through culture (Blommaert 1999 ; Suleiman 2013).

Thus, this chapter is situated within the framework of colonial linguistics (Errington 2008; Makoni and Pennycook 2007). Colonial linguistics provides a robust analytic-interpretive framework for the study and critique of linguistics as a colonial enterprise implicated in the construction of a particular cultural representation of non-Western societies and individuals. As a research programme, colonial linguistics can be used as an analytical framework to investigate the nature of language in postcolonial contexts. In this chapter, we apply this framework to examine the history of vernacular construction in the context of the Anglo-Egyptian Sudan, with a specific focus on the Rejaf Language Conference of 1928 (RLC). The conference was held 9–14 April in Rejaf, a small town on the bank of the Nile in South Sudan. In analysing some aspects of the RLC report, we contend that the conference's outcome contributed to the construction of racial and regional differences and has significantly shaped the history of Sudan and South Sudan. We explore the discursive strategies utilized by the conference attendees to create social and political distinctions (cf. Makoni , Dube and Mashiri 2006; Makoni and Pennycook 2007; Meeuwis 2011; Seghers 2004).

In the second section of the chapter, we intend to, first, show that although one of the aims of this conference was to develop a common writing system for (presumably pre-existing) local languages for educational purposes, the choice of a unified orthographic system was a contested ideological act. The history of the choices made (e.g. between the Lepsius system and an

IPA-based orthography) shows that the objectified native people themselves were a point of struggle between competing systems of representation. In the third section of this chapter, we contextualize the RLC socio-historically. We critically examine the participants' contributions and interventions and their positioning. Our analysis is thematically selective in that we highlight the main contributions and points of contention that emerged as a response to the set agenda and frame through the lens of the tyranny of expertise (Easterly 2013). Our aim is to provide an understanding of how a dialogically constructed text within a particular locality is shaped by wider ideological, historical and sociopolitical agendas.

2 Social stratification in the Anglo-Egyptian Sudan (1899–1956)

Sudan was a British colony, although the colonial system was symbolically termed the Anglo-Egyptian Condominium (1899–1956). For socio-economic convenience, the Condominium initially governed the country as a united entity. The northern part was controlled with a particular 'regime of language' (Kroskrity 2000), in which Arabic and Islam were instituted as the official policies in the north, while other symbolic resources, including English, were scaled down. At the same time, Christian missionaries were allowed open access to the southern part of the country, which was conceptualized as pagan and as relatively underdeveloped compared to the northern part.

Shortly thereafter, however, the British colonial system changed its agenda and divided the country into two selfcontained spaces with antagonistic sociocultural systems: the Arabic-speaking Muslim North versus a vernacularized Christian South (with English as a lingua franca), who construed themselves as experts even of contexts with which they were rarely familiar. Although we concentrate on Sudan, such 'splittist' policies were the norm in British colonies and the differentiation of people along ethnic, linguistic and religious lines was seen, for example, in Nigeria (Muslim Northerners vs. Christian Southerners), India (Muslims vs. Hindus), Ceylon (Tamils vs. Sinhalese, see Chapter 7 in this book[2]) and Cyprus (Greek Cypriots vs. Turkish Cypriots) (Mazrui and Mazrui 1998).

The splittist policy in Sudan came to be known as the Southern Policy (1920–46). The 'special identity' of the North was recognized through administrative interventions, including the adoption of Friday as a public holiday, honouring of Muslim feasts and the adoption of Arabic as the official language (Miller 2003). As a result of these actions, Arabic was invested with prestige and power. Notwithstanding its orthographically well-harmonized status, the institutionalization of Arabic as a 'monoglot standard' (Silverstein 1996) in Sudan has its roots in the British colonial system. In effect, Arabic became a hegemonic ideology that enacted a relatively high social status, anchored to specific spaces within colonial and then postcolonial sociolinguistic regimes. This discursive image still ideologically mediates the geopolitical relations between Sudan and South Sudan.

In the South, in contrast, colonial rule was aided by Christian missionaries preoccupied with translation of the Bible into local idioms, intended to help 'build up a series of self-contained racial or tribal units' (see Abdel-Rahim 1965: 20-23). Coercive measures restricted the movement of Arabic-speaking 'Northerners' to the South and provided for the deportation of Arabic-speaking merchants and officers from the region (Abdelhay et al. 2011). The policy required top-down, discursive control of diversity (e.g. through official language educational policies) to construct a politically united, internally pluralized southern front, rooted in language and religion. This project also required the implementation of a distinctive Southern education system (a key vehicle of sociocultural reproduction; Bourdieu and Passeron 1977). To deal with the issue of linguistic standardization and unification of various orthographic conventions, the colonial government coordinated and funded the RLC.

---

[2] See footnote 1 above.

3 The RLC and the construction of ideological categories of interaction

Conferences were central to the method used by missionaries in their 'invention' of African languages, making Christianity and colonialism mutually constitutive (Fabian 1983). These conferences provided space for 'descriptive appropriation' (Fabian 1986: 10) of African languages.

Participants in the RLC were all either Christian mission representatives (e.g. American Mission, Church Missionary Society, Italian Catholic Mission, Africa Inland Mission) or colonial officials (e.g. from Sudan, Uganda, Belgian Congo; RLC 1928: 5). The key participants in the conference were the Secretary for Education and Health in the colonial administration J.G. Matthew who called the conference together and acted as its chair, Archdeacon Archibald Shaw of the Church Missionary Society and 'expert adviser' Diedrich Westermann, Director of the International Institute of African Languages and Cultures in London.

Not only were 'native voices' conspicuously absent, but also the inconsistency and contradictions of participants' positions were not foregrounded. The agenda of the conference, as articulated in the statement of objectives in the memorandum (dated 30 October 1927) by Secretary Matthew, contains the following items:

1. 'To draw up a classified list of languages and dialects spoken in the Southern Sudan.'
2. 'To make recommendations as to whether a system of group languages should be adopted for educational purposes and, if so, what languages would be selected as the group languages for the various areas. In this connection, the following considerations will arise: -
    a. Whether owing to their kinship two or more languages or dialects can share a single literature.
    b. Whether a local vernacular can be expanded, particu-

larly in the matter of borrowing words from foreign sources, to convey new meanings.
c. Whether any particular vernacular is worth adopting and developing on the grounds that there is a definite demand for education among the people speaking it.
d. To consider and report as to the adoption of a unified system of Orthography. It is suggested that the most practical means of attaining this end is to consider and report as to whether the Memorandum issued by the International Institute of African Languages and Cultures can be adopted with or without modification.'

3. 'To make proposals for co-operation in the production of textbooks, and the adoption of a skeleton grammar, reading books, and primers for general use.' (RLC 1928 : 4)

Matthew's memorandum, with its institutional authority, marks the active intervention of government in language-in-education planning, formerly the exclusive responsibility of the missionaries. It also uses key cultural metaphors, including 'languages', 'dialects', 'local vernacular' and 'literature', as self-evident concepts. In colonial linguistics, the distinction between these terms is based on an idealized version of writing, and, thus, this perspective confuses writing with speech (for which concepts like 'dialect' and 'vernacular' are appropriate). Metalinguistic categories, such as 'language' and 'dialect', as used in traditional Western philology, overlook potentially more appropriate meta-terms about language practices that emerge from non-Western contexts (for discussion of language ideologies, generally, see Blommaert 1999 ; Kroskrity 2000 ; Silverstein 1996). Language practices are a manifestation of the impact and influence of the tyranny of expertise.

The first objective of the RLC implies that languages and dialects pre-exist linguistic classification, and the technical task is 'to draw up a classified list'. The expectation of accurately capturing languages 'out there' elides that the terms being used in themselves create and invent languages (Makoni and Pennycook 2007), partly arbitrarily, partly culturally/ideologically and only partly empirically. In our view, analysis of collateral damage that arises from language policies (globally) is crucial but frequently overlooked even within colonial linguistics, as attention is restricted to (synchronic) textual analysis of policy statements rather than their historical trajectories and conditions.

The second objective signals that observed linguistic variation in the South was conceptualized negatively (e.g. 'whether any local particular vernacular is worth adopting and developing'). The system of group languages that the memorandum recommended for educational purposes and to manage linguistic diversity in the South constitutes an illegitimate simplification of polyglot contexts – religious and cultural as well as linguistic, with a major material sociopolitical consequence: a graphically scripted pluralism (group languages that are anchored to localities or formally demarcated missionary spheres of influence). Indeed, although the South is presently seen as multilingual, it is still constructed through colonial lenses as a single front against the Arabic-speaking North.

The memorandum also mentioned Westermann who made significant contributions to the colonial archives of non-Western languages and peoples but did so from the perspective of a particular linguistic ideology in the service of a particular theology. He already had been in the south of Sudan (August–November 1910) to study the Shilluk, including their language, a trip commissioned by the United Presbyterian Church of North America (Westermann and Hermann 1912: vii). The point is that the relationship between Western linguistics and theology in the colonial context is extensive (see Zimmermann and Kellermeier-Rehbein 2015).

3.1 Engineered absence of a perceived indigenous lingua franca in the South

The conference opened with a message from the Governor-General of the Sudan, read by Matthew, that stressed the significance of creating a unified system of orthography for pedagogic ends. The Governor-General noted a lack of consensus over how languages should be selected from 'the large number of dialects' (as distinct from those constructed or codified as standards). Graphic harmonization was presented as 'essential' for schooling, with the role of language as viewed in technical terms: Education could not be carried out without language, and language use in itself was a form of education; this was in contrast to 'dialects', which did not qualify as media of instruction. One consequence of this linguistic ideology, which is still very much present today, is that 'language education' is misleadingly reduced or restricted to the 'domain of the school', and the function of the education system becomes to make learners first 'unlearn' (or forget) their inherited knowledge about their culture's communicative forms and 'relearn' normative speech according to the school's legitimate language (Bourdieu 1991).

Matthew emphasized the need for 'a classified list of languages and dialects spoken in the Southern Sudan' (RLC 1928 : 8), noting that 'a preliminary list of languages and dialects and their distribution has been compiled from the replies to the questionnaire and other sources' (RLC 1928: 8). Regarding the basic principles for choosing a means of instruction, Matthew approvingly quoted the recommendations of the US-based Phelps-Stokes Commission's report *Education in East Africa*, developed during a tour of East Africa in 1924 at the request of missionary societies and with British government cooperation, based on the following considerations:

1. 'that every people have an inherent right to their Native tongue';
2. 'that the multiplicity of tongues shall not be such as to deve-

lop misunderstandings and distrust among people who should be friendly and co-operative';
3. 'that every group shall be able to communicate directly with those to whom the Government is entrusted'; and
4. 'that an increasing number of Native people shall know at least one of the languages of the civilized nations'

(RLC 1928: 9)

The Commission's recommendations for language education in Africa, which emerged from those considerations, were as follows:

1. 'The tribal language should be used in the lower elementary standards or grades';
2. 'A lingua franca of African origin should be introduced in the middle classes of the school if the area is occupied by large Native groups speaking diverse languages';
3. 'The language of the European nation in control should be taught in the upper standards'. (RLC 1928 : 9)

These principles thus create a hierarchy of linguistic resources that reflect users' social status, with European languages at the top and local languages at the bottom, or local, level. This reduction of education to a process of producing a limited number of Sudanese clerks who are moderately literate in European languages was needed to keep the colonial apparatus running, always reluctantly and pragmatically, as a necessary evil. This ambivalence was illustrated in White missionaries' treatment, in some ways, of native missionaries as equals and, yet, always as mediators between them and native communities and facilitators of White missionaries' proselytizing projects.

Thus, as seen above, linguistic diversity ('the multiplicity of tongues') was discursively correlated with 'misunderstanding' and lack of 'co-operative' interaction in terms of the Phelps-Stokes Commission's educational policy. This view stemmed from a denotational ideology of language: (Mis)understanding was attributed to a variety's intrinsic structure, not its social use.

Further, the evaluative metaphors with which Matthew (and the RLC) inter-textually aligned were invested with specific indexical values. Finally, the epistemological basis of Phelps-Stokes's education policy for Africa was 'naturalist' and 'essentialist' (e.g. the right to 'native tongues' was viewed as 'inherent', an ethnicizing ideology also implicit in the current mainstream theory of language rights). The teaching of European languages was to be restricted to 'upper standards' (high school), implying also that language was largely defined by its written form (an *Ausbau* view). This policy framework was intended to produce a select class of natives who were competent in colonial languages and who could enable colonial rule (see Hungwe 2007 ; Seghers 2004).

A third significant point is that the Phelps-Stokes Fund's philosophy of education was entirely racial in orientation, modelled on a version of social Darwinism predicated on the 'inferiority' of blacks. Seghers (2004: 463-464) stated that its policies were modelled on the conviction that 'education had to be "adapted" to the limited intellectual capacities of black men and limited possibilities of the "Negro world"'.

The Phelps-Stokes Fund's educational policy was trans-locally entextualized into guiding principles for the RLC and became a significant instrument for the creation and reproduction of unequal race relations between the South and the North and between the (entire) colony and the metropole. Further, the basis of the RLC's metadiscursive 'enumeration of forms', that is, languages and, through them, racial/tribal identities, in the South was unclear; Matthew himself admitted, 'there is little doubt that some of the tongues conventionally enumerated as separate languages are in reality local variants of a common form of speech, and that the names by which they are known are tribal rather than linguistic' (RLC 1928: 10). This process was, of course, repeated by European colonizers all over Africa; missionaries and officials were not simply 'discovering languages' (whether separate or grouped) but, rather, actively inventing them, using their own ideological definitions of what a language and its speakers should look like. The ways in which these Orientalizing self-image-creating strategies were grounded in a particular cultural world view determined the nature and goal of education policies.

For Matthew, management of linguistic diversity for the sake of education meant a reduction of 'the multiplicity of tongues by selecting one of the dialects as the basis of a literary medium for the whole group' (RLC 1928: 10). Inspired by the Phelps-Stokes Fund's policy that a lingua franca should be 'indigenous', he opposed pidgin Arabic, which he viewed as not of African origin, notwithstanding its prestige (in whatever '-lect') in the South. Thus, Matthew detemporalized Arabic by categorically denying it any communal functionality in the social biography of at least some southern districts. Thus, he believed, there was no need to teach or even develop a language of intercommunication for Southern Sudan at this stage.

To justify that Arabic was not a desired lingua franca in the South, Matthew stated that it was official policy 'that English should as soon as possible become the language of official correspondence in the Southern Sudan' (RLC 1928: 10). His statement also indicates that Arabic had indeed been the government's preferred lingua franca in the Southern Sudan before the issuing of the splittist Southern Policy. However, some RLC participants noted that, even if English were established as the official language, this would not warrant the eradication of Arabic from the South. Some speakers even suggested Bangala, Swahili or English as a lingua franca for the South, despite the fears of others that if English were used, it would 'almost certainly degenerate to something approaching the pidgin English of the West Coast' (RLC 1928: 22–23).

Thus, neither the missionaries, nor (yet) the government, was interested in the imposition of English on the South but, rather, in the artificial, abstract categories of 'group languages' and standardized versions of 'local vernaculars'. Matthew's view that it was not necessary to develop a lingua franca in the South became the consensus, as did the corresponding rejection of Arabic. Most importantly, the instrument of language grouping and the planned replacement of Arabic by English effectively resulted in the engineered absence of a lingua franca perceived as 'indigenous' in the Southern Sudan. Further, because the locals were managed physically and linguistically as self-contained tribal units, the possibility of an inter-ethnic communicative language, apart from Arabic, was not likely to emerge bottom-up.

3.2 A Eurocentric design for African languages

Matthew suggested three main options for developing a unified orthography, all based on the Roman alphabets: (1) a phonemically based alphabet with certain distinctions disregarded and left to the reader to recognize from the context; (2) a Roman alphabet with dots and diacritical marks (the Lepsius system); or (3) an International Phonetic Alphabet (IPA)-based orthography adapted for African languages with new additional letters and shapes such as ɛ and ɔ for vowels and ŋ and ɣ for consonants which came to be known as the 'Africa Alphabet'. The choice between the latter two was a site of intense conflict, broadly speaking, between missionaries, on the one hand, and professional linguists, on the other (although the reality of the opinion was more nuanced). The system that used diacritics had been designed by Egyptologist Karl Richard Lepsius (1810–84) at the request of some British missionary societies (RLC 1928) and the IPA-based system was developed by the International Institute of African Languages and Cultures.

Regarding educational materials, Matthew said:

We should, I think, not only consider the educational requirements of the native, but also the needs of the Government Official and the Missionary studying a vernacular. We urgently require a series of grammars and vocabularies to assist the ever-increasing number of those wishing to learn native languages. (RLC 1928: 12)

Ideological discussions about African languages and their framing were conducted among missionaries and colonial officials, with Africans shut out. This was emphasized in the final resolution of the conference, which suggests that existing standardized 'local vernaculars' in the South were viewed as artificial inventions within this colonial economy of education. The very construct of the 'native speaker' in the local sociolinguistic regime was provided mainly by European Christian missionaries; consequently, the output of meta-pragmatic activities would be technically conceived versions of 'mother tongues' for 'natives', anchored to specific localities. In other words, the RLC was a mechanism for the cultural production not only of languages but also of places with specific indexical configurations (a similar strategy was applied in the Nuba Mountains; see Abdelhay 2010; Salih 1990).

The group languages that were believed to exist prior to the conference were (1) Dinka Nuer; (2) Shilluk Acholi; (3) Bari Latuko; (4) the Bahr el Ghazal languages, excluding Dinka; and (5) Madi (RLC 1928: 14). Each language group was assigned a committee, and a committee was created to produce textbooks. We contend, however, that these languages and language-groups were brought into existence by the very institutional naming practices performed by missionaries and by officials such as Matthew. The tendency to use terms such as *Shilluk-Acholi* and *Bari-Latuko* indicates an implicit assumption of the validity of these ethno-linguistic categories.

Westermann addressed the conference on the topic of orthography and noted that a unified system was possible because 'we are dealing with a definite group of African languages' that were interrelated and spoken in a circumscribed geographical area (RLC 1928: 14). He made the following significant statement:

> The script we want to introduce is intended for use by Africans, not for use by Europeans who want to learn the language. We should keep this constantly in mind. It means that we should try to look at the problems from the African's point of view, not from our own. His difficulties are not always ours; we are to remember that our views on orthography are always hopelessly restricted by the historical orthography of our European languages. (RLC 1928: 14–15)

The statement above appears to be an outright rejection of Matthew's argument that the European idea of the literary language should be a frame of reference for the development of written African languages. It also was a rejection of Matthew's view that the primary intended users of the orthographies should be government officials and missionaries and that the guiding principle should be the actual structure of the African linguistic forms, complemented by perspectives of their actual users (i.e. Africans). Westermann defended the use of the African-adapted Roman script in the phonetic (IPA) version. The principle of the phonetic script, he explained, was to use new letter forms instead of diacritical marks to express sounds, including those salient to group languages in the Southern Sudan (RLC 1928: 15).

Further, Westermann urged participants to agree on the main orthographic features, which would be applicable to most of the language groups, before proceeding in their respective committees to discuss in detail the sound system of the relevant language. Most of the proposals were accepted by the delegates; however, representation of long/short vowels stirred controversy. The epistemic conflict became heated when Matthew asked the conference to accept the memorandum and to avoid diacritical marks (the Lepsius system). At this point, Archdeacon Shaw and Bishop Kitching, also of the Church Missionary Society, who supported the diacritical system, 'both felt it to be inconsistent on the part of those responsible for the memorandum to object to diacritical marks below the letter while using such symbols as the glottal stop, the mark indicating nasalisation' (RLC 1928: 19). Matthew responded that the memorandum 'had already been adopted in other parts of Africa, and it was to be feared that by rejecting it we would fall behind the times'; he suggested that, 'if this Conference found itself unable to adopt it, it should have weighty reasons for such a refusal' (RLC 1928: 19–20).

Shaw responded, stating, 'The alphabet was based on that of the International Phonetic Association; that is to say, on an alphabet produced by scientists for the use of scientists, in which Greek letters were used and other letters were turned upside down' (RLC 1928 : 20). He added that Christian missions already had long been conscious of the importance of creating a uniform writing system for African languages and that the IPA-based system was impractical in the African context. He explained that, at the Arua Conference in 1918, the missions had carefully studied the IPA system and rejected it, instead developing a simple diacritical system. The Arua system did not allow the use of letter combinations to represent a single sound, as the IPA-based one did; that role was instead filled by diacritical marks, not defined as letters. Shaw argued that 'the Natives' themselves had pointed out the necessity of certain diacritical marks; in addition, he noted, 'the Arua system could easily be used on typewriters' (RLC 1928: 21). He disputed the calligraphy of the letters, which he said should be suitable not just for scientists but also for ordinary people. The missionaries, whose fundamental goal was to Christianize Africans, were strongly against the use of modern European educational materials and products, including the IPA (Meeuwis 2011); Shaw rejected Westermann's argument that the IPA had been a success in West Africa. In response, Westermann agreed that the IPA system was not specifically developed for Africans but rejected Shaw's claim that it was suitable only for scientists.

Both linguists and missionaries, however, assumed that, as European experts, they knew more about African languages than did the speakers of those languages, a perceived gap magnified by the power differential: the more powerful parties were secure in the reputation of expertise that was, to some degree, unearned, while the less powerful were not recognized as well informed, even on their own experiences and culture – a type of 'authority reversal' (Gilmour 2006: 111). Stated differently, knowledge possessed by colonial powers was privileged, and indigenous knowledge was devalued as, in Foucault's (1980 : 81) term, 'subjugated knowledge'. Nonetheless, missionary reactions were ambivalent: In some cases, they treated local languages as tribal and used them as evidence of the rudimentary status of African languages, while, in other cases, they were impressed by the 'genius of native languages'. Whether African languages were treated as primitive or sophisticated was largely a function of the missionaries' racial attitudes (that varied from time to time even within individual missionaries).

Generally, African languages were categorized and perceived in ways that legitimated some of their attendant knowledge-systems and illegitimated others. The categorization also exposed an intriguing distinction between experts and local informants; the corpus-planning activities of the missionaries, who included some professional linguists, effected a carefully controlled form of meta-language and meta-discourse through which they were (self-)defined not just as preachers but also as 'language experts'. In the same way, as missionaries in their practice 'imagined' language through writing, they institutionalized what 'counted as language'. Suleiman (2013: 20) stated that 'script and script variations are effective ways of making visible

– of constructing – differences between languages', which may include these languages.

3.3 Ideologies in the production of textbooks and grammars

Matthew suggested that the medium of instruction at the primary education level should be the vernacular, with English used for higher education. This suggestion adhered to the Phelps-Stokes Fund's stance. It was generally noted that, in certain districts in the Southern Sudan, Arabic was used not just as a lingua franca but also as 'the vernacular of a community' (RLC 1928: 23). Although some diehards, such as Father Crazzolara of the Italian Catholic Mission in Sudan, denounced the Arabic teaching school that operated at Malakal, Matthew defended the use of Arabic in some districts if it was the community's vernacular, while Shaw emphasized the necessity of using Arabic as a medium of instruction in primary schools in districts where Arabic was spoken as a mother tongue. A number of speakers emphasized the importance of using Roman script for the teaching of Arabic in these schools (RLC 1928: 26). Thus, it could be noted that the proposed condition (to Romanize it under a new orthographic system) for the use of Arabic as a medium of instruction in places where it was the vernacular was to 'de-Arabicize' it, that is, to decouple it from Arabs, Islam and Arabic script. The participants also discussed the role of mission authorities in the selection and design of teaching materials. Matthew suggested that it be resolved that 'the Education Department should work in collaboration with the Mission authorities' (RLC 1928: 24), and Shaw noted that missionary societies in England might help with costs.

In relation to the proposal on alphabets for particular languages, there was considerable discussion of the use of diacritics. Although Shaw's request to use < ṭ >, < ḍ > and < ṇ > instead of < th >, < dh > and < nh > respectively, had been accepted by the Shilluk Committee and the Nuer part of the Dinka-Nuer Committee, it was ultimately defeated, despite the fact that, as Shaw pointed out, 'if the orthography now recommended were adopted, Missions would be put to a considerable expense in printing new text-books which they could not easily meet' (RLC 1928: 28–29); he again brought up the possibility of government help.

As these discussions and concerns show, a complex system of participation at various scales was involved in the material production, circulation and uptake (eg local, regional, global) of educational materials in local languages, and the economic assistance from missions for their production was not unconditional. Westermann and Hillelson expressed the need for people with linguistic expertise in African phonetics, linguistics and anthropology for producing materials 'for the use of Missionaries and Officials' (RLC 1928: 24).

3.4 The RLC resolutions: Language grouping and the construction of a pluralistic society

The first resolution recommended that Westermann should be asked to draw up a revised list of group languages taking into consideration the information gathered and any other sources of information. The second resolution stated:

> The Conference is of the opinion that the following group languages are suitable for development and that the preparation of text-books in these languages for use in the elementary vernacular schools of the Southern Sudan is a matter of urgency:
>
> Dinka. Bari.
> Nuer. Latuko.
> Shilluk. Zande.
>
> Acholi and Madi are in a different category, as only a very small proportion of the people speaking these languages live in the Sudan. Literature for these lang-

uages must therefore be drawn from elsewhere. It is recognized that in sub-grade schools the use of other vernaculars may still be necessary. Colloquial Arabic in Roman script will also be required in certain communities where the use of no other vernacular is practicable. (RLC 1928: 30)

The third resolution recommended the adoption of a memorandum of the International Institute of African Languages and Cultures on 'Practical Orthography of African Languages'. The final resolution of the RLC adopted the Text-book Committee's recommendations: (1) consultation with a 'specialist' regarding a 'model grammar' for use in preparation of vernacular grammars; (2) collaboration between the Education Department and mission societies on selection and compilation of textbooks; (3) attention to cost-effective and convenient printing; and (4) availability of books for study of 'important group languages' by missionaries and government offi cials (RLC 1928: 31).

Aside from its immediate practical goals, the production of these textual artefacts was a necessary meta-pragmatic activity to circulate and stabilize the constructed categories of languages and language-groups. Because these historically established language groupings were the basis of the local education system, the official pluralistic image of the society was itself an artefact of the colonial imagination, an observation that we also might make of multiculturalism in general, as a product of institutional intervention and engineered division of social and material labour.

4 Conclusion
In this chapter, we have examined the language-making processes established by the RLC, a key colonial language-making event in the Anglo-Egyptian Sudan, and have sketched their wider historical context. The conference served as a political platform for the deployment, enumeration and definition of

metalinguistic categories for the analysis of African languages. The philosophical basis of native education policy broadly reflected the Phelps-Stokes Fund's philosophy of racial categorization. Using colonial linguistics as an analytic framework, we argued that these language constructs did not pre-date the colonial social practices that produced them and that their intended audience was primarily missions and government officials. The 'native voice' was strikingly absent. Arabic was rejected in its functional role as a lingua franca, yet accepted in a Romanized version as a medium of instruction in primary schools in districts where it was the vernacular. This shows how script choice can be manipulated to create or efface social and spatial differences.

The creation of language groups tied to localities and the Romanization of Arabic and/or its broad replacement with English as a medium of inter-ethnic communication effected the planned absence of an indigenous lingua franca for the Southern Sudan, even as artefactualizing processes of group language and language group formation produced a pluralistic image of society. The process of choosing a unifying orthographic system was a contested ideological action. The discursive contest between the theological and social-scientific linguistic discourses served as a vehicle for their complementary and contradictory effects, dialectically operant within a supposedly coherent regime of sociolinguistic governance.

The chapter showed that, during the colonial period in Sudan, languages were developed by missionaries, often supported by professional linguists, to the planned exclusion of locals themselves capturing the effects of foreign expertise. Two methodological–epistemological questions about the nature of 'the local voice' or 'local resistance' that should be raised are: (1) What linguistic practices pre-dated the colonial linguistic policy intervention, and how do they complicate or contradict the Western representation of what should count as 'local' in this context? and (2) What happens if we locate similar strands of resistance in our own time and find evidence of (dis)continuities with the colonial moment? In other words, because the resistant local is inaccessible in this colonial archive, how do we find it; how do we reconstruct it; and what is the status of its traditions and theories today? This leads to a third question: (3) Is local resistance 'then' legible 'now'? These questions boil down to the nature of the non-Western cultural discourses within which the local voice is constructed. To recover this voice, we need to reconstruct the entire discursive bundle. But this leads to further questions: Is this possible, given the absence of (unregulated) non-Western materials from this period? How do we avoid the essentializing trap of relying inappropriately on our own ideological discourses, moulding the local body into an image that conforms with our own preconceptions? To what extent does this reconstituted local under Western Orientalizing epistemology still remain local? And local for whom? What is the discursive tradition within which this reconstruction is performed? And who does it? In whose interest?

Our work has contemporary relevance in several ways. First, the dynamics of intellectualization and the politics of epistemological power relations are evident in contemporary scholarship, where global hegemonic power still imposes its understanding of phenomena that indigenes are expected to accept regardless of their contextual (in)appropriateness. To understand the ideological positions of missionary linguistic work, it must be contextualized within the larger trajectory of (African) missionary linguistics as well as the exigencies of individual contexts.

A lack of awareness of the politics and history of the notion of indigenous languages has led scholars to argue for the promotion of indigenous languages as such, not taking full consideration that some of them, particularly written languages, are simplified and denatured versions of the languages they purport to represent. Elites who promote indigenous languages must take into account the importance of this rewriting. Clarifying the roles of African elites is complicated due to the multiple and inconsistent uses of the term 'elites' in African contexts (Makoni and Meinhof 2003), and it is important to emphasize its contingency and contested nature in African scholarship (and indeed that of indigenous scholarship as well). The questions that we have asked here are intended to liven up the debate on the local voice in colonial Africa – inevitably a discursive construction; otherwise, the entire project of African cultural studies would immediately collapse.

Acknowledgements
This chapter builds on work we have published in the *Journal of African Cultural Studies* (Abdelhay et al. 2016). The analysis was by and large based on an analysis of the original Rejaf Language Conference Report. We would like to thank the reviewers and editors for their useful comments on the early draft of this chapter.

References
Abdelhay, Ashraf (2010), "The politics of writing tribal identities in the Sudan: the case of the colonial Nuba policy" *Journal of Multilingual and Multicultural Development* , 31(2): 201–13 .
Abdelhay, Ashraf, Abu-Manga Al-min and Catherine Miller (2015), "Language policy and planning in the Sudan: from local vernaculars to national languages" in *Multidimentional Change in Sudan (1989-2011): Reshaping Livelihoods, Conflicts and Identities* , edited by Barbara Casciarri , Munzoul Assal and Francois Ireton , 263–80, Oxford : Berghahn Books .
Abdelhay, Ashraf, Busi Makoni and Sinfree Makoni (2010), "The politics of linguistic indigenousness in Sudan ', in *Sudan's Wars and Peace Agreements*, edited by Jay Spaulding, Stephanie Beswick, Carolyn Fluehr-Lobban

and Richard Lobban, Jr., 17–56, Newcastle-upon-Tyne: Cambridge Scholars.

Abdelhay, Ashraf, Busi Makoni and Sinfree Makoni (2016), "The colonial linguistics of governance in Sudan: The Rejaf Language Conference, 1928" *Journal of African Cultural Studies*, 28(3): 343–58.

Abdel-Rahim, Al-Lamin M. (1965), *Fourteen Documents on the Problem of the Southern Sudan*, Khartoum, Sudan: Ministry of Foreign Affairs.

Blommaert, Jan, ed. (1999), *Language Ideological Debates*, Berlin: Mouton de Gruyter.

Blommaert, Jan (2008), "Artefactual ideologies and the textual production of African languages" *Language and Communication*, 28(4): 291–307.

Bourdieu, Pierre (1991), *Language and Symbolic Power*, edited by John Thompson, translated by Gino Raymond and Matthew Adamson, Cambridge: Polity Press.

Bourdieu, Pierre & Jean-Claude Passeron (1977), *Reproduction in Education, Society and Culture*, London: Sage.

Edwards, John (2009), *Language and Identity*, Cambridge: Cambridge University Press.

Errington, Joseph (2008), *Linguistics in a Colonial World: A Story of Language, Meaning, and Power*, Oxford: Blackwell.

Easterly, William (2013), *The Tyranny of Experts: Economists, Dictators, and the Forgotten Rights of the Poor*, New York: Basic.

Fabian, Johannes (1983), "Missions and the colonization of African languages: developments in the former Belgian Congo", *Canadian Journal of African Studies/Revue Canadienne des Etudes Africaines*, 17(2): 165–87.

Fabian, Johannes (1986), *Language and Colonial Power: The Appropriation of Swahili in the Former Belgian Congo 1880-1938*, Berkeley: University of California Press.

Foucault, Michelle (1980), *Power/Knowledge: Selected*

Interviews and Other Writings, 1972–1977, edited by Colin Gordon, translated by Colin Gordon, Leo Marshal, John Mepham and Kate Soper, New York: Pantheon.

Gilmour, Rachelle (2006), *Grammars of Colonialism,* Houndmills: Palgrave Macmillan.

Hungwe, Kedmon (2007), "Language policy in Zimbabwean education: historical antecedents and contemporary issues" *Compare: A Journal of Comparative and International Education,* 37(2): 135–49.

Kroskrity, Paul (ed). (2000), *Regimes of Language: Ideologies, Polities, and Identities,* Oxford: James Currey.

Makoni, Sinfree, Busi Dube and Pedzisai Mashiri (2006), "Zimbabwe colonial and postcolonial language policy practices" *Current Issues in Language Planning,* 7(4): 377–414.

Makoni, Sinfree and Ulrike Meinhof (2003), "Introducing Applied Linguistics in Africa" *AILA Review* 16: 1–13.

Makoni, Sinfree and Alastair Pennycook (eds) (2007), *Disinventing and Reconstituting Languages,* Clevedon : Multilingual Matters.

Mazrui, Ali and Alamin M. Mazrui (1998), *The Power of Babel: Language & Governance in the African Experience.* Oxford: James Currey; Chicago: University of Chicago Press .

Meeuwis, Michael (2011), "The origins of Belgian colonial language policies in the Congo" *Language Matters,* 42(2): 190–206 .

Miller, Catherine (2003), "Linguistic policies and the issue of ethno-linguistic minorities in the Middle East" in *Islam in the Middle Eastern Studies: Muslims and Minorities,* edited by A. Usuki and H. Kato, 149–174 , JCAS Symposium Series 7, Osaka: JCAS.

Rejaf Language Conference (1928), *Report of the Rejaf Language Conference,* London: Sudan Government .

Salih, Kamal Osman (1990), "British policy and the accentuation of inter-ethnic divisions: the case of the Nuba Mountains Region of Sudan, 1920–1940" *African Affairs*, 89(356): 417–436.

Seghers, Maud (2004), "Phelps-Stokes in Congo: transferring educational policy discourse to govern metropole and colony" *Paedagogica Historica: International Journal of the History of Education*, 40(4): 455–477.

Silverstein, Michael (1996), "Monoglot "standard" in America: standardisation and metaphors of linguistic hegemony" in *The Matrix of Language: Contemporary Linguistic Anthropology*, edited by Donald Brenneis and Ronald Macaulay, 284–306, Oxford: Westview.

Suleiman, Yasir (2013), *Arabic in the Fray: Language Ideology and Cultural Politics*, Edinburgh : Edinburgh University Press.

Warnke, I. H. and T. Stoltz (2013). "(Post-)Colonial Linguistics, or: What is the colonial in dominated colonial discourses? *Zeitschrift fur Semiotik* 35(3–4): 471–495.

Westermann, Hermann and Diedrich Hermann (1912), *The Shilluk People, Their Language and Folklore.* Philadelphia : Board of Foreign Missions of the United Presbyterian Church of North America.

Zimmermann, Klaus and Birte Kellermeier-Rehbein (2015), "Preface" , in *Colonialism and Missionary Linguistics*, edited by Klaus Zimmermann and Birte Kellermeier-Rehbein, pp.i–x. Berlin and Boston: De Gruyter.

VII

Toward Black Linguistics
(with Geneva Smitherman, Arnetha F. Ball, and Arthur K. Spears)

This book foregrounds contributions to research on Black languages by Black scholars in Africa and the Americas. It identifies key epistemological and political underpinnings of what we are here calling "Black Linguistics": a postcolonial scholarship that seeks to celebrate and create room for insurgent knowledge about Black languages. Black Linguistics is committed to studies of Black languages by Black speakers and to analyses of the sociopolitical consequences of varying conceptualizations of and research on Black languages. The overall goal of Black Linguistics is to expunge and reorder elitist and colonial elements within language studies. In so doing, Black Linguistic scholarship will contribute to a rethinking of the discipline. By challenging conventional constructs such as multilingualism, indigenous languages, linguistic human rights—and even the term "language" itself—Black Linguistics research will contribute to the formation of a new intellectual climate. Black Linguistics seeks to argue that a notion such as multilingualism, unless handled carefully, becomes a plural variant of monolingualism, that indigenous language is itself a product of colonial language ideology, and that it is unrealistic to imagine that social equality can be realized through linguistic human rights when notions about "language" and "rights" are both open to contestation. In this introductory essay, we examine the effects of a Black Linguistics perspective on the nature and type of research we conduct and the ways we communicate our work to our constituencies in and outside of the Academy.

Although this book is on Black languages, it has not been written in a Black language. As Black scholars from varying ethnolinguistic backgrounds, English is the language we have in common. The use of English in writing and communication between Black scholars is here a counter-hegemonic move: an attempt to challenge the hegemony of English by using English to create an intellectual counter-discourse in language studies (Pennycook 1994, 2001).

Within the study of Black languages by Black scholars, there are, of course multiple perspectives. The aim of this book is to bring these multiple voices together to explore the significance of their work for mainstream theoretical and applied language studies.

Despite the range and different types of Black social and linguistic experiences, numerous scholars, either explicitly or implicitly, speak to the commonalities of these phenomena in their research. Yet, no "Black Linguistics" perspective, *per se*, has emerged from the literature in the way in which Black scholars in other fields—e.g. psychology, sociology, literary criticism—have formulated well-established perspectives and paradigms. This book seeks to create opportunities to demonstrate similarities in the work we do, to relate our common shared experiences as scholars on/in the margins and to reflect on issues that consume Black language and communication scholars.

Most of our examples of Black languages in Africa are drawn from "sub-Saharan Africa." However, we do not subscribe to an elevation to epistemological status of this and other similarly divisive, demeaning, balkanizing categories, such as "Francophone," "Anglophone," or "Lusophone" Africa. While we use such terms for communicative convenience, we insist that these terms be used circumspectly because they are not particularly illuminating as conceptual tools. For example, on the one hand, "Anglophone," "Francophone," and "Lusophone" Africa have a good deal of language, social practice, and ethnocultural history in common, clearly much more than is implied by the colonial distinctions "Anglophone," "Francophone," and "Lusophone" Africa. On the other hand, these conceptual categories conceal substantial sociolinguistic diversity within these regions of Africa.

The term "Black languages" covers languages of Africa and the Diaspora. In this book, however, we are restricting ourselves to the Western Hemispheric Diaspora. These languages and those in Africa are grouped together because the problems and possibilities associated with these languages are similar. All exist in social contexts of white supremacy and resource expropriation characteristic of neoimperialism and internalized oppression. In the various communities in which these languages are spoken, there exist similar problems and possibilities. The social settings of Black languages are typically different from those of other languages in the so-called "Third World." For example, in comparison to Latin America, Africa has a greater degree of multilingualism, and it is spread over wider areas and in key administrative centers—e.g. capitals, ports, and manufacturing and mining areas. In fact, African multilingualism exists among such a high percentage of the population that Fardon and Furniss suggest that "multilingualism is the African lingua franca" (1994: 4). Further, a majority of the people in Latin America speak some form of the official language—Spanish or Portuguese—and even those who don't have speaking proficiency have at least receptive competence (understanding) in Spanish or Portuguese. By contrast, only a minority of the various creole language populations have spoken proficiency in the official ex-colonial language (although many may have a high degree of receptive competence in the official language, for example English in Jamaica).

"Black languages" are generally construed to include pidgins and creoles in Africa and the Caribbean; African American (Vernacular) English in the US (also known as US Ebonics, African American Language, Black English); standardized and non-standardized African languages; and "vehicular" languages emerging in urban African centers (Childs 1999). The names of the languages which fall under the broad rubric of Black languages may at times be different from the names used by speakers of these languages. For example, speakers of US African American English refer to what they speak as "English"; the creole in Jamaica is referred to as "Patwa" by Jamaican speakers; in Haiti, it is "Kreyol," which is increasingly being replaced with "Haitian"/"Haitian language" (Devonish 1986; Winford, this volume[1]). And in "sub-Saharan Africa," there are speakers who simply refer to what they speak as part of being human, "chivanhu." For example, in Southern Africa those who do not speak Shona are regarded as not speaking "chivanhu," the human language. In SiSwati, it will be said that "abatsefuli sintvu." In Zulu, it will be "abathethi isintu." In all cases what is being asserted is that the person(s) does not speak the human language. Rarely is the name of the language given.

It may come as a surprise to many that some speakers of Black languages do not have a specific name or label for their form of speech. However, languages without names are not an oddity. Naming languages is a type of consciousness, an artifact embedded in the consciousness of Western formal education. Communities with limited or very little formal Western educa-

---

[1] Donald Winford, "Ideologies of language and socially realistic lingustics" which appeared as chapter 1 (pp.21-39) in the original publication for which this essay served as the introduction: Sinfree Makoni, Geneva Smitherman, Arnetha F. Ball and Arthur K. Spears (eds.), *Black Linguistics: Language, Society, and Politics in Africa and the Americas*. London; New York: Routledge, 2003.

tion sometimes do not possess the type of consciousness of which language naming is a component (Romaine 1984). Naming, or more accurately namelessness, is not a criterion for excluding or categorizing a language as a "Black language." What is of central importance in Black Linguistics is that we describe and analyze the ways members of communities relate to their speech, so that we do not rely exclusively on outside analytical categories. Thus, if communities do not have distinct names for their languages, we take into consideration their "folk" terminology, rather than creating and superimposing categories and labels on their behalf, however convenient that might be for us intellectually. Our interest in taking into consideration the categories of language users arises from our concern for local-level perspectives. Further, in Black Linguistics we are acutely aware that even when a given language does have a name shared by linguists and members of the local communities, there may be vast differences in the conceptualizations of that language, in terms of where the linguistic boundaries are situated, the linguistic spaces within that language, and the social constructions of that language by its speakers (LePage and Tabouret-Keller 1985).

    The naming and appropriation of languages is of crucial significance because of the conceptual complexity in the way in which language, ethnicity, and culture are compounded. The conceptual clustering of language, ethnicity, and culture has vast political significance. The injunction early on, by anthropological linguist Franz Boas, against incorrectly conflating language, culture, and race is important in dealing with Black languages. For example, the South African apartheid regime clustered the relationships between language, ethnicity, and culture in a very specific way such that the languages used by different groups became "metonyms" (Cook 2002) for their rights, status, and privileges (or lack of privileges for the vast majority of the speakers).

There are two key themes in the languages we are analyzing. Irrespective of whether the languages are drawn from "sub-Saharan Africa," the Americas, the Caribbean, or elsewhere in the Diaspora, all are spoken and used largely by communities that were institutionally disadvantaged, at one time or another, by colonization, imperialism, and white supremacy. Indeed the formation of some of these languages was an active reaction to colonization and extreme forms of domination. Black languages in some of these contexts are a product of postliberation whereby "new" urban speakers attempt to forge new identities, with their new languages functioning as anti- or counter-languages (LePage and Tabouret-Keller 1985). A very recent example is the adoption of US African American English by Sudanese youth in Canada who are imagined and have begun to construct themselves as "Black" in North America (see Ibrahim, this volume[2]).

A book of this nature is now possible because of the substantial number of Black critical scholars working on Black languages, both as trained professional linguists and as native speakers in the Black communities where they are working *in*, *for*, and *with* Black languages. Several challenges relating to epistemological frameworks confront these scholars. The problem is well articulated by Skinner who writes:

> One of the major problems facing scholars and lay people of African origin is to be able to develop and use paradigms that are based on their experience. They must insist that if the paradigms are to be useful to them, they must be filtered through the African experience before being judged truly universal and not simply hegemonic. (Skinner 1999: 450)

---

[2] Awad El Karim M. Ibrahim's essay "'Whassup, homeboy?' Joining the African Diaspora: Black English as a symbolic site of identification and language learning" which appeared as chapter 9 (pp. 169-185) in the original publication for which this essay served as the introduction (see footnote 1).

Because of the increasing presence of Black scholars in language scholarship, language study can no longer be read as if it were a "whites only" preserve. This volume explores the implications and consequences of the "darkening" of language studies. It should be seen as the naming of a strand of language research, done by Black scholars on Black languages and written either fully or in part by these scholars.

The roots of Black Linguistics can be traced to a few monumental but institutionally marginalized works by scholars such as Devonish (1986), whose book is appropriately entitled *Language and Liberation*, and Williams (1975), whose edited volume *Ebonics: The True Language of Black Folks*, represented an interdisciplinary effort by Black scholars to treat Black language from a Black perspective. The emergence of a strand of Black language scholarship is not an anomaly. As mentioned above, there is a relatively robust tradition of Black research in areas such as psychology and anthropology (Harrison 1991a). What is different about language scholarship is that debates about the desirability of and necessity for such an approach have not (yet) emerged. One of the objectives of this volume is to generate such a debate, to force the issue onto the language scholarship agenda.

Because Black languages are used by people who have historically been colonized and who are socially disadvantaged, their languages have been and are often used as a source of discrimination against them (see Ball, Baugh, this volume). Black Linguistics has had to confront the legacy of colonization and continued oppression manifest in several forms in the social lives of Black people—notably, limited access to resources, power, and education through a race-based hierarchy.

To the extent that we can talk at present about a Black Linguistics, it involves four main principles:

1. membership in or life experience with the communities whose languages we research and analyze;

2. use of an ideological orientation designed to analyze and expose the workings of ideology in research *on, about,* and *for* Black languages;
3. race as a defining feature of our linguistic autobiographies as Black language scholars;
4. analysis of language as social practice with a keen eye/ear attuned to its sociohistory, changes and continuities in the "categories of thought," and the historiography of linguistic analyses of Black languages at different historical periods.

Membership/sociological affiliation
As Black scholars we are anthropologically members of or sociologically affiliated with the communities we are working in. Our research as Black scholars is on behalf of and in collaboration and consultation with local communities. We are seeking to impact positively on speakers of Black languages in these communities. We are therefore very much concerned about the relevance and application of our work. "The socially responsible researcher acknowledges his or her responsibility to individual participants and to his or her community. Social responsibility also precludes short sighted, self-aggrandizing research that does little more than imitate or perpetuate negative stereotypes" (Harris 1996: 30).

The impact of our work might range from raising awareness about the language basis of discriminatory practices and the disempowering nature of descriptions of language in mother tongue education in Africa, to the ways language abilities are used to exclude people. Our insider status impacts on different facets of what we do, ranging from the selection of topics to be investigated and our preferred methodologies to the analysis and dissemination of results. The selection of research topics originates in the proposition that Black Linguistics must contribute toward an understanding of the nature of oppression and strategies for conquering it, or at the very least for containing it. The selection of topics of intellectual inquiry in Black Linguistics is not a mere academic exercise. Rather, it is motivated by what the communities themselves feel is the key problem confronting them. The research topics are defined in collaboration between linguists, as "organic intellectuals" (Gramsci 1971, quoted in Dombrosky 1989: 330), and those directly affected by the "problem." For example, research on language and health in late life has traditionally focused on dementia and Alzheimer's disease. However, after conducting a series of focus group discussions with older persons from Black communities, it was clear to us that the concern of older African Americans was not dementia or Alzheimer's, but diabetes and its effect on language and cognition. The shift in focus from a preoccupation with Alzheimer's disease to diabetes research in older African Americans is an example of how our research agenda shifted to accommodate the perspectives of the communities. The shifts demonstrate the extent of our social sensitivity arising from feelings of social responsibility. Social sensitivity is also an excellent basis for good science. For example, it is increasingly being shown that a large majority of older people within ethnic minorities who subsequently get dementia have diabetes; thus diabetes is a high-risk factor for dementia.

Not only is the research topic defined in collaboration with the speakers directly affected, but also the research results are validated through the participation of the community. For example, in a research project on communication and health among speakers of African American (Vernacular) English, we ran a series of workshops and presented the data and results to the community as part of a postexperimental debriefing procedure. This has proven to be a powerful way of exploring the extent to which research interpretation resonates with the experiences of members of the communities in which the research was conducted.

Working within the paradigm of Black Linguistics, our role is clear: we are both professional linguists and members of the speech communities we work in. We are creole speakers, or speakers of Venda (a South African language), or African American Language speakers, and/or speakers of other Black languages. Because of our sense of social responsibility, we seek to bring our analytical expertise together with the social experiences of our communities. Our analysis benefits from and draws on our expertise as linguists and our insights as members of local speech communities. This dual role enables us metaphorically (to) "see out of more than one eye" (Harrison 1991b: 91), or to see more out of each eye, a welcome intellectual double vision.

Applying the notion of "double consciousness" (DuBois 1903), we argue in Black Linguistics that our double, or more accurately "multiple," consciousness arises from our professional membership in Western-dominated areas of study and anthropological membership in communities with histories and remnants of oppression. Multiple consciousness plays a key role in our struggle to develop a decolonized science of humankind in which language and communication sciences play a significant role. Concurring with Worsley (1984: 36–7), Harrison states:

> Multiple consciousness and vision are rooted in some combination and interpenetration of national, racial, sexual, or class oppression. This form of critical consciousness emerges from the tension between, on the one hand, membership in a Western society, a Western dominated profession, or a relatively privileged class or social category, and, on the other hand, belonging to or having an organic relationship with an oppressed social category or people . . . the conjuncture of multiple subaltern statuses and bases of Otherness, combined with the apparent irreconcilability between them and the ideals and normative expectations of the "free world" of capitalism, the American dream, or middle class privilege, may heighten and intensify our counter-hegemonic sensibilities, vision and understanding. (Harrison 1991b: 90)

Our double vision or multiple consciousness enables us to metaphorically code-switch into the living and lived experiences of our communities, hence providing us with access to particular forms of data which might be difficult for outsiders to access. Examples in this volume include Alim's research on the language of Hip Hop artists, Pollard's analysis of the language of Rasta music, and Ball's analysis of the voices of Black teachers in the US and South Africa.[3] Because we can metaphorically code-switch into the lived and living experiences of the communities, we are "best positioned to provide insights that may escape scholars unfamiliar with the intricacies of local contexts" (Roy-Campbell, this volume[4]). This metaphoric code-switching creates conditions for fruitful lines of communication between Black linguists and members of local communities, as illustrated, for example, in Baugh's research on linguistic profiling (see Baugh, this volume[5]), in Spears's (1999a) work treating language within the larger framework of race and ideology, and in Smitherman's language activist work, e.g. in *King* (the 1977–9 "Black English" Federal court case, in which Black parents filed a lawsuit against the Ann Arbor School District for using the children's language as a basis for denying them their right to an equal education).

The advocacy work we are trying to describe here is not without potential problems, particularly when the positions we want to advocate conflict with deeply held views of our local community. Under such circumstances, if we cannot change the views and practices of the community to share our professional positions, our strategy should be to follow the lead of the com-

---

[3] For the volume mentioned here, see footnote 1.
[4] Zaline M. Roy-Campbell "Promoting African languages as conveyors of knowledge in educational institutions" which appeared as chapter 4 (pp.83-102) in the volume to which this essay was the introduction (see footnote 1 above.)
[5] John Baugh "Linguistic profiling" which appeared as chapter 8 (pp.155-168) in the volume to which this essay was the introduction (see footnote 1 above).

munity and to mitigate the potentially negative effects that may emanate from the community's decision. A striking example of a context in which a language policy position held by language activists conflicts with the community's position on language can be cited from South Africa, where language activists are experiencing resistance from local communities about the use of African languages as media of instruction for schoolchildren. The linguists are well aware of the long-established, voluminous research from around the globe about the advantages of mother tongue education. However, these South African communities have expressed an explicit preference for English as the language of education.

This "pressurizing for English" (as South Africans refer to it) is exerted perhaps more intensely in South Africa's Western Cape than in any of the country's other eight provinces. According to Pluddemann, the "pressurizing" has already begun by first grade (2000: 40). In some schools, even teachers may exert such pressure (although it is well documented that teachers encounter severe pedagogical difficulties when teaching through English, primarily because they are not fully proficient in English themselves). The pressurizing for English is not a "love" for English *per se*. Rather it reflects a sharp sensitivity to the social and economic disparities between schools. English-language schools receive more and better resources, and they have a higher level of professionally qualified teachers than African-language schools. Owing to the disparity in educational quality between African-language and English-medium schools, most advocates of African-language schools do not send their children to these schools! Because we are unlikely to change the deeply entrenched position of the communities on language in education, we should thus focus our attention on improving current teaching practices with English as the medium of instruction and on ways of reducing the educational disadvantage of students being taught in a foreign medium (Ferguson 2000). When there is a difference between our professional position on a language issue and the position of the community we work in, our strategy should be based on a "critical engagement with the wishes of the communities, their desires and histories, that is, a way of thinking that pushes one to question rather than to pontificate" (Pennycook 1998: 343).

That Black Linguistics cannot merely be an "academic" language exercise is neatly captured by Gordon when he writes:

> Intellectual production which is not instrumentalized through praxis has no liberating effect. The knowledge and truths unveiled by critical intellectuals in conjunction with the community must be assimilated by the people, turned into concrete strategies and ultimately into activities which move the collectivity towards liberation. (Gordon 1991: 155)

He further notes that activism moves the decolonizing of anthropology to an anthropology of liberation. Whether the issue is addressed explicitly or implicitly, liberation is foremost in the thinking and intellectual practices of Black Linguistics. It serves and promotes the interests of the oppressed (Gordon 1991) and seeks to contribute toward social liberation.

In the course of promoting the interests of the communities of Black-language speakers, Black Linguistics has the potential for advancing and enhancing the field of language studies. In our efforts to take the linguistic affairs of our own people into our own hands, we as intellectual activists, trained in the methods and theories of the human sciences, may also uncover, discover, recover concepts that end up generally advancing knowledge in the field. For example, Alim's research in Hip Hop has implications for notions about language variation and code-switching (see Alim, this volume[6]). Vaughn-Cooke's

---

[6] H. Samy Alim, "'We are the streets': African American Language and the strategic construction of a street conscious identity" which appeared as chapter 2 (pp.40-59) in the volume to which this essay was the introduction (see footnote 1 above).

(1987) theorizing about the need for time-depth studies of African American English as a counter to notions about its postmodern "divergence" from white varieties of American English resurrected theories about longitudinal data collection research. The work of linguists in the "Ebonics Movement," dating back to 1973, and the coining of the term "Ebonics" by Black psychologist Robert Williams, has led to a reexamination of the whole notion of what constitutes a "language" (see e.g. Blackshire-Belay 1996; Smith 1998; Fasold 1999; Nehusi 2001; Palacas 2001). Similarly, in South Africa, the recent emergence of urban vehicular African languages is raising fundamental issues about the conceptualization of language (Cook 2002; Makoni, this volume[7]).

Ideological orientation in Black Linguistics

Any intellectual enterprise is ideological (Joseph and Taylor 1990; Cameron *et al.* 1992; Blommaert 1999). Black Linguistics is, therefore, ideological. The fruitful line of inquiry to pursue in Black Linguistics is not whether Black Linguistics is ideological or not—that is taken for granted—but what type of ideological orientation is a useful line to pursue in Black Linguistics. Our preoccupation is with the conditions and purpose of the production of knowledge about Black languages. Interest in an analysis of the conditions under which knowledge of Black languages is produced is justifiable because of the wide range of scholars working on Black languages and the historiography of intellectual thought in the production of knowledge about these languages. For example, historically knowledge production within Creole Studies occurred during an era when speakers of the language were considered less than human. The early work on

---

[7] Sinfree Makoni, "From misinvention to disinvention of language: multilingualism and the South African Constitution" which appeared as chapter 7 (pp. 132-152) in the volume to which this essay was the introduction (see footnote 1 above).

African languages was, by and large, carried out by white missionaries and linguists with limited expertise in the languages they were describing and inventing as part of empire building. Because of the less than ideal conditions under which some of the work on Black languages began, it is logical to raise questions about the current nature of the conditions under which knowledge of these languages is being produced.

Because of our ideological orientation, our analysis of language and language varieties becomes inseparable from the sociohistories which created them. For example, an analysis of the emergence of vehicular languages in urban Africa requires an understanding of the emergence of urban youth identities. The youth seek to deliberately distance themselves from rural identities seen as "backward," and to forge a new identity and create new languages which best define them.

An important aspect of the ideological orientation of Black Linguistics is its global and comparative perspective, unlike the tendency of much of the work done on Black languages which has been to focus on the social and linguistic phenomena of individual Black communities to the exclusion of Black experiences outside a given community—for example, work on US Ebonics that ignores creoles and African languages. Because of enslavement, slavery, wars, colonization, and the continuing migration *en masse* of Continental Africans to North America, there has been a global dispersal of Black communities. Black researchers have emerged from these communities with perspectives growing out of circumstances experienced in many societies around the world. These circumstances have led to the development of a research perspective that looks at local phenomena with global vision. The comparative thrust in Black Linguistics is consonant with that in other social science research which deals with aspects of Blackness in the Diaspora (Fredrickson 1999; also comparisons of the political and economic histories of Blacks in South Africa and the US, e.g. Walters 1993; Fredrickson 2001). Winford (this volume[8]) provides such a linguistic perspective in his analysis of African American (Vernacular) English and Caribbean creoles. Other examples are analyses of language policies and provisions for higher education for Blacks in South Africa and the US (Smitherman 2000; Ball 2003[9]).

Race as a defining feature of Black Linguists

That race is not a scientific concept but socially constructed is well known. What is less well known is how this non-scientific construct impacts on our scientific work as Black researchers of Black languages. Current research by Ibrahim (1999, this volume[10]) illustrates that even areas of linguistics such as language learning, which some scholars might feel is psychologically oriented, are not color blind. We work in communities in which color, and indeed variations in color, are perceived and endowed with social meanings (Harrison 1991c).

In Black Linguistics we explore the intellectual consequences that our identities, including those which we select and those which select us (those attributed to us), have on our academic research. We seek to examine the various ways in which our identities as scholars are implicated in our epistemologies, in the work we do, and in the research orientations we adopt. The central issue which we address in Black Linguistics is what *being Black*, or *becoming Black*, means in language scholarship. One critical thing that it means, as this volume demonstrates, is that the Black Linguistics perspective asks "fundamental-liberation oriented" questions and candidly seeks to provide language solutions to problems. In Africa and the Caribbean, particularly, language issues are central in the social lives of Black communi-

---

[8] For this reference, see footnote 1.
[9] Arnetha F. Ball, "US and South African teachers' developing perspectives on language and literacy: changing domestic and international roles of linguistic gate-keepers" which appeared as chapter 10 (pp.186-214) in the volume to which this essay was the introduction (see footnote 1 above).
[10] See footnote 2 above.

ties. More so than in the US and other "developed" countries, language in African and Caribbean communities is an integral part of the nature of statecraft and governance (Devonish 1986). Solutions to language problems in these communities vary depending on the nature and magnitude of the problem. For example, in some cases we argue for the appropriacy of linguae francae as media for education, while in other cases we call for extended use of standard languages and the establishment of common orthographies as possible solutions to the language-in-education problem.

Language as social practice
The general thrust in Black Linguistics is to conceive of language as social and communicative practice, conceptualized within a wider framework than formalistic theories of language. Contrary to Chomskyan linguistics, which treats grammar as neutral (e.g. Newmeyer 1986), in Black Linguistics language is conceived of as socially embedded. Grammatical patterns have to be deconstructed and understood within the social and political contexts in which they are used.

From the vantage point of Black language as social practice, our analyses of language and language varieties become inseparable from the communities and the sociohistories which created these languages and varieties. This mandates a perspective and an analytical framework that go beyond the now common methodologies and scholarly practices of quantitative sociolinguistics, which, like Chomskyan linguistics, tends to dichotomize language and speaker and to focus on the former, rather than both the former and the latter. Black Linguistics is keenly attuned to the fact that we are producing knowledge about both the creation (language) and the creator (Black people). It is thus imperative that our scholarship reflects the histories, social circumstances, political economies, aspirations—and voices—of the people whose language we study.

We bring this discussion to a close by stating that Black Linguistics is concerned not only with analysis but with why the analysts are doing the analysis; concerned not only with results, but with the impact of the dissemination of the results on audiences both in and outside of the Academy.

[The descriptions of the individual chapters of the volume for which this was the introduction and which followed in the original publication have not been reprinted here.—Ed.]

References
Blackshire-Belay, C.A. (1996) "The location of Ebonics within the framework of the Africological paradigm," *Journal of Black Studies*, 27 (1): 5–23.
Blommaert, J. (ed.) (1999) *Language Ideological Debates*, Berlin: Mouton de Gruyter.
Cameron, D., Frazer, E., Harvey, P., Rampton, B., and Richardson, K. (1992) *Researching Language: Issues of Power and Method*, London: Routledge.
Childs, G. Tucker (1999) "The status of Isicamatho, a Nguni based urban variety of Soweto," in A. Spears and D. Winford (eds) *The Structure and Status of Pidgins and Creoles*, Amsterdam and Philadelphia, PA: John Benjamins, 341–370.
Cook, S. (2002) "Urban language in a rural setting: the case of Phokeng, South Africa," in G. Gmelch and W. Zenner (eds) *Urban Life Readings in the Anthropology of the City*, Prospect Heights, IL: Waveland Press, 106–113.
Devonish, H. (1986*) Language and Liberation: Creole Language Politics in the Caribbean*, London: Karia Press.
Dombrosky, R.S. (1989) *Antonio Gramsci*, Twayne Publishers.
DuBois, W.E.B. (1903) *The Souls of Black Folk*, New York: Dover.

Fardon, R. and Furniss, G. (1994) *African Languages, Development and the State*, London: Routledge.

Fasold, R.W. (2001) "Ebonic need not be English," in J.E. Alatis and A. Tan (eds) *Language in our Time: Bilingual Education and Official English, Ebonics and Standard English Immigration and the Unz Initiative* (Georgetown University Round Table on Languages and Linguistics 1999), Washington, DC: Georgetown University Press, 262–280.

Ferguson, G. (2000) "The medium of instruction in African education: the role of the applied linguist," in S. Makoni and Nkonko Kamwangamalu (eds) *Language and Institutions in Africa*, Cape Town: Centre for Advanced Studies of African Society, 95–111.

Fredrickson, G. (1999) "Reform and revolution in America and South Africa freedom struggles," in D.C. Hine and J. McCleod (eds) *Crossing Boundaries*, Bloomington, IN: Indiana University Press, 71–87.

Gordon, E. (1991) "Anthropology as liberation," in F.V. Harrison (ed.) *Decolonizing Anthropology: Moving Further toward an Anthropology for Liberation*, Washington, DC: American Anthropological Association, 149–68.

Harris, J. (1996) "Issues in recruiting African American participants for research," in G.K. Alan, K.E. Pollock, and L. Joyce (eds) *Communication Disorders in African American Children: Research Assessment and Intervention*, London: Paul Brookes Publishing Company, 19–36.

Harrison, F.V. (1991a) "Anthropology as an agent of transformation. Introductory comments and queries," in F.V. Harrison (ed.) *Decolonizing Anthropology*, Washington, DC: American Anthropological Association, 1–15.

Harrison, F.V. (ed.) (1991b) *Decolonizing Anthropology: Moving Further Toward an Anthropology for Liberation*, Washington, DC: American Anthropological Association.
Harrison, F.V. (1991c) "Ethnography as politics," in F.V. Harrison (ed.) *Decolonizing Anthropology: Moving Further Toward an Anthropology for Liberation*, Washington, DC: Association of Black Anthropologists/ American Anthropological Association, 88–110.
Ibrahim, A. (1999) "Becoming Black: Rap and Hip Hop, race, gender, identity and the politics of ESL," *TESOL Quarterly*, 33: 349–65.
Joseph, J.E. and Taylor, T.J. (1990) *Ideologies of Language*, New York: Routledge.
LePage and Tabouret-Keller, A. (1985) *Acts of Identity*, Cambridge: Cambridge University Press.
Marley, B. (1980) "Redemption Song," Bob Marley Music Ltd B.V.
Nehusi, Kimani S. (2001) "From Medew Netjer to Ebonics," in C. Crawford (ed.) *Ebonics and Language Education of African Ancestry Students*, New York: Sankofa World Publishers, 56–122.
Newmeyer, F. (1986) *The Politics of Linguistics*, Chicago: University of Chicago Press.
Palacas, A. (2001) "Liberating American Ebonics from Euro-English," *College English*, 63(3): 326–352.
Pennycook, A. (1994) *The Cultural Politics of English as an International Language*, London: Longman.
Pennycook, A. (1998) *English and the Discourses of Colonialism*, London: Routledge.
Pennycook, A. (2001) *Critical Applied Linguistics*, Mahwah, NJ: Lawrence Erlbaum.
Pluddemann, P. (2000) "Education with multilingualism in

South Africa: an overview," in E. Ridge, S.B. Makoni and S. G. Ridge (eds) *Freedom and Discipline: Essays in Applied Linguistics*, New Delhi: Bhari.

Romaine, S. (1984) *The Language of Children and Adolescents: The Acquisition of Communicative Competence*, Oxford: Blackwell.

Skinner, E. (1999) "Hegemonic paradigms and the African world: striving to be free," in C. Hine and J. McLeod (eds*) Crossing Boundaries*, Bloomington, IN: Indiana University Press, 45–71.

Smith, E. (1998) "What is Black English? What is Ebonics?," in T. Perry and Lisa Delpit (eds) *The Real Ebonics Debate: Power, Language, and the Education of African American Children*, Boston, MA: Beacon Press, 49–58.

Smitherman, G. (2000) "Language and democracy in the United States of America and South Africa," in S. Makoni and Nkonko Kamwangamalu (eds) *Language and Institutions in Africa*, Cape Town: Centre for Advanced Studies of African Society, 65–90.

Spears, A.K. (1999a) "Introduction," in A.K. Spears (ed.) *Race and Ideology: Language, Symbolism and Popular Culture*, Detroit: Wayne State University Press, 11–58.

Spears, A.K. (ed.) (1999b) *Race and Ideology: Language, Symbolism and Popular Culture*, Detroit, MI: Wayne State University Press.

Vaughn-Cooke, F. (1987) "Are Black and White vernaculars diverging?," *American Speech*, 62: 12–32.

Walters, R.W. (1993) *Pan Africanism in the African Diaspora*, Detroit, IL: Wayne State University Press.

Williams, R.L. (1975) *Ebonics: The True Language of Black Folks*, St. Louis, MO: Institute for Black Studies.

Worsley, P. (1984) *The Three Worlds: Culture and World Development*, Chicago: University of Chicago Press.

VIII

Regional and international perspectives on language activism
(with Marika K. Criss)

This special issue is written in honor of the late Joshua Fishman, specifically, his life and academic contributions.

Joshua Fishman (1926–2015) taught at a number of institutions, including the University of Pennsylvania and Columbia University, and held the position of visiting scholar at a number of universities around the world. He is regarded, in some circles, as the founding father of the sociology of language. He concentrated on a number of aspects of the sociology of language, including language policy and planning, language and identity, and language and ethnicity as well as others. He viewed the sociology of language through a minority lens and framed scholarship as a form of social action, influencing scholars and researchers worldwide. In light of Fishman's interest in social action and activism, we decided to compile a special issue on language activism. Consistent with his global perspectives on the sociology of language and the status of minority languages, we invited scholars from different regions of the globe, including Canada, New Zealand, and Africa. We view issues of language activism through different lenses, including minority and indigenous languages, such as Maori in New Zealand and Khoi-San in southern Africa. We explore the multiple ways in which language activism is understood in different contexts across the globe and the positive and negative impacts of activism and how paradoxically in some cases language activism may reinforce social class differences between language activists (the advocates) and the communities on whose behalf they are advocating. Activism may accentuate differences within the language communities because not all segments of the community will benefit equally from the efforts of language activists. If language activism in some cases entails promoting a specific (male) variety of language, members of the community who are least proficient in the standard, or have a different gender identity, may find themselves in a less favorable position as a consequence of language activism than before the language advocacy campaign began.

Drawing on the literature of language activism, in this introduction, we seek to address the following questions:

1. Who is a language activist?
2. What are the different dimensions of language activism?
3. What are the effects of language activism on local communities?
4. What do language activist who succeed in their quest to enshrine their own language do with former rival language communities?

At a general level, language activism is a form of linguistic, political, and social intervention whose major objectives are to revive, promote, and develop languages and, in some cases, reverse language loss. Language activism frequently occurs in indigenous and other marginalized communities (Fishman 1997). Language activism is carried out by groups and individuals, including missionary organizations such as the Summer Institute of Linguistics (SIL); linguists from the local communities or, at times, from other communities, but both of whom generally receive training in Western countries; and scholars from western countries, including the United States. Another group of language activists includes indigenous peoples who are part of language academies or local associations with an interest in the preservation and documentation of indigenous languages.

The most powerful and widely pervasive institutions for the promotion and revival of languages are language academies, sometimes referred to as language boards. In some cases, the language academies that provide institutional support for language activists may be constitutionally determined, while, in other cases, they arise organically from the interests and concerns of local communities. In some cases, they may be driven by one individual only. Some of the most prominent academies are the Arabic Language Academies, the Pan South African Language Board, Académie française (The French Academy), and the Portuguese Camões Institute. Although all these academies play prominent roles in the preservation of languages, including the imposition of what may be regarded as correct forms of writing and speaking, these language academies also can develop into powerful political institutions.

Whether language activities are educated in Western countries or locally trained, they share a belief in the need to preserve and understand standard languages. In this regard, speakers are linked in extremely complex ways to other individuals and members of society in terms of gender, race, generation, social class, and other social categories. As such, interventions on behalf of a threatened minority language that leave intact all other aspects of social evolution that link the community with the world have generally resulted in failure. The contributors to this volume are acutely aware of these complex relationships and these interventions. They understand that language activists are likely to succeed only if they resist framing languages as free-standing (Edwards 2010), independent, asocial entities. Language activism is a type of language advocacy, a form of political social intervention in which boundaries between pure scholarship and ideological engagement are tenuous. As noted, advocates can be members of the community or outside individuals who value a certain community. In this volume, Ka'ai is a Maori who advocates for the promotion of Maori in a manner which echoes Fishman's strong and passionate interest in advocating on behalf of one's own ethnicity (Fishman et al. 1985).

To succeed, language activists must be sensitive to their Western ideology of social engagement. In this ideology, the objective of language activism is for the communities to subsequently be autonomous and to manage and carry out issues related to activism, including developing teaching materials for language use in education. Nevertheless, some local communities might feel that, because language activism was initially instigated by outsiders, their withdrawal reflects the outsiders' lack of interest in the projects, which may cause a concomitant loss of interest by the local communities. In most cases, however, communities are interested in and advocate for their languages. The success of language policies will be partially dependent on whether the language is viewed in a positive light by those who speak it, as is the case with the Maori community in this volume.

Language activism, whether it is aimed to reverse language shift, revive a language, or preempt language death, cannot succeed if the interventions of the communities who are expected to use that language do not regard using or reviving that language as meeting their needs or if they do not regard the language activists or language advocates as legitimate. In this regard, the right to language choice includes the right to choose against a language. The concept of language revival also must be understood in view of local social practices and issues and their associated communication practices. Communicative practices, such as the songs, dances, rituals, and ways of linguistically addressing each other, carry symbolic meanings. This means that any politics of language revival also must be seen as politics of social practices, reinforcing the deep relationship between language and discourse. Languages, therefore, are evolving products of historically modes of sharing life together. Understanding of and respect for all modes of linguistic practices is an important political and ethical issue for any language activist.

Language activists are engaged in a wide range of activities. Language activists can also succeed in having their own languages enshrined as official languages as happened in Quebec in which after winning elections they made French an official language, thereby enhancing the status of French. Paradoxically, the French separatists are intolerant of other minority languages. Language activists may engage with communities as a means to develop the expertise of local community members. For example, in language documentation, activists need to develop the expertise of local linguists so that they can document their own languages (or decide not to). This local documentation, however, must not include an imposed linguistic framework, and local concepts and methodologies, resulting from a dialogue between top-down and bottom-up policies, must be taken into consideration. Further, in claiming the importance of local protagonism in language activism, we also must recognize that power relations in modern societies may create some difficulties for such protagonism. One example is the capturing of indigenous languages in Brazil for the purpose of constructing a Brazilian cultural reference that takes into account nationalism, territorialization, and politics of cultural heritage. Because this process involves power asymmetries, it must include a dialogue between the local people and intellectuals.

[The descriptions of the individual chapters of the volume for which this was the introduction and which followed in the original publication have not been reprinted here.—Ed.]

Acknowledgements: We would like to extend our heartfelt gratitude to Abigail Kahn for starting this project, Kseniji Ajdinović za njen doprinos tokom projekta, aussi bien que Richard Bourhis pour ses commentaires au cours du processus.

References

Edwards, John (2010). *Minority languages and group identity: Cases and categories*. Amsterdam & Philadelphia: John Benjamins Pub. Co.

Fishman, Joshua A. (1997). *In praise of the beloved language: A comparative view of positive ethnolinguistic consciousness*. Berlin: Mouton de Gruyter.

Fishman, Joshua A., Esther G. Lowy & Michael H. Gertner. (1985). *The rise and fall of the ethnic revival: Perspectives on language and ethnicity*. Berlin: Mouton de Gruyter.

IX

An argument for ethno-language studies in Africa
(with Ulrike Meinhof)

"Africa's language problem, like its problem of 'tribalism', is imagined at the extreme as a condition of plenty, its fate is to suffer from oversupply, in short, Africa seems to be marked by death or glut, but never a just or appropriate measure". We focus on the so-called "language problem" which—it is claimed—arises out of Africa's complex multilingualism underwitten by "oligolinguistic" tendencies in language planning (Fardon and Furniss 1994:1; Blommaert 1999: 179). We analyse the assumptions made about "language" in Africa whch encourage this perspective. Given the breadth and diversity of Africa this is an enormous task which we consider necessary, since any analysis either of a geographical region or individual nation/state is sociolinguistically untenable (Adegbija 1996; Samarin 1996:389).

Language use in Africa is best analysed in terms of transitional and transnational networks—something analogous to "imagined communities" or the "narration of the nation", and on the basis of a (pre) literate and literate continuum (Anderson 1991; Hall 1997). Such a continuum enables us to examine the ways in which "languages" are constructed and the role of literacy in shaping the assumptions made about them. We are restating the argument that linguistic theory in Africa is more a theory of literacy than of language. Until recently, the "language problem" was conceptualised as the existence of too many languages in Africa. In terms of language planning the solution proposed to "overcome" the over-supply of "languages" was to advocate the use of a single "European" language as a national language, because African policies were predicated upon a one nation = one language policy (Bamgbose 2000).

The rhetoric of multilingualism construes the existence of many languages not as a problem but as an asset, a "resource" (Bloch 2002: 24), a notion which may be regarded as somewhat insensitive by impoverished multilinguals. To such persons it is of little comfort to be told that multilingualism constitutes a form of cultural wealth. If we are to convince lay people about the validity of our arguments it s important to formulate alternative ways of speaking about the issues we address.

But how different are the monolingual models and the multilingual approaches from each other in their assumptions about "language"? Both conceive of "language" in a similar way. From both perspectives multilingualism is a variant of monolingualism if one is referring to "different" languages which are expressions of inter-translatable languages, such as, for example, Xhosa/Zulu, Ndebele/Zulu. Plural monolingualism is of reduced value.

In this article we illustrate how languages are socially constructed and the consequences of these constructions for our own understandings of language. However, we resist the temptation of assigning victory to particular perspectives about language, but instead hold the different views about language in mind without "suppressing" any, because, as Nagel (1986:2) states: "there is no view from Nowhere".

We examine the assumptions about "language" made in Africa in the contexts of colonialism and post-independent (class-apartheid) Africa, and how they may match or at times distort prevailing language practices. The issue is important both linguistically and ethically. "All solutions to language problems have knock-on effects to the conditions of people's lives", so ethical issues inevitably emerge (Brumfit 2004). Linguistic descriptions in that sense constitute a form of socal intervention. Misrepresentation of these realities can have harmful effects, even if the descriptions are well intentioned (Grace 1981). Hence, development of a "standard" in African languages that was too different from any variety actually spoken, or of a standard that was oversimplified inhibited the development of literacy, rendering it more difficult than necessary (Irvine 2001: 169). Such disabling repercussions for literacy and creative writing are the material consequences arising from some assumptions about language.

Processes in the Social Construction of Language
But what do we mean by saying that African languages are social constructions? We mean that a language is an invention, a construction just like other categories such as "time." Speaking of time as a construction does not dispute the geophysical fact that the earth rotates on an axis, but it means that the signification of time has a social and variable base. In a similar vein what is socially constructed in languages is "a language", and not a natural category "Language". A capacity for language is natural in humans, but "languages" are a product of social and historical intervention.

There are three processes underpinning the social construction of languages: iconisation, fractal recursivity and erasure (Irvine and Gal 2000). "Iconization imputes to a linguistic feature or system the inherent nature of the social group indexed by it. A linguistic feature is iconic if it is treated as if it portrays the group's essence" (Irvine & Gal 2000:38). For example, clicks have an iconic status with speakers of Nguni languages even though clicks are Khoisan in origin. Fractal recursivity is the projection of an opposition, salient at some level of relationship, onto another level. When such oppositions are reproduced within a single person, they do not concern contrasting identities so much as oppositions between activities or roles associated with prototypical social persons. In any case, "the oppositions do not define fixed or stable social groups... Rather, they provide actors with the discursive or cultural resources to claim and thus attempt to create shifting "communities", identities, selves, and roles, at different levels of contrast within a cultural field" (Irvine and Gal 2000:38). By adopting clicks Nguni speakers "create lexical substitutions that were absent in everyday speech". The substitutions of clicks for everyday words produced an avoidance register, *Hlonipha* (Irvine & Gal 2000). Erasure explains away facts that are inconsistent with the ideological scheme. In addition to the three processes we include a literacy narrowly defined as production and reception of "written texts". Texts such as marriage certificates and labour passes were significant in so far as they had an impact on how Africans constructed the ontological status of African languages. It was the "reduction" of these speech forms to writing and their use in literacy and instruction which led to the "emergence" of African languages—not only in Africa but in other parts of the world as well (Samarin 1996: 390).

Literacy had an impact not only on the emergence of these languages, but also on the social meanings which Africans had of their "own" languages and other languages, notably English and French. When we argue that the colonial encounter facilitated the "emergence" or the "springing up" of languages in Africa, we are not saying that prior to colonialism and literacy there was no speech in Africa or that there was any less "talk" before colonialism, but that the "shredding" of these speech forms into languages and some of our current ways of thinking about language in Africa are a product of literacy and colonialism. We can see this, for example, in the connection between Christianity, literacy, and language, including English. Schools that taught English also taught literacy and Christianity, so "perforce" engagement with one led to an engagement with the other, an engagement reinforced by the dual status of teachers as preachers (Summers 2002).

If applied linguistics is to address "real" world issues then we have to examine our assumptions, because most of the concepts were neither conceived with African contexts in mind nor aimed at addressing African "language" problems. Adjusting our categories to suit the problem is necessary because practical problems require the use of categories appropriate to their solution. For example, it is frequently repeated that additive bilingualism is cognitively, socially, and linguistically beneficial (Webb & Kembo-Sure 1999). The bilingualism which the analysts usually have in mind includes a European language and an African language, and rarely African languages only, even though the latter form is more widespread than the former.

Our focus here is not whether or not binigualism does indeed have such effects but on how the construction of language in (additive) bilingualism falls into the trap of "objectivising" languages as "if (they) were akin to having access to clean water, fuel, or food so that accessing them would produce cognitive and material benefits" (Pennycook 2004: 149; see also Makoni & Meinhof 2004). The objectivisation of language encourages policy makers to think in terms of who has languages, of how many people can be persuaded to use them, or of how people can be given these languages.

Efforts to determine the nature of language problems in Africa are complicated by the fact that "language" as an object is different depending on how we look at it. Furthermore the assumptions to describe language are typically couched in conceptual metaphors. Hence if we are to avoid being held captive by "our own semiotics" and categories (Halliday and Brumfit, personal communication) an analysis of these metaphors is necessary.

Language in Applied Linguistics and the Lay Public in Africa

In applied linguistics "language" raises different expectations for linguists, who construct language in terms of rule-governed generative systems, as against psychologists, preoccupied with the use of symbols for the realisation of meaning, or sociologists, concerned with the ideological implications of structures of shared meanings (Brumfit 2001). In applied linguistics we must not only take into account the assumptions about "language" made by different sub-disciplines, but we must also understand how the discourses about language are understood by language users, reflecting the complications that arise as applied linguists serve the "lay" public. Lay people do not necessarily have categories corresponding to those of applied linguists, and even if they did the meanings for the same categories would be different. For example, Bamanankan, a language in the Republic of Mali, has no lexical distinction between "language" and "dialect". The Shona in Zimbabwe do not define themselves in terms of the language they speak but in terms of the geographical space which they occupy (*vana vevbu*)—children of the soil. For the Shona, the notion of language—if it exists at all—is subordinate to geography (Dwyer 2002). "The vocabulary of the dictionary in Africa is synonymous with the vocabulary of the language—a vocabulary which no speaker can actually "know" independently of the printed record" (Liddicoat 2000: 425). It becomes an objectified and authoritative "thing" whose supreme authorities are the "book" and the expert, held in reverence even amongst those who can neither read nor write. Language becomes a text whose meanings cannot be negotiated and adapted to context. Lists of words are far more common than grammars in Africa, reflecting an orientation towards understanding "language" as the use of words rather than speech.

... And Then There Were Languages: The Emergence of Languages in Africa and Applied Lingustics in Africa

In a review of languages in sub-Saharan Africa, Samarin writes: "The map of Africa we would start with would be white, or gray, or black—whatever best iconized a 'clean slate'. A continent without languages. Yes, a continent without languages. Of course, Africans used language in a linguistic sense to communicate with each other..." (Samarin 1996: 390). Samarin is suggesting that prior to colonisation and the introduction of Christian evangelism and literacy, the notion of "language" as a marker of social identity did not exist. Although their speech forms shared common linguistic structures they did not constitute common languages because there was no shared identity. Shared identities based on language only emerged with the introduction of colonisation and Christianity. Is Africa unique in this regard? Heryanto (1995; 2005), with his mind on Indonesia, writes:

> Once the success of the European project of invention was established, other empires sought to emulate it: The newly acquired meanings of Bahasa were derived from one or more modern European languages. At least in the two most widely spoken and influential languages in Indonesia (Malay and Javanese) there was no word for "language", and no need for expressing its idea until the latter part of the past century.

Indeed, Heryanto argues that Bahasa Indonesia was introduced into "language-free communities".

In speaking of "language-free communities" the point is not that these contexts involved any less language use, but rather that we need to view this through a different lens (Makoni & Pennycook 2005). Prior to nationalism, Germany and Italy could be described as "language-free-communities". Even though nationalism played a role in the emergence of "languages" in Europe, in Africa literacy rather than nationalism played a more crucial role in bringing about the notion of separate languages. Languages (and not language) and the meta-languages emerged literally as part of the Christian colonial project. The project of socially constructing languages is ongoing, continuing under the guise of the Summer Institute of Linguistics. Within a Christian framework language proficiency is understood as the ability to translate from one langage to another, rather than as verbal communication (Fabian 1986).

At a philosophical level an analysis of the language categories is germane if applied linguistics is construed as a subject within African studies. African scholarship is thus subjected to a double critique. In the contexts of "tribalism", African scholarship has been criticised for discarding concepts because they have fallen out of favour in Euro-American centres. On the other hand, it has been criticised for not rejecting inappropriate European models such as nation state in language planning (Fardon and Furniss 1994; Lucko and Wolf 2003).

Although we question the validity of some of the western assumptions about the African langauge situation which form the basis of some of our thinking, we urge caution in the use of "local knowledge" as an alternative foundation for African applied linguistics in postcolonial Africa (Geertz 1983). How valid is "local knowledge" as an alternative basis for framing ethno-applied linguistics in postcolonial Africa? There is a tradition of critiquing western theories of colonial and postcolonial Africa best exemplified in philosophy, religion and history texts (Hountondji 1977, 1995; Towa 1979; Mudimbe 1998). The critiques of rationality have succeeded insofar as they have weakened the "rational" hold which the West exerts epistemologically over postcolonial Africa's knowledge production (Bates, Mudimbe, & O'Barr 1994). At another level, they had limited success because they replicated the mind set which they were challenging.

If we are dealing with the real world issues in which language is implicated, it is necessary to re-examine the descriptions of Africa so as to explore whether it is possible for applied linguistics to formulate conceptualisations about language outside Eurocentric frameworks. When Mudimbe posed the same question wth a focus on history, his answer was a qualified yes. In this paper we raise the same question for applied linguistics. There are a number of recurring assumptions about Africa's linguistic situation which we now review.

Assumption 1: The Primary Function of Language Is to Convey Factual Information

Imagining language via the "conduit metaphor" assumes that its primary function is to convey factual information. The conduit metaphor has a strong hold over our thinking about language as is apparent from some language planning discourses in Africa embedded within the nation state paradigm. For example, arguments have been advanced about the validity of using "indigenous" languages as the medium of instruction (Bamgbose 1976, 1984; Rubagumya 1990; Fafunwa et al. 1989; Webb 1999). The concept of a "medium" is widely used in academic literature on applied linguistics in Africa as can be seen from recent publications. For example in a book entitled *New Language Bearings in Africa: A Fresh Quest* (2004), Muthwii & Kioko (eds) have a chapter entitled "Challenges of using English as medium of instruction in the multilingual contexts: a view from Ugandan classrooms". This notion of language as a medium is not restricted to Africa. Such widespread use in current writing on Africa shows that contrary to what Brumfit (personal communication) argues, "the 'medium' is not a 'dead' metaphor". In this section we are arguing that the construct of medium of instruction—however misleading it might be—still has currency. The continued use of the metaphor has consequences for our conceptions about language. Rather than debating whether "indigenous" languages can be a panacea to Africa's complex educational problems, our paper will comment on the metaphors underlying the notion of indigeneity and critically examine the notion of "medium of instruction". The focus on the medium metaphor is not to deny the existence of other more humanistic conceptualisations of language, particularly those shaped by the thinking of Paolo Freire. The issue is that the humanistic conceptualisations of language may be widspread in creative literature but are rare in discussions about language planning.

The Relevance of Indigenous Languages as Christian Languages to Applied Linguistics in Africa

It is easy to construe "indigenous" languages as authentic. Hence unproblematic repositories of African cultures which contribute towards the formation of a nation state—a view influenced by Anderson's (1991) *Imagined Communities*—unfortunately regard "languages as essentially unproblematic" (Joseph 2004). The interest in the "invention" of national heritages foregrounds the socal dimension of custom and ethnicity and leads us to question the naturalness implied in terms such as "indigenous" languages (Spear 2003:4). There is an increasing number of studies focussing on how "indigenous" languages such as Tswana, chiShona, and Tsonga were socially and linguistically constructed (MacGonagle 2003; Cook 2002). Our understanding of the social construction of "indigenous" languages is analogous to Blommaert's (1999: 104) "discovery attitude" or what Said (1985:156-7) calls "being there", which arises from the simple fact of having been present in Africa, the Middle East, and South East Asia. Irrespective of length of stay or nature of association, having been there is deemed adequate to claim "knowledge" of the native languages and cultures.

The fact that "indigenous" languages were socially constructed is relevant to applied linguistics in Africa. The argument is not that we should dispense with the concept of separate languages but rather that we need to be aware of what lies behind it. Since languages are socially constructed they need to be deconstructed from time to time, with the goal of making the reconstructed languages as comprehensive as possible so that the standard approximates to the student's usage. Like Shirley Brice Heath (1998) in the US, we suggest that the language of schooling should change so that it corresponds with that of upbringing. However, such a correspondence can only be approximate, so some students will still be left out. The alternative would be to build sociolinguistic awareness into the curriculum so as to get across the idea of differential functional appropriateness of various usages. The argument for such a procedure is not entirely unlike one which promotes a standard language for institutional use in general, but gives full recognition to variant forms in other domains. The other alternative is to experiment with using language teaching materials based on authentic texts from different varieties. If such an educational strategy were pursued, African language speakers would be relieved of extreme pressure to make their language approximate a standard (Makoni & Meinhof 2004).

The orthography for such a language can be constructed in a way which allows maximum variation within it. African languages do not necessarily have to be standardised to be teachable.

If the teaching of indigenous languages is to be effective, it will be necessary to minimise the disjuncture not only between the "medium of instruction" and home language practices but more importantly to reduce the differences between pedagogy as practised in schools and pedagogy as understood in "traditional" African societies. Traditional African educational thought and practice is characterised not only by its concern wth the "good person", however defined, but by its interweaving of social, economic, political, cultural, and educational threads into a common tapestry. There is extensive literature on African educational practices rarely tapped by those who write on indigenous languages in Africa (Cheikh Anta Diop 1962; Fafunwa et al., 1989; Abdou Moumouni 1968).

This is not to say that there is no research into educational practices in African societies, but rather that such research constitutes research into western education in non-western contexts. Western education research in non-western contexts subjects non-western educational practices to a treatment analogous to "Orientalism" by framing it as socialisation.

The "indigenous" languages have changed under the impact of Christianity because old words assumed new meanings, following the tendency within Christianity to use existing words to describe Christian concepts, rather than opt for neologisms. It also influenced the "indigenous" concepts of time when it introduced "salvation", which was future-oriented. Prior to the onset of Christianity, indigenous conceptions of time referred to the past and present and not the future. Christianity, by using old words to convey new meanings, pre-empted its own message in the African context.

But how "authentic" are these indigenous languages? Fardon & Furniss (1994: 26) suggest that intellectuals' and politicians' accounts of authenticity are unconvincing to rural people since they feel that proponents of such a view are living in a comparatively splendid, but inauthentic, style, appropriating the signs of authenticity from the villages they have left. Furthermore what elite Afrcan intellectuals define as authentic is inauthentic to the rural poor. It is thus important to situate authenticity within wider African discourses. Unfortunately, the discourses of authenticity to which those of indigeneity are aligned were appropriated by Mobuto Sese Seko, the ex-Zairean dictator, as *authenticité* in the 1970s, and recently by Robert Mugabe in his historiography of "Patriotic History" (Crossman 2004: 22; Ranger 2004).

Assumption 2: Languages Exist Ontologically Outside the Communicative Event

The assumption that language/s exist ontologically outside and prior to a communicative event reinforces a structuralist view of language. Harris (1981; 1990) in his critique of modern linguistics refers to this as a segregationalist orientation, as opposed to an "integrationist" perspective, which examines the complex interdependence between forms of communication and "the multitude of environmental factors" (Mühlhäusler 1996:8). The structuralist tradition in African linguistics reflects strong beliefs about how languages were thought to be spoken and not how they were or are actually spoken. Within this structuralist/segregationalist perspective "grammar" is a pre-requisite of speech, not as Hopper (1987) might say a by-product of communication. Previous discourses are today's language; today's discourse is tomorrow's language. A perspective of grammar as existing ontologically prior to a communicational event has implications for language use in the real world within postcolonial Africa, since once established the grammatical rules were portrayed as operating autonomously of their creators. Their person-made origins were occluded and they were conceived as givens operating according to the laws of science (Harris 1987:43). "Because of pressures for 'objectivity' in linguistic science, the personal, or socially situated character of authors and speakers disappeared—or was made to disappear—at both the speaker and the linguist end, in pursuit of a science of a language" (Irvine 2001). Within an African context, the constructed knowledge was to be subsequently presented as natural knowledge, and the natural knowledge transformed into an official description of the language in question. The notion that grammar exists prior to communicative events also has further sociolinguistic implications in an African context in that it encourages a more normative approach to language description. This redefines what constitutes language expertise as the capacity to write grammatical rules of so-called languages. Since most of the linguistic analysts in Africa are either European or American professional linguists who more often than not have learnt African languages as second languages, or western-educated Africans, native speakers are displaced as legitimate experts of their "own" languages, influenced by a descriptive appropriation: a process which reveals the "essentially defensive nature of codfications and formulations in the fields of language study and language policy" (Fabian 1986: 136).

Assumption 3: Languages Are Made up of Discrete Units and Dual Linguacism

Another problematic assumption about language reinforced by census ideology is that language is made up of discrete systems (Makoni & Pennycook 2005). Some of the language assumptions in census ideology are problematic. That we cannot say with any confidence how many languages there are in Africa and indeed in the world at large suggests that African languages (indeed language) do not divide neatly into individual entities. Yet this is precisely how they are represented in censuses when used by governments to articulate categories, gather data and to put them to work. We are also focusing on censuses because in addition to the language provisions in constitutions they are amongst the most powerful ways in which "official" views about the construction of "language" in Africa and other categories such as ethnicity and race can be gleaned.

There is also no clear answer to the question to which language the utterances belong. For example, it's not clear whether the following utternaces are in Shona or English or both. The examples are taken from the section on obituaries and memorials in the *Herald* and *Sunday Mail*, national newspapers in Zimbabwe.

1   *Baba* (Father) it's been 6 long years. *Tave nherera* (we are not orphans). Rest in peace. *Vana venyu* (your children).

2   I long for the time we spent together. The lord gives, the Lord will take away, *Rudo rwangu haruperi rwakakura samakomo* (My love is endless it's as big as a mountain), *rwadzama samadziva* (as deep as a river), *rugosimba kunge rufu* (is as strong as death). Till we meet again. (October 1999)

The problem of determining which language the writing is in extends into the area of fiction as well. Some African novelists provide an excellent example of the problem of determining the language from a fictional writing perspective. Determining to which language an utterance belongs is not a problem peculiar to less well-known languages but is also experienced with "major" languages such as English. For example, when the 15-part series of the Story of English was televised, many of the dialects were subtitled, because they were not mutually intelligible. Nearer home, speakers of what linguists call pidgins insist that what they are speaking *is* English. So are their utterances in English or Pidgin? Perhaps the problem is the assumption that all utterances are necessarily in a "language".

Our critique of languages as discrete entities should not be construed to mean that we are simple repeating the familiar observation about the existence of geographical continua between German and Dutch on the border between the Netherlands and Germany, or are arguing for a simple chain model in whch each individual is located wth a particular social and geographical location. We are making a different argument.

African languages, like European languages, represented varieties which are not spoken by anybody, but for different reasons. In the standardisation of European languages, the representation was base on the continuum, while in Africa they were combinations of speech forms aggregated by the missionaries and linguists. In some cases this entailed combining the speech forms of different "ethnic" groups (Harries 1987)—that is to say compiling an "inventory" of speech forms as Harries describes it. The language now called "Tsonga"—which means in Zulu "The language of the conquered"—is an example of such a compilation.

Census ideology forms the basis of one of the enumerative modalities which arose in the colonial period, and has continued in postcolonial Africa. The unitary language is "not something given (*dan*) but is always in essence posited (*zadan*)—and at every moment of its life it is opposed to the realities of heteroglossia" (Bakhtin 1934 [1981]: 270). The enumerative modality is based on the assumption that the languages could be separated from other forms of behaviour and enumerated in terms of the number of speakers for each language. The problematic nature of censuses in dealing with real world issues can be illustrated using South Africa as a case study.

In nineteenth and twentieth century South Africa censuses were held at ten year intervals and at five year intervals since 1991. Both the 1980 and 1991 censuses were based on questionnaires in English and Afrikaans only and included ethnic/race and language questions. For selecting race (or population group as it was referred to) the respondent had four options: "White/Coloured/Asian/Black". The "language" question asked the respondent to indicate whether they could communicate, read, and/or write any of the following languages: "English/Black Language/Other".

Two additional questions were posed:

State which language each person most often speaks at home and if more than one language is usually spoken at home, state the other language which is spoken

The 1996 census, unlike earlier censuses, was available in eleven languages and also added more ethnicity options: African/Black, Coloured, Indian/Asian, and White.

The censuses had some flaws because only the first home language was included, so no data were available for languages other than the first home language spoken at home. Dialects such as Pretoria Sotho, and languages of recent African immigrants Yoruba and Swahili were excluded. We adopt a different perspective from that of Broeder et al. We analyse how censuses shed light on government views of language, race, and ethnicity. Censuses thus offer categories that have the effect of making up people, or engendering the existence of groups of people and languages.

If censuses nominated people and languages into existence it means censuses do not only describe prevailing realities but create realities useable for "governmentality", "erasing" other competing realities. For example, it is difficult to infer from the censuses the extent to which people may communicate by using different languages, i.e. a Zulu speaker interacting in Zulu wth a Tswana speaker responding in Tswana. Dual linguacism is thus elided by a government view of sociolinguistics.

Jeater and Hove (undated) describes how evangelists in contemporary Zimbabwe use isiZulu when speaking to Ndau speakers, and indeed descibed isiZulu as the "own tongue" of the Ndau speakers. The definition of isiZulu as the own tongue of Ndau speakers is important in so far as it marks a radical departure of what constitutes a mother tongue, namely to include the language which one "hears" and not necessarily what one is able to speak. Dual linguacism is not restricted either to historical or contemporary Africa (see Dwyer 2002 for examples of dual linguacism in Europe).

It is possible that the categories used by ordinary speakers do not correspond to official ones. For example, in the 1981 South African census African languages nominated into existence were simply referrerd to as "Black" Languages. In the 1996 census the racial categorisation had been dropped and replaced with "first mother tongue" moving away from an overtly race-based category towards a more linguistic one. The "official" accounts of language which can be gleaned from censuses are different from those used by other public bodies, such as the media. For example, the most popular radio channel in South Africa was the one which produced English programmes, followed by a channel simply called "multilingual".

The multilingual channel contrasted with other channels which broadcast in Setswana, Sepedi, Sesotho, and Xitsonga.

Multlingualism is construed wthin the South African Broadcasting Corporation (SABC) as a language, a "lingua franca" (Fardon and Furniss 1994:4). To us the official categories are interesting because of what they tell us about the government beliefs about language.

The general tendency in both the SABC and the official censuses is to treat "languages" as if they were discrete entities, and independent social actors. This may produce unintended effects in which rights are attached to languages, and not people, and where languages are treated as "killer" languages (Mufwene 2004). The census ideology, with its emphasis on languages as discrete units, exaggerates the linguistic heterogeneity of the African sociolinguistic situation because "varieties of the same language(s) are given different labels and described as full blown languages in their own right" (Djite 1988:1).

The exaggerated complexity makes language planning more difficult than it should be. It creates an image of an African sociolinguistic situation made up of numerous discrete units and artificial boundaries which do not correspond to social and functional realities, particularly of speakers who have verbal repertoires made up of fragments from many "languages" and do not focus exclusively on genetic classifications.

What we need to do is to move beyond a perception of Africa as made up of linguistic "things" to a description of the social and linguistic experiences of the language users. Such a view of language is possible if our thinking about language and African languages is predicated upon the whole language experience of the person, including the ability to translate from one language to another.

The metaphor which aptly describes what we have in mind here is that of "language" as a multilayered chain which offers an individual a set of options to be used in the immediate environment and a "steadily diminishing set of options to be employed in more distant interactions, albeit a set that is always liable to be reconnected more densely to a new environment by rapid learning, or the development of new languages" (Fardon & Furniss 1994: 4). The use of highly symbolic speech in the poor housing estates in France are an excellent example of fine layering in "language" in which the focus is not on language per se but on communicational activities.

Assumption Four: Languages Have Names
Literacy and politics played a key role in the naming of African languages. Naming was initiated by non-Africans literate in European languages and Arabic when they wanted to know to whom they were talking. This resulted in some cases in over-differentiation: for example Kanre (or Pana or Tali) in the Central African Republic were named as separate languages. The converse also occurred when speech forms were compiled and fused into the same language. The emergence of Tsonga is an excellent example (Harries 1987). The names given to African languages were not new, but had completely different meanings. For example, the terms KoreKore and Zezuru were nicknames for highlanders and northerners which were subsequently used as linguistic and ethnic labels (Chimhundu 1992).

The naming contributed to a conflation of ethnicity and language proficiency: a Zulu speaker spoke Zulu, a Yoruba spoke Yoruba (Rampton 1995; Blommaert 1992). To us what is even more important than the political nature of the naming is that it was founded on a categorisation of "language" predicated upon a botanical or animal world perception about language (Blommaert 1999: 176).

Naming was also relevant to applied linguistics since research into language attitudes was predicated on naming practices. Prior to the naming of the speech forms as languages it was not feasible to have language attitudes, hence the argument that language "attitudes were brought to Africa" (Samarin 1992: 390). The study of language attitudes in Africa began with the emergence of "languages" as a phenomenon that could be identified with certain groups (Samarin 1992: 390).

If western representations of African realities are open to question, the fundamental question then becomes about using "local" knowledge as a foundational discipline. Is it possible to conceptualise African applied linguistics outside Anglo-American frameworks? It is to this question that we now turn.

From Local Knowledge to Ethno-Applied Linguistics
"Local knowledge" is made up of beliefs and "vernacular" discourses not legitimated by any institution (Geertz 1983; Canagarajah 2002: 243). Because "local" is endogenous practice and not a body of knowledge, we avoid developing essentialised, romantic, and gendered views of knowledge (Makoni & Meinhof 2004). It is site specific, and pluralistic. Such an orientation to knowledge enables us to understand some of the problems with which linguists are confronted in Africa and indeed in other parts of the world such as Papua New Guinea, namely, how to come to terms with the problem arising when linguists are claiming that the speech forms constitute different languages, while the speakers suggest that they belong to the "same" language (Romaine 1992). For example, in Côte d'Ivoire Djite (1988) suggests that speakers of Guere and Wobe regard the two languages as the same language while linguists define them as different languages. The Guere/Wobe issue demonstrates that the external perspective of the linguists may not necessarily coincide with the inside perspective of the speakers. Resolving the problem is complicated because "language" on the one hand differs from the quests for knowledge in other areas in that the object of study "language" is not given in advance. On the other hand "linguists risk only developing a partial understanding of a linguistic situation if we dismiss popular perceptions outright because they contradict scientfic data or we cannot easily access them" (Joseph 2004: 160).

We therefore need to take into account the "lay" person's "stories" about what they speak, their beliefs about what they think they speak, how they think they should talk, and not necessarily restrict ourselves to how they speak (Cook 2002). Ignoring the perceptions of the users may produce negative results when applied linguists intervene, a problem which is however not unique to postcolonial Africa.

Historically, there has always been a "struggle" to determine which type of knowledge about African languages should be accepted. The trend to discount certain types of knowledge arose from sustained contact with speakers of African languages in the nineteenth century and developed when African linguistics as practiced in the metropolitan centres sought to become "objective". In its quest for objectivity the "language accounts of missionaries who were now participating in the academy in the metropole were discarded as unsystematic and "biased"—the metropole was not to be ruled from the periphery" (Irvine 2001: 87).

If in the metropole the debate was between missionaries and European linguists, in contemorary Africa the debate revolves around the role and status of what has unfortunately been disparagingly called "folk" linguistics. The notion of "local" applied linguistics situates "folk" linguistics within an anthropological approach to language. Incorporating a lay person's views is problematic because the views have to be ferreted out, and even when that is done it will still be necessary to demonstrate that an applied linguistics programme can be based on the local ideas.

Conclusion

In this article we have focused on "language". Our main interest has been to deconstruct the assumptions held about language with a special focus on Africa. Our argument is that those who view language from the perspective of governments and nation-state understand language differently from those who by adopting local level perspectives try and capture the user's experiences of those languages. Descriptions of language useable by governments may seem insensitive, if not coercive to local level language practices, while detailed local level descriptions of language practises may seem impractical from a nation state-government perspective. The interest in "language" is important in an ethno-applied linguistics which analyses the ways in which language is understood. An analysis of these ways is necessary because the descriptions have an impact on language users.

An examination of perceptions about language is also necessary if any social intervention is to achieve desired results. Because there are multiple and at times conflicting ways in which language is constructed, any intervention has to take into account the multiple ways in which these communities comprehend "language". Such an approach requires more rather than less "mediation" from applied linguistics. Therefore in a sense although the construct of ethno-applied linguistics is new, the notion of applied linguistics which underpins—"mediation"—is not. It is a return to an earlier and more conventional view of applied linguistics as "mediation". There is however one major distinction between the mediation of applied linguistics in earlier eras (Corder 1973; Brumfit 2001, 2004) and "mediation" as understood in ethno-applied linguistics. Mediation entails much more than interfacing between different disciplines. Applied linguists can only mediate when it interprets the different constructs of "language", for which the applied linguist has to use her own taxonomy. That taxonomy subsequently shapes other points of view, introducing "other values" and other ways of understanding "language". Mediation therefore also brings to the discussion perspectives of language other than those of applied linguists. The first obstacles to "mediation" are applied linguists themselves. This is inevitable, since as Nagel (1986:6) argues, "But since we are who we are, we can't get outside of ourselves completely. Whatever we do, we remain subparts of the world with limited access to the real nature of the rest of it and of ourselves. There is no way of telling how much of reality lies beyond the reach of present or future objectivity or any other conceivable form of human understanding".

References

Adegbija, E. (1994). *Language Attitudes in Sub-Saharan Africa.* Clevedon: Multilingual Matters.

Anderson, B. (1991). *Imagined Communities: Refections on the Origin and Spread of Nationalism.* London: Verso.

Bernstein, B. (1971). *Class, Codes and Control, Vol. 1. Theoretical Studies Toward a Sociology of Education.* London: Routledge.

Bakhtin, M. (1934 [1981]). *The Dialogic Imagination* (ed. M. Holquist) Austin: University of Texas Press.

Bamgbose, A. (2000). "Language planning in West Africa" *International Journal of the Sociology of Language* 14(1): 101-117.

Bates, R., Mudimbe, V.Y., O'Barr, J. (eds.) (1993). *Africa and the Disciplines: The Contributions of Africa to the Social Sciences and Humanities.* Chicago: University of Chicago Press.

Bloch, C. (2002). "Nurturing biliteracy through interactive writing" *Reports on Mother-tongue Education, Project for the Study of Alternative Education in South Africa, Occasional Paper* No.8: 23-31.

Blommaert, J. (1999). "Reconstructing the sociolinguistic image of Africa: grassroots writing in Shaba (Congo)" *Text* 19(2): 175-200.

Bokamba, E. (2002). *African Language Program Development and Administration.* Madison, Wisconsin: NARLC Press.

Breckenbridge, C. and P. van der Veer (eds.) (1993). *Orientation and the Postcolonial Predicament: Perspectives from South Asia.* Philadelphia: University of Pennsylvania Press.

Broeder, P. et al. (2002). *Multilingualism in South Africa: With a Focus on KwaZulu-Natal and Metropolitan Durban.* Cape Town: University of Cape Town. PRAESA Occasional Papers, 7. Accessed 1 August 2020: http://www.praesa.org.za/wp-content/uploads/2017/01/Paper7.pdf

Brokensha, D., D. Warren and O. Werner (1980). *Indigenous Knowledge Systems and Development*. Lanham, Maryland: University Press of America.
Brumfit, C. (201). *Individual Freedom in Language Teaching*. Oxford: Oxford niversity Press.
Brumfit, C. (2004a). "Applied linguistics in 2004: unity in diversity" *AILA Review* 17(1): 133-136.
Brumfit, C. (2004b). "Colloquium: Applied Linguistics and Real World Problems" American Association of Applied Linguistics, Portland, Oregon.
Canagarajah, A.S. (2002). "Celebrating local knowledge on language and education" *Journal of Language, Identity and Education* (1(4): 243-261.
Chimhundu, H. (1992). "Early missionaries and the ethnolinguistic factor during the invention of tribalism in Zimbabwe" *Journal of African History* 33: 87-109.
Chiwome, E. and J. Thondhlana (1992). "Sociolinguistics and education: a survey concerning attitudes on the teaching of Shona through the media of Shona" in R. Herbert (ed.), *Language and Society in Africa: The Theory and Practice of Sociolinguistics*. Johannesburg: Witwatersrand University Press, 247-263.
Cook, S. (2002). "Urban language in rural setting, the case of Phokeng in South Africa" in G. Gmlech and W. Zenner (eds.), *Urban Life: Readings in the Anthropology of the City*. Prospect Heights: Waveland Press, 106-113.
Corder, S.P. (1973). *Introducing Applied Linguistics*. Harmondsworth: Penguin.
Crossman, P. (1999). *Endogenisation and AfricanUniversites: Initiatives and Issues in the Quest for Plurality in the Human Sciences*. Belgian Administration for Development Corporation.
Crossman, P. and R. Devisch (2001). "Endogenous knowledge: an anthropological perspective" in C. Odora-Hoppers (ed.), *Towards a Philosophy of Articulation: IKS and its*

  Integration of Knowledge Systems. Cape Town: New Africa Education Publisher, 96-125.
Diop, C.A. (1962). *The Cultural Unity of Negro Africa.* Paris: Presence Africaine.
Djite, P. (1988). "Correcting errors in language classification: monolingual nuclei and multilingual satellites" *Language Problems and Language Planning* 12(1): 1-11.
Dwyer, D. (2002). *The Language Dialect Problem.* http//www.msu.edu/:course/426
Ela, J.-M. (1998). *Innovations sociales et renaissance de l'Afrique noire.* Paris: Harmattan.
Fabian, J. (1986). *Language and Colonial Power: the Appropriation of Swahili in the Former Belgian Congo, 1880-1938.* Berkeley and Los Angeles: University of California Press.
Fafunwa, B.A., I. McValualey, J. and J.A.Sokoya (1989). *Education in the Mother Tongue: the Primary Education Research Project (1970-1978).* Ibadan: University Press.
Fardon, R. and G. Furniss (1994). "Introduction: Frontiers and boundaries: African languages as political environments" in Fardon, R. and G. Furniss (eds.), *African Languages, Development and the State.* London: Routledge, 1-29.
Geertz, C. (1983). *Local Knowledge: Further Essays in Interpretive Anthropology.* New York: Basic Books.
Grace, G.W. (1981). *An Essay on Langage.* Columbia SC: Hornbeam Press.
Hall, S. (1997). "The local and the global: globalization and ethnicity" in A.D. King (ed.), *Culture, Globalization and the World System.* Minneapolis: University of Minneapolis Press, 19-40.
Harris, R. (1981). *The Language Myth.* London: Duckworth.
Harris, R. (1990). "On redefining linguistics" in H.Davis and T.

Taylor (eds), *Redefining Linguistics*. London: Routledge, 18-52.

Harries, R. (1987). "The roots of ethnicity: discourse and the politics of language construction in South Africa" *African Affairs*, 87(346): 125-152.

Heath, S.B. (1998). "Working through language" in S. Hoyles and C.T. Adger (eds.), *Kids Talk: Strategic Language in Later Childhood Years*. New York: Oxford University Press, 217-240.

Heryanto, A. (1995). *Language of Development and the Deelopment of Language: the Case of Indonesia*. Canberra: Department of Linguistics, Australian National University. Pacific Linguistic Series, D-86.

Hopper, P. (1998). "Emergent grammar" in M. Tomasello (ed.), *The New Psychology of Language: Cognitive and Functional Approaches to Language Study*. London: Lawrence Erlbaum Associates.

Hountondji, P. (1977). *Sur la 'philosophie africaine': critique de l'ethnophilosophie*. Paris: Maspero.

Hountondji, P. (1995). "Producing knowledge in Africa today" *African Studies Review* 38(3): 1-10.

Irvine, J. (1993). "Mastering frican languages: the politics of linguistics in 19th century Senegal" *Social Analysis* 33: 27-44.

Irvine, J. (2001). "Genres of conquest: from literature to science in colonial African linguistics" in K. Knolauch and H. Kottholf (eds.), *Verbal Arts Across Cultures: the Aesthetics and Proto-aesthetics of Communication*. Tübingen: Gunter Narr Verlag, 63-89.

Irvine, J. and S. Gal (2000). "Language ideology and linguistic differentiation" in Kroskrity, P.F. (org.) *Regimes of Language: Ideologies, Politics and Identities*. Santa Fe: School of American Research Press, 35-84. School of American Research advanced seminar series.

Jeater, D. and C. Hove (n.d.). "And the God was made word:

exploring the limitations of translation and power" (undated manuscript)

Joseph, J. (2004). *Language and Identity: National, Ethnic, Religious*. Palgrave: Macmillan.

Kashoki, M. (2003). "Language policy formulation in multilingual Southern Africa" *Journal of Multilingual and Multicultural Development* 24(3): 184-194.

Kroskrity, V. Paul (ed.) (2000). *Regimes of Language: Ideologies, Politics and Identities*. Santa Fe: School of American Research Press School of American Research advanced seminar series.

Liddicoat, A.J. (2000). "The ecological impact of a dictionary" *Current Issues in Language Planning* 1(3): 424-430.

Lucko, P., L. Peter and Hans-Georg Wolf (eds.) (2003). *Studies in African Varieties of English*. Frankfurt: Peter Lang.

Makoni, S. and U. Meinhof (2004). "Western perspective in applied linguistics in Africa" *AILA Review* 17: 77-104.

Makoni, S. and A. Pennycook (2005). "Disinventing and reconstituting languages" *Critical Inquiry in Language Studies: an International Journal* 2(3): 137-156.

Masolo, D. (1994). *African Philosophy in Search of Identity*. Bloomington, Indiana: Indiana University Press.

McWhorter, J. (1998). *The Word on the Street: Fact and Fable about American English*. New York: Plenum Press.

MacGonage, E. (2002). *A Mixed Pot: History and Identity in the Ndau Region of Mozambique*. PhD Thesis, Michigan State University.

Moumouni, A. (1968). *Education in Africa*. New York: Praeger.

Mudimbe, V.Y. (1988). *The Invention of Africa: Gnosis, Philosophy and the Order of Knowledge*. London: James Currey.

Mufwene, S. (2004). "Multilingualism in linguistic history: creolization and indigenization" in T. Bhatia and W. Ritchie (eds.), *The Handbook of Bilingualism* (pp.460-488). Malden: Blackwell.

Mühlhäusler, P. (1996). *Linguistic Ecology: Language Change and Linguistic Imperialism in the Pacific Region.* London: Routledge.

Muthwii, Margaret Jepkirui and Angelina Nduku Kioko (eds). (2004). *New Language Bearings inAfrica: A Fresh Quest.* Clevedon: Multilingual Matters.

Nagel, T. (1986). *The View from Nowhere.* New York: Oxford University Press.

Pennycook, A. (2004). "Language policy and the ecological turn" *Language Policy* 3:213-239.

Rampton, B. (1995). *Crossing: Language and Ethnicity Among Adolescents.* London: Longman.

Romaine, S. (1992). *Language, Education and Development.* Oxford: Oxord University Press.

Ranger, T. (2004). "Nationalistic historiography, patriotic history and the history of the nation: the struggle over the past in Zimbabwe" *Journal of Southern African Studies* 30(2):15-24.

Rubagumya, C. (ed.) (1990). *Language in Education in Africa: a Tanzanian Perspective.* Clevedon: Multilingual Matters.

Said, E. (1985). "An ideology of difference" *Critical Enquiry* 12(1):38-58.

Samarin, W. (1996). "Review of Adebija Efuroshina, *Language Attitudes in Sub-Saharan Africa: A Sociolinguistic Overview*" *Anthropological Linguistics* 38(2):389-395.

Scollon, S. (1977). "Language, idiolect and speech community: three views of the language at Fort Chipewyan, Alberta" *Working Papers in Linguistics, Department of Linguistics, University of Hawaii* 9(3): 65-76.

Spear, T. (2003). "Neo-traditionalism and the limits of invention in British colonial Africa" *Journal of African History* 44:3-27.

Spivak, G. (1987). *In Other Worlds: Essays in Cultural Politics.* London: Routledge.

Summers, C. (2002). *Colonial Lessons: Africans' Education in Southern Rhodesia, 1918-1940*. Portsmouth: James Currey.

Towa, M. (1979). *L'idée d'une philosophie négro-africaine*. Yaoundé: CLE.

Wallerstein, I. (1999). "The social sciences in the twenty-first century" in *World Social Science Report 1999*, Paris: UNESCO.

Webb, V. and Kembo-Sure, (eds.) (1999). *African Voices: An Introduction to the Languages and Linguistics of Africa*. Cape Town: Oxford University Press.

X

Conflicting reactions to chi'ixnakax utxiwa: A reflection on the practices and discourses of decolonization

I have read the article by Cusicanqui, who is a feminist sociologist, historian, and subaltern theorist who draws upon anarchist theory in combination with indigenous Quecha and Aymara cosmologisms in her analytical work. Because Cusicanqui focused on Bolivia, the article provided me with an opportunity to view African Global Southern sociolinguistics through the experiences of a different site in the Global South and to compare, philosophically, sociolinguistic practices in two sites of the Global South, Bolivia and Africa.

In a series of articles (see Severo & Makoni, 2014; Makoni & Severo, 2015, 2017), Severo and I compared Brazil and an African nation, Angola, and were able to illustrate, at least to our satisfaction, that, even though both Brazil and Angola shared Portuguese colonial experiences, their current political linguistic dispensations were radically different, underscoring the importance of not viewing the Global South as a homogeneous entity. The diversities within the Global South, for example, in Africa, also are likely to have an impact on knowledge production and circulation. For example, at international conferences, one is more likely to meet scholars from South Africa than from other African countries because it is easier to secure funding and visas for travel by South African scholars than it is for African scholars in other regions of Africa. Scholarship on Africa is, therefore, strongly skewed toward South Africa. The Global North also should be construed as a hierarchized space.

This is not to deny the analytical value of the Global North/Global South distinction but, rather, to draw attention to the importance of diversity within each entity (Mignolo & Walsh 2018). Methodologically, it may, therefore, be inadequate to simply state that we are dealing with either the Global North or the Global South. It is more appropriate to emphasize the sociological, economic, and historical configurations of the sites in which the analysis is situated.

Our social location has a bearing on our knowledge production and the research we conduct and the answers we are amenable to accept. I perceive myself as a Black male intellectual migrant who is working on the sociolinguistics of African languages, at a major, yet rural, university in the Global North, while retaining relatively strong personal and professional connections with institutions in the Global South. It is conceivable that, had I been a non-nomadic scholar, I would not have developed a substantial interest in how knowledge is produced in diverse contexts and interpreted or how ideas circulate, and, more importantly, I would not have sought to address issues related to conceptually mediating philosophies between the Global North and Global South. The fact that I am working in a major institution in the Global North while engaging in a sociolinguistics of African languages, a research area of marginal interest in the institution and department with which I am affiliated, has created both positive and negative aspects in how I engage with scholarship generally.

From a positive perspective, the marginality within the major rural institution with which I am affiliated has rendered it feasible to develop "border thinking". In this regard, I am critical of the Eurocentric thinking that may permeate some aspects of the sociolinguistics of African languages while, at the same time, wary of the Third World fundamentalisms that are typically couched as African perspectives or Afrocentric orientations to scholarship and are characteristic of some decolonial approaches to contemporary African scholarship.

My personal history as a scholar from the South, which has a colonized and racialized history, adds an additional intellectual wrinkle to my positionalities, which manifest themselves in an interest in *colonial linguistics, raciolinguistics, Black linguistics*, and other areas of sociolinguistics that seek to address issues of discrimination – that said, it may be possible that I may not be as subjected to comparable forms of discrimination as are African Black female sociolinguists whose work is rarely acknowledged in African sociolinguistics, either in the Global North or Global South.

Distinctions can be made between centre and periphery institutions in the Global North, and there are different hierarchies of power even within centre institutions because not everyone within these institutions wields the same amount of power or even wants to. Being on the periphery has its advantages, however, as it has led me to envisage scholarly opportunities that I might not have readily been aware of if I were not confronted with challenges of demonstrating my own relevance due to my being on the periphery of a powerful institution. Over the years, I have been aware that, in rural universities, at least in the United States, African languages do not "sell", while, at the same time, study abroad programs are the "in" thing in U.S. academia. Thus, the tying of courses in the sociolinguists of African languages to study-abroad programs has proved to be productive. The success of the programs, however, has, unfortunately, been a product of the exocitization of Africa by either White Americans or Americans of Black descent.

In addition to this, and because one can carry out research from either a Southern perspective in the Global North or from a Northern perspective in the Global South, we need to distinguish between geographical location and epistemological orientation (Blommaert, Collins & Slembrouck, 2005). For example, African philosopher Hountondji (1996), in what he calls "extraversion", outlines theoretical approaches in which the main aim is to elicit data to confirm or disconfirm pre-packaged theoretical positions, typically from the Global North. Critical Discourse Analysis (CDA) has frequently employed the notion of extraversion in the Global South when the main objective has been to illustrate the nature of power dynamics within the local contexts more so than contributing towards a reframing of CDA. If Northern epistemologies can be used in the Global South, the opposite does occur as well. For example, Southern epistemological orientations may be evident in research into the interactional dynamics of refugees, migrants, and other vulnerable communities in the Global North.

But scholarship from the Global South needs to develop alternative perspectives that widen the intellectual repertoires of scholarship. A powerful example is the concept of *Vivir Bien* (*Buen Vivir*), which, loosely translated, means "plentiful life", "sweet life", "harmonious life", "sublime life", "inclusive life", or "know how to live". *Vivir Bien* has been used as alternative to development framework. The concept has been integrated into the Bolivian and Ecuadoarian constitutions. *Vivir Bien* envisages a continual life for decolonization. The Spanish conquest initiated, 500 years ago, a new cycle that did not end with independence; the cycle continues under post-colonialism and is consolidated by new forms and structures of domination. The major criticism against *Vivir Bien* is that it has been co-opted and so vaguely construed by the state that it has now been mobilized to serve "neo-liberal" and capitalists interests and not the Bolivian and Ecuadoarian indigenous peoples.

A concept that Cusicanqui describes that has relevance to African sociolinguistics is how logic is handled in Western scholarship. Aymara philosophy is based on a trivalent logic as opposed to a binary one in Western logic; it is based on the "inclusion" of a third concept: A is not B, and B is not A, but there are times when A and B are the same thing. In binary logic, one excludes the other. This trivalent logic can be extended to complex decolonial contexts and is analogous to Woolard's (1999) *bivalency* in African sociolinguistics. For example, the same speech form may be defined as belonging to different languages simultaneously – in binary logic, the same speech form cannot belong to different categories or languages because one excludes the other. When you have inclusion, you have enormous possibilities for intercultural action, I believe.

The indigenous cosmologies that I have outlined above deal with issues of language and life on land and, unfortunately, exclude indigenous seascape epistemologies. Indigenous seascape cosmologies can be defined as modes and ways of knowing through a multiplicity of senses that include, but are not restricted to, visual, spiritual, intellectual, and embodied literacies. Indigenous seascape cosmologies should include an awareness of the complex and intricate nexus between the sea and land. Cosmologies about the land are important because colonial exploration, colonization, and forced migration produce diverse pluriversal knowledges, contact zones, and languages, including creole and pidgin languages.

I would like to conclude this forum piece by engaging with Cusicanqui's point on the importance of activism in scholarship. From an applied linguistic perspective, one could say that research into minority languages, language planning, and, to some extent, some regimes of teaching are forms of activism in which we seek to change the state of social affairs, ideally for the better, even if the goals are not explicitly stated. The goal of scholarship should be to bring about change and to avoid the curse of the *gatopardismo* in which everything changes but remains the same. However, the rise of applied linguistics, with its capitalist orientations, has led to precisely that. Applied linguistics, like other forms of scholarship in both the Global North and the Global South, has been accompanied by an accentuation of power differences between Blacks and Whites, Caucasians and minorities, males and females, those who receive a paycheck for employment and those who rely on public benefits, and those who are part of the tenure system and those who are on contractual appointments.

The increase in the precarity of one's employment status has a bearing on the nature and type of sociolinguistic research that one is willing to risk conducting. If one's employment status is precarious, one is not likely to want to invest much time and energy into long, drawn-out research projects, but may prefer, instead, short-term projects or to reanalyse secondary data. We all are worse off if the sociolinguists and applied linguists find themselves in more precarious situations. Funding agencies are instrumental in shaping scholarship, as research agencies decide what is worth investigating and what is not.

I treat this Forum piece as a contribution to a decolonial scholarship. It is decolonial for two reasons. First I have tried to illustrate how my thinking is decolonial, in so far as it takes colonialism, "empire, and racism", as important empirical and discursive objects of study. In other words, the Forum piece is decolonial because in it I have sought to explore alternative ways of thinking about the world, and alternative forms of praxis (Bhambra et al., 2018: 2). Decoloniality is still however, a very contentious strategy because the term means different things to different people. Furthermore, as a strategy to initiate change it has generated substantial resistance to it.

References

Bhambra, G. K., Gebrial, D., & Nisancioglu, K. (2018). "Introduction: Decolonising the university?" In: *Decolonising the university*. London: Pluto Press.

Blommaert, J., Collins, J., & Slembrouck, S. (2005). "Spaces of multilingualism" *Language and Communication*, 25, 197–216. https://doi.org/10.1016/j.langcom.2005.05.002

Hountondji, P. (1996). *African Philosophy: Myth and Reality*. Bloomington, MI: Indiana University Press.

Makoni, S., & Severo, C. (2015). "Lusitanization and Bakhatinian perspectives on the role of Portuguese in Angola and East Timor" *Journal of Multilingual and Multicultural Development* 36(2), 151–162. https://doi.org/10.1080/01434632.2014.909441

Makoni, S. & Severo, C. G. (2017). "An Integrationist Perspective on African philosophy" In Pablé, A. (Ed.) (2017), *The Integrational Turn in Philosophy of Language & Communication* (pp. 63–76) London: Routledge.

Mignolo, W., & Walsh, C. (2018). *On Decoloniality: Concepts, Analytics, Praxis*. Durham, NC: Duke University Press. https://doi.org/10.1215/9780822371779

Severo, C., & Makoni, S. B.. (2014). "Discourses of language in colonial and postcolonial Brazil" *Language and Communication* 34, 95–104. https://doi.org/10.1016/j.langcom.2013.08.008

Woolard, K. A. (1999). "Simultaneity and bivalency as strategies in multilingualism. *Journal of Linguistic Anthropology*, 8(1), 3–29.

XI

In response to "New Englishes"

Abstract
This paper argues that interest in "New Englishes" reflects a kind of proprietary interest in varieties of English, an interest which should be explained within a multidimensional approach which takes into account historical, economic, political and linguistic factors. Historically, the development of local varieties of English can be traced back to the British colonial language policy which encouraged the development of local languages and local varieties of English. Because of the nature of British colonial language policy, interest in "New Englishes" should be seen as part of the African scholar's attempt to react to her colonial inheritance.

Economically, interest in '"New Englishes" is an attempt by African scholars to reduce their financial contributions to the British economy. African economies unintentionally subsidise the British economy when they rely heavily on language teaching materials and tests designed by British native speakers of English. Politically, when African scholars are documenting local varieties of English, they are striving to create a sense of national identity. National identity is an important issue in post colonial Africa because most African countries are states not nations. Linguistically, documentation of "New Englishes" is aimed at changing the varieties through corpus planning and, more importantly, it is a vote for restricted proficiency. Unfortunately, by describing localised varieties of English as nativised, linguists are depriving the "New Englishes" of the very legitimacy which they want to confer on them through their description. The term "nativised" is not only part of colonial discourse, but is also pejorative. The term has not yet been sufficiently rehabilitated in post colonial discourse in Africa for it to confer legitimacy.

Introduction
The paper argues that in order to appreciate why African scholars have been fascinated for some time, and continue to be fascinated by "New Englishes", their scholastic activities have to be placed in a wider context which takes into account the impact of historical, economic, political and linguistic factors.

The historical aspect of the paper has three major aims. First, it outlines some of the factors which have given English its current position. Second, it argues that an understanding of "New Englishes" is enhanced by examining the role of British colonial language policies. Thirdly, it demonstrates that the attempt to define "New Englishes" on the basis of the popular EFL/ESL distinction is unsatisfactory because of the inconsistencies in the way the terms are employed.

Guardians of standard English are not keen to legitimate localised varieties of English because this would threaten some of the economic advantages which accrue to them as native speakers of English. Politically, African scholars view their description of "New Englishes" as part of their contribution towards nation building. Linguistically, the description of "New Englishes" is part of language standardisation and IS a quest for legitimacy. The paper concludes by examining the implications of the arguments outlined above for Zimbabwe.

1 New Englishes and the problem of the ESL/EFL divide
"New Englishes" is the term used to describe the English used in ESL countries (Kachru 1983). It is common practice in

Britain to draw a distinction between ESL and EFL countries, with the label "New Englishes" restricted to countries labelled as ESL.

The term ESL is used to describe the English used in countries such as Zimbabwe, Nigeria, Kenya and Zambia. In such countries, although English is not a native language for the majority of the population, it is widely used in government, administration and creative writing. Another characteristic feature of ESL countries is the emergence of local varieties of English attributed partly to the widespread use of English and the absence of English native speaker influence. English is a foreign language in former Portuguese and Francophone colonies such as Mozambique and the Ivory Coast where it is taught as a subject, but is not the medium of instruction.

The attempt to define "New Englishes" with reference to ESL is most welcome because the distinction has educational and social significance. Unfortunately, the terms are used inconsistently (Phillipson 1991; 1992). One may cynically argue that the distinction between the terms is blurred because of their social and educational significance. It seems more accurate to speak of the various EFL/ESL situations in a particular area of the country rather than attempt to categorise the whole country.[1]

The categorisation of countries as either ESL/EFL is further complicated by the fact that some situations which are described as ESL may be recategorised as EFL depending on the ideological persuasion of the individual analyst. For instance, the Director of the Organization of African Unity of Inter-African Languages labels English and French as foreign languages

---

[1] Zimbabwe is generally categorised as an ESL country (Ngara 1982), but the label unfortunately, overlooks the diversity of the sociolinguistic contexts within which English is used and learnt in that country. In urban Zimbabwe, on the one hand, the amount of English school-going children are exposed to is so rich and diverse that the situation is best described as an ESL situation. The situation is radically different in rural communities, where exposure is restricted exclusively to the classroom. In Zimbabwe, the ESL/EFL divide therefore corresponds to an urban/rural divide.

(Mateene 1985 cited in Phillipson 1991). The description of English as a foreign language emphasizes English's alien nature because of its connection with British colonialism. Obviously, the labelling of English as a foreign language overlooks the degree to which English was used in African liberation struggles and continues to be used in the fight for a more democratic Africa (Bloor and Bloor 1990).

As pointed out earlier, another characteristic feature of "New Englishes" is the emergence of localised norms of usage, attributed in part to the absence of English native speaker influence. The absence of English native speaker influence in the so-called localised norms is more of a fiction than a reality. Although there are very few native speakers in most countries in which "New Englishes" are evolving, the physical absence of native speakers should not be construed to mean that there is no native speaker influence. The native speaker of English has been disembodied and technologised. Her physical presence is no longer necessary, because through the influence of institutions like the BBC and the Voice of America, the use of English in Africa is stronger than would have been the case if the native speaker were physically present. Commenting on the role of the BBC in promoting English native influence, Whitley (1971: 4) aptly observes:

> The English language is to be used to bind together the ruling bourgeoisie of the countries which Britain wishes to retain within her orbit of influence, whereas vernaculars are to be used to instigate counter-revolution in countries attempting to build socialism. Is this the reason that the BBC continues to use Swahili in its broadcasts to East Africa?

2 English in its African and global context

In order to understand the various sociolinguistic positions English currently occupies in the African context and the world, it is necessary to appreciate the current status English enjoys as an international language. English has a dominant though not exclusive position in science, medicine, computers and international diplomacy.

> From a minor language in 1600, English has in less than four centuries come to be the leading language of international communication in the world today. This remarkable development is ultimately the result of the 17th, 18th and 19th century British successes in conquest, colonisation and trade (Troike 1977:2).

Not only is the presence of English in Africa an outcome of British colonialism and the spread of international capital, it is also a product of the concerted efforts of organizations such as the American Ford Foundation and the British Council. For instance, the British Council was set up in 1934 and granted a royal charter in 1940 "for the purposes of promoting a wider knowledge of the UK and the English language abroad and developing closer cultural relations between the UK and other countries" (Whitely 1971:4). The British Council not only spread English, but perhaps fuelled the myth of the native speaker as the ideal language teacher—a myth which is widespread and goes largely unchallenged because of the economic advantages which accrue to native speakers of English from it.

The status of English was boosted by the emergence of the USA as a major military and technological power in the aftermath of World War II. The technological might of the USA was felt not only in the spread of English, but in the type of language teaching methods which were used. For instance, audiolingualism had the strongest impact in countries which were technologically weak (Phillipson 1990), in as much as the impact of American capital was particularly felt in the poorest countries. Not only was English being spread, but particular language teaching methods and myths were also being promoted.

Contrary to the view Davies (1986) and Wardhaugh (1987) take, after gaining independence from Britain, African governments pursued policies which were only superficially different. The policies ranged from a complete retention of English as a medium of instruction in Kenya and Zimbabwe to a limited retention in Tanzania because of the latter's policy of Swahilization.

But the differences between the language policies of these countries, in spite of their ideological differences, were more apparent than real. English was a requirement for top jobs and university education, even in Tanzania in which English was for some time replaced by Swahili in primary and early secondary education.

Evidence of the continued importance of English is the increasing number of African elite whose children are acquiring English as a mother tongue, a phenomenon which has been observed in countries as far afield as Zimbabwe and Ghana (Makoni 1989; Chinebuah 1981). This challenges the argument that the English native speaker is on the retreat in Africa. The increasing number of African native speakers of English led Mazrui (1975) to predict (rather optimistically) that by the year 2000 there will be more Black people who speak English as a mother tongue in Africa than in Britain. What is interesting about Ali Mazrui's observation, however, is not the accuracy of his prediction but the sociolinguistic implications of language spread implied in his prediction. In some instances the spread of English is replacive and not additive, resulting in "linguicide" (Spolsky 1991).[2]

---

[2] English is not only competing with some African languages as a mother tongue, it has also begun to win recruits from European languages in Africa such as Portuguese and French. Mozambique has increasingly begun to realise the advantages of English over Portuguese for full participation in some of the regional organisations. A majority of Mozambique's neighbours are English speaking, for example Zimbabwe, Zambia, South Africa, etc.

Arguably, interest in "New Englishes" was forced on the agenda of language scholars by their realisation that the sun might not set on the "Empire of English". Through their documentation of "New Englishes", language scholars were unintentionally reinforcing the permanent status of English in Africa.

3 New Frenches

The situation of the French language in Africa is in many respects comparable to that of English, but there is one major difference. Both French and English are Languages of Wider Communication (LWC), partly because of their continued use in their former colonies, and their dominant role in international trade, diplomacy and academia.

There is, however, one major difference between French and English as LWCs. Interest in "New Frenches" in French applied linguistics is neither comparable to that of "New Englishes" in British applied linguistics, nor is the study of localised varieties of French as respectable an "area of academic enquiry" as the study of localised Englishes. This difference can be attributed to a large degree to the nature of British and French colonial language policies.

4 Colonial language policies

The disparity in the statuses of former colonial languages in their non-European contexts (i.e. in situations in which non-localised varieties are either evolving or have been institutionalised) can be traced to differences between British and French colonial policies, particularly where they related to language. The French pursued a policy of direct rule which placed emphasis on French, which was considered the language of "high culture". Local languages were treated with contempt (Wardhaugh 1987).[3]

---

[3] The French, however, were not consistent in the implementation of their policy. Phillipson (1991) points out that the French encouraged the development and use of local languages even in sub-Saharan Africa, particularly in

On the other hand, the British pursued a policy which, although similar to the French in aiming at distinguishing the coloniser from the colonised, encouraged the development of local languages in early educational instruction and literacy activities. In 1950, for instance, there were ten vernacular literature bureaux or committees in British Africa for the production of teaching and reading materials. Colonial officers were also encouraged to learn at least the African language of the region (unlike some of their modern British Council counterparts, who appear to be proud of their ignorance of the L1 of the countries to which they are posted). The recognition of local languages in British Africa was taking place in a triglossic situation in which standard English was the high form vis-a-vis the localised varieties of English. The latter, in turn, were regarded as more prestigious than the local indigenous languages. Interest in "New Englishes" is, arguably, an attempt by an African scholar to come to terms with her colonial intellectual inheritance.

5 Language standardisation

Standardisation may also play an important role in generating interest in "New Englishes". One dimension along which languages may differ is whether they are standardised or not. Even after being standardised, languages differ in the degree to which they are standardised, with the process of standardisation itself never fully complete, because languages are inherently dynamic. The extreme standardisation of the French language may be due to the functions of the French Academy (Academie Française).

The extreme standardisation of French manifests itself in the insistence by the French on a metropolitan standard, which creates an "intolerance of dialects and languages within national borders, xenophobic national linguistic purity and an expansionist urge externally" (Phillipson 1991: 89). The legal measures employed by the French parallel those employed by Fascist reg-

---

countries such as Mali. As a rule, however, the French did not encourage the use of local languages.

imes in Italy, Germany, and Spain. It is a sobering experience to realise that a country may be democratic, but its language policies fascist.

The high degree of dialectal intolerance in the standardisation of French created an atmosphere which militated against the recognition of local dialects of French in former French colonies.[4]

6 The creation of new states and the emergence of "New Englishes"

Wardhaugh's (1987) observation that "the reality of the modern world is that most states are not nations" is relevant to postcolonial Africa, where states were arbitrarily created during European colonialism. One of the many consequences of the arbitrariness with which colonial boundaries were drawn is that the same ethnic group would find itself split and consequently compelled to identify with groups drawn from diverse backgrounds—a sure recipe for national instability. Examples of groups split across many political boundaries abound in Africa.

Because of the diversity of ethnic groups within each state, feelings of national consciousness are at times salient by their absence. The absence of national feelings is an important

---

[4] If interest in "New Frenches" is difficult to cultivate because standardisation creates languages which are "pathological in their lack of diversity" (Hudson 1980: 34), it is possible to argue that "localisation" of English is likely to occur in those areas of English which are less standardised, because there is no language which is uniformly standardised.

Spelling, according to Stubbs (1986) is the most highly standardised area of the English language. Standard spellings are listed in major dictionaries. There are two major types of spelling, British and American. There are no studies to my knowledge into the nurture of spelling in "New Englishes". The majority of studies into New Englishes have concentrated on areas which are not highly standardised. Because use of the lexicon and pronunciation are less highly standardised, they permit a great deal of variability, hence are more susceptible to localisation. A considerable amount of work in "New Englishes" has focused on the lexicon and vocabulary (Sey 1973; Platt, Weber and Ho 1984; Criper-Freedman 1991; Bokamba 1991).

element contributing to the frequent attempts at secession—a phenomenon quite common in Africa. The Nigerian and Ugandan civil wars and the military confrontation in Southern Zimbabwe in the mid-eighties were attempts at secession.

In a bid to manufacture feelings of national identity, African governments have frequently invented symbols such as national flags and anthems. The symbols are part of the attempts by African governments to convert states into nations. Nation formation, as Brass (1974) aptly observes, requires a "pool of symbols" and, arguably, "New Englishes" are part of the repertoire of symbols.

If the politicians reacted to the absence of feelings of national identity by creating national symbols, the academics responded in different ways to the quest for national identity, depending on their area of academic expertise. Just as historians chronicled the great achievements of past African states, such as tracing the origins of present day Zimbabwe to the Mhunhumutapa Empire, so language scholars have begun to identify patterns in oral and written texts which, if taken collectively, mark the text as either Ghanaian, Nigerian, Zimbabwean or African (Bokamba 1982; Owusu-Ansah 1991).

Although the documentation of "New Englishes" is linguistic, the functions which the documentation serves are political: it is a response by language scholars to the absence of national identity and an attempt to create one. In other words, the documentation of "New Englishes" is a linguistic task firmly rooted in nationalistic consciousness and sentimentality. Arguably, the attempt to alter the status of "New Englishes" through description parallels what British and American linguists sought to achieve through their description of non-standard dialects of English. Stubbs (1986: 20) expresses the point quite forcefully when he says:

> Descriptions of social reality become persuasive as soon as people become aware of them. For example, the atten-

tion that linguists have given to non-standard dialects of English, community languages in Britain, and British and American sign language has changed the status of these languages. Sometimes this has been the overt aim: to attack the notion that such language varieties are in any way "primitive". **But they mean that description becomes prescription due to dissemination** .... there is no such thing as pure research on language and society. (The emphasis is mine.)

The description of fragments of "New Englishes" is an exercise in manipulating status planning through corpus planning.

7 Localisation
Localisation may contribute towards some of the interest by African scholars in "New Englishes". Localisation is an extremely powerful factor in most newly independent African countries. Localisation in some instances manifests itself as Africanisation.

Localisation operates on at least three different levels: staffing, content and approaches to content. In terms of staffing, most newly formed governments seek to replace the expatriate staff with locally trained personnel. Consistent with the localisation of staff, or strictly speaking as a result of it, is the localisation of content (subject matter). In most former British colonies this involves de-Europeanising the curriculum, hence the emergence of subjects such as African literature and African history. Interest in "New Englishes" is part of the general concern with studying something which is typically African or non-European.

Research into localised varieties should be interpreted as an attempt by language scholars to achieve a level of linguistic localisation analogous to that found in African literature, and African history. But there is one major difference which is in danger of being overlooked between content subjects and language. There are native speakers of English, but there cannot be native speakers of African history and African literature etc. (unless one is using "native speaker" in a specialised sense to refer to "expertise in" as Paikeday 1989 does). Localisation of language cannot proceed in the same way as localisation of content subjects because of the native speaker. The absence of native speakers of history and literature facilitates domestication of those disciplines. Conversely, the presence of native speakers of English constrains its localisation in African contexts.

8 The democratisation and ownership of English

As pointed out above, linguistically, the "LOCALISATION" of English aims to achieve a level of linguistic independence commensurate with political independence. The idea of Zimbabwean English began to be mooted, as MacGinley (1987) points out, a number of years after the attainment of independence by Zimbabwe in 1980.

Studies into localised varieties of English constitute an attempt to break away from the subordinate position which the emerging varieties occupy, if the view that English is "owned" by native speakers of English is maintained in Western Scholarship; hence the argument that "there is no national right of ownership attached to English. Any language is the property of the speech community that utilises it and English is now the property of many communities that transcend national boundaries and include native and non-native speakers alike" (Bloor and Bloor: 41). Bloor and Bloor's argument is echoed by a number of scholars including Strevens (1983) and more recently Greenbaum (1991).

Crystal (1985) puts the number of English native speakers in the core countries at about 350 million. The number of non-native speakers outside ranges from 300 to 1000 million. The "numbers game" is part of what Quirk (1989) cynically calls "liberation linguistics". The "numbers game" is designed to appeal to the democratic sentiments of the academic community, because, as the argument goes, if there are as many non-native speakers as there are native speakers, then the non-native speakers have as much right to English ownership as the native speakers do. Legally, the "numbers game" is designed to draw attention to the language rights of the non-native speaker. The language rights of the non-native speaker are part of the speaker's cultural and social rights. Expressed more emphatically, ownership of non-native varieties by second language users is as much part of their constitutional rights as are their social and cultural rights. In spite of the powerful nature of the "liberation linguistics" argument, one wonders how the putative number of speakers of English was arrived at, because census figures, which may be the potential source of such information, are notoriously unreliable in Africa. Furthermore, those who happily cite the number of non-native speakers of English do not identify what the minimum level of proficiency is that one has to acquire before being counted as a user of English. It is highly questionable to regard all users of English as having the right to own English irrespective of their proficiency in it.

9 Economic considerations
Sir Richard Francis, Director General of the British Council argues:

> Britain's real black gold is not the North Sea oil but the English language. It has long been at the root of our culture and now is fast becormng the global language of business.

English has grown into one of Britain's major economic resources because of its status and role in international business. In order for Britain to fully exploit the status of English for the benefit of the UK, the native speaker is placed at the centre of English language teaching. The Director of the international house in London aptly summarises the situation in a brochure when he writes:

> Once we used to send gunboats and diplomats abroad; now we are sending English teachers (p. 42 Economic Intelligence Unit).

Quirk (1989) reflects a similar view when he comments that some of the English teachers are qualified "through accident of birth, that they happen to be native speakers of English".

The financial benefits accruing to the UK, the USA etc, are threatened if Africa can claim "ownership" of the emerging varieties, for two reasons. Firstly, the language teaching materials meant for Africa will not be described with reference to standard English. Secondly, the English language examinations offered by the University of Cambridge will no longer be appropriate, and there are at least a quarter of a million candidates takmg the Cambridge exams annually (Spolsky 1991).

During a period of recession such as is currently being experienced by the UK and the USA, the recognition of "New Englishes" in education in Africa could have adverse effects on the native speaker of English who benefits from the expanding English language teaching business. From an African perspective, interest in "New Englishes" is an attempt by African linguists to save African governments from unintentionally subsidising the UK and the USA.

10 Education and the indigenisation of the teaching force

In Zimbabwe, as elsewhere in Africa, the advent of independence after a prolonged period of colonial rule brought with it a rapid expansion in education, at least at the primary school level. Makoni (1989) points out that Zimbabwean primary education expanded tenfold in 1989. The rapid expansion in education has resulted in the majority of the pupils' being taught by non-native speakers of English whose proficiency in the target language is very low. One way of rendering the variety of English the speakers are using sociolinguistically respectable and educationally acceptable is to argue that the teachers are using a localised variety. The teachers themselves therefore become experts in the variety of English they are using, and consequently attempts to compare the local variety with standard English become misplaced. In Zimbabwe, it is not without sociolinguistic significance that the term "Zimbabwean English" gained popularity in some circles at the same time as some people began to complain about the falling standards of English (McGinley 1987).

Talk of "Zimbabwean English" or more boldly educational interest in the functional adequacy of English, it would appear to me, is an attempt to avoid addressing the issue of language in education, something which was not an issue earlier because there was very little education available.

The term "Zimbabwean English" is also ambivalent—an ambivalence which might be absent in the use of terms such as "Nigerian English" or "Ghanaian English". In Zimbabwe the term might refer not only to the English used by Africans, but to the English used by Zimbabweans of European descent—two types of English one might usefully keep separate.

11 The illegitimacy of "New Englishes"

A considerable amount of research effort is spent on documenting new varieties of English as a way of establishing their legitimacy. The description of these varieties as "the Other Tongue" or as "nativised" does, contrary to the expectations of the analysts, deprive these very varieties of the legitimacy which the analysts seek to achieve through their interventionistic descriptions which alter the objects of their description. Rampton (1990) succinctly sums up the situation when he suggests that by describing "New Englishes" as "the Other Tongue", Kachru and others are reinforcing the subordinate position of "New Englishes", because they describe the "New Englishes" using standard English—something which, theoretically, they would like to avoid, but in practice, reinforce.

The illegitimacy of the term "nativised" can be seen when it is contextualised in history. Makoni (1991: 18) contextualises the term thus:

> During the colonial period, Africans were described as "natives" (see Phimister 1985). This is a term comparable in its pejorative force to "Kaffir", a term used by the South African White government to refer to the Blacks. From a Southern African perspective, it is a contradiction to argue that the English used by Africans is given legitimacy if it is called nativised. Nativisation of English delegitimises it.

Support for the existence of "New Englishes" comes from groups with conflicting ideological interests. The first group, as pointed out earlier, is made up of African academics who are interested in "New Englishes" for nationalistic reasons. The second group is made up of English purists who feel that non-native speakers cannot acquire standard English, so there is nothing to lose from encouraging the development of localised varieties of English because the varieties are not bona fide parts of the English language. Thus, the development of "New Englishes" is in itself a testimony to their inability to master English. The forging of an alliance between the extreme right and extreme left is not unique to the "New Englishes" controversy but is also characteristic of mother tongue teaching in the UK.

The rejection of localised varieties of English at the grassroots level arises from an awareness of TWO important factors:

1 Those who champion the cause of "New Englishes" are themselves experts in using standard English, as demonstrated by their ability to champion the "New Englishes" cause through standard English in international journals.

2 The common person at the grassroots level feels that if "New Englishes" are used as language teaching models, she would be deprived of access to a variety which is used in academic and technological literatur.

12 Conclusion

This paper has sought to identify political, historical, economic and linguistic factors which may partly account for the continued interest by African scholars in "New Englishes". It has been argued in this paper that central to the whole debate is a kind of proprietary interest by linguists, teachers and other establishments. Another factor which is frequently overlooked in the debate about the legitimacy of "New Englishes" is the sociolinguistic significance the common person attaches to "New Englishes" in promoting her social advancement.

References

Bloor, Merriel and Thomas Bloor (1990). "The role of English in resurgent Africa" In *Language and Power, British Studies in Applied Linguistics* 5:32-44.

Bokamba, Eyamba G. (1983). "The Africanisation of English. In Kachru, B.B. (Ed), *The Other Tongue: English Across Cultures.* Urbana IL: University of Illinois Press:72-79.

Bokamba, Eyamba G. (1991). "Sociolinguistic theories in the African context: An agenda for the 1990's" Paper presented at the Sixth Biannual International Conference; University of Port Elizabeth, South Africa.

Chineua, Isaac K. (1981). "Language policy and practice in education in Ghana" *AILA Bulletin* 2(30):8-36.

Criper-Freedman, L. (1990). "The tone system of West African Coastal English" *World Englishes,* 9(1):63-77.

Davies, Alan (ed). (1982). "Introduction to special issue on language and identity" In *Journal of Multilingual and Multicultural Development,* 3(3).

Davies, Alan (ed) (1986). *Language Education in Africa.*

Seminar proceedings No. 26, Centre for African Studies, University of Edinburgh.
Hudson, R. (1980). *Sociolinguists.* Cambridge, U.K.: Cambridge University Press.
Kachru, B.B. (ed). (1983). *The Other Tongue: English Across Cultures.* Urbana: University of Illinois Press.
Makoni, Sinfree B. (1989). *Planning Variability in Second Language Acquisition.* Unpublished PhD dissertation, Department of Applied Linguistics, University of Edinburgh.
Makoni, Sinfree B. (1991). "Post graduate researching in applied linguistics: reflections on applied linguistics post-graduate experience in the U.K."
Mazrui, Ali (1975). *The Political Sociology of the English Language: an African Perspective.* The Hague: Mouton.
McGinley, Kevin (1987). "The future of English in Zimbabwe" *World Englishes,* 6(2):159-164.
Ngara, Emmanuel (1982). *Bilingualism and Language Education.* Harare, Zimbabwe: Mambo.
Owusu-Ansah, Lawrence (1991). "Is it or is it not interlanguage: a head-on confrontation with non-native English" *Edinburgh Working Papers in Applied Linguistics,* 2:51-62.
Paikeday, T.M. (1985). *The Native Speaker is Dead.* Toronto and New York:Paikeday Publishing.
Phillipson, Robert (1990). *English Language Teaching and Imperialism.* Tronninge, Denmark: Transcultural.
Phillipson, Robert (1991). "Some items on the hidden second/foreign language acquisition" In Phillipson, Robert, Eric Keelerman, Larry Smith, Michael Sharwood Smith and Merrill Swain (eds), *Foreign/Second Language Pedagogy Research.* Clevedon: Multilingual Matters: 38-52.
Phillipson, Robert (1992). *Linguistic Imperialism.* Oxford: Oxford University Press.
Phimister, Ian (1988). *An Economic and Social History of Zimbabwe.* London and New York: Longman.

Platt, John, H. Weber and M.L. Ho (1984). *The New Englishes.* London: Routledge and Kegan Paul.

Quirk, Randolph & Henry G. Widdowson (eds). (1985). *English in the World: Teaching and Learning the Language and Literature.* Cambridge: Cambridge University Press.

Rampton, Ben H. (1990). "Displacing the native speaker: Expertise, affiliation and inheritance" *English Language Teaching Journal,* 44(2):97-101.

Romaine, Suzanne (1984). *The Language of Children and Adolescents: The Acquisition of Communicative Competence.* Oxford: Blackwell.

Sey, Kof A. (1973). *Ghanaian English: An Exploratory Survey.* London: MacMillan.

Stubbs, Michael (1986). *Educational inguistics.* London: Basil Blackwell.

Strevens, Peter (1983). "The localised forms of English" In

Kachru, B.B. (ed.), *The other Tongue: English Across Cultures.* Urbana IL: University of Illinois Press: 23-31.

Spolsky, Bernard (1991). "English and endangered languages" Paper read at a conference on Language in Venezuela.

Troike, R. (1977). "The future of English" Editorial in *The Linguistic Reporter,* 14 February 1982.

XII

On speaking multilanguages: urban lingos and fluid multilingua francas
(with Busi Makoni and Alastair Pennycook)

Introduction
The chapter is based on an analysis of the award-winning South African film, *Tsotsi*, in which multiple languages and entwined semiotic resources are used. By analysing the film, we explore the nature and type of an emergent multilingualism associated with plurilingual and multicultural societies depicted in both song and dialogue. The multilingualism is emergent because it is always in a state of becoming (Otsuji & Pennycook 2010) and has no clearly discernible target which it is approximating unlike concepts such as transitional bilingualism in which there is an implicit target language (Garcia 2003). Although there is a tendency to regard emergent multilingualism as novel, a product of accelerated urbanisation, the assumption cannot be supported by historical evidence and is a conceptual consequence of maintaining too firm a distinction between synchronic and diachronic (socio-) linguistics, urban and rural, tradition and modernity.

The aim of the chapter is to contribute to an understanding of language use in urban contexts in South Africa, to a more general reconsideration of multilingualism, and to an understanding of the role of popular culture in sociolinguistic research. Multilingualism has often been understood in terms of top-down enunciations which are based on languages as distinct codes that can be counted, crossed (Rampton 2006), switched or mixed. Recent research has shown that such boundaries or distinctions are a product of specific language ideologies. Yet in complex multilingual contexts such as urban centres, language use shows borderlessness. Thus, an analysis of language practices from below reflects instances of 'borderless language use' (Otsuji & Pennycook 2010: 3) wherein features are symbiotically integrated to form a lingua franca that is 'fluid'. Even though this shifting or fluid language practice is evident in urban centres, owing to cyclical migration and modem media such practices can be found in rural areas (Cook 2009). Specifically, it investigates whether valuable insights can also be gained which may have an impact on our conceptualisations of 'fluid' multilingualism in plurilingual contexts and the adequacy of the theoretical apparatus in sociolinguistics for dealing with entwined systems. Attention to the linguistics of film not only brings together various linguistic aspects through talk, but also through the semiotics of body movement and other visual modalities which might be missed by a disembodied linguistic analysis.

The rise of new urban multilingualism presents numerous challenges for sociolinguistics and the study of multiple language use. Based on a long history of European concepts of languages, where languages have come to be seen as discrete entities, and bi- or multilingualism is seen as the addition of one or more of these to an individual repertoire or social context, sociolinguistic approaches to multilingualism do not have ready tools for dealing with the new urban language varieties emerging across the world, particularly in the contexts of the rapid urbanisation and social change in many parts of Africa (Makoni & Pennycook 2005). These urban varieties can be characterised by a number of features: they draw on and use a wide range of linguistic resources; they are constantly in flux; they are predominantly oral; they are street languages; and they are often linked to popular culture, crime and urban unrest (Spitulnik 1998). To speak these languages requires not only a multilingual capacity as commonly conceived (the ability to use distinct linguistic codes), but also a facility for handling a mobile multilanguage. These urban languages are also multilanguages in themselves, diverse, shifting, and variable according to who is using them with whom, at what point, and to what effect. In fact, these urban languages are an example of multilingualism from below which challenges 'the idea that languages are systems of communication that are used by people in different contexts... in favor of a view of language as a local practice whereby languages are a product of the deeply social and cultural activities in which people engage' (Pennycook 2010: 1).

The perspective that the 'mixing' or use of multiple languages in one site is a recent phenomenon is a consequence of the a-historical character of most code-switching literature from Africa. The existence of multiple languages in one site preceded colonialism. That being so, the phenomenon of using multiple languages or for that matter, 'mixing' of languages, is not a post-colonial phenomenon. Cities in precolonial Africa contained people from diverse historical and linguistic backgrounds. The phenomenon of linguistic assemblage was largely hidden from view because sociolinguists in Africa were preoccupied with controversies about which language to use and not with the variety of African languages (see Makoni et al. 2010, Cook 2002).

Each ensemble arising from multiple language use is composed of linguistic items drawn from multiple resources which reflect both the speaker's personal and social experiences and the contextual configurations of language possibilities. The use of these multilanguages is thus a result both of the complexity of multilingual environments and the creativity of language users as they create and remix language resources. Multilanguages – temporary, fluid configurations of language resources –

take on properties that from a conventional perspective none of the source languages possessed. Speaking multilanguages is therefore *less an instance of using different languages* as commonly construed and more akin to what Jørgensen (2008: 166) calls *polylingualism*, where 'speakers use features and not languages', or what Otsuji and Pennycook (2010) have termed *metrolingualism*, which describes the ways in which people of different and mixed backgrounds use, play with and negotiate identities through language, particularly in urban contexts. All these terms avoid assumed connections between language, culture, ethnicity, nationality or geography, and seek instead to explore how such relations are produced, resisted, defied or rearranged. The focus is not on *language systems* but on *languages as emergent from contexts of interaction and how language is constituted by as well as constitutive of its locality* (Pennycook 2010).

Code-switching in sociolinguistics

There is extensive literature on linguistic code-switching (CS) in Africa and other parts of the world (see Myers-Scotton 1998; Ferguson 2003, 2009; Bullock & Toribio 2009), and in this section we make a brief exposition of this literature in order to highlight the main argument of the chapter: the problematic nature of conceptualisation of language as discrete boxes, which leads to a view of multilingualism as plural monolingualism, or multiple 'solitudes', which is what top-down approaches assume. The CS literature is predicated on the assumption that the speakers are using different languages which they sometimes mix. From a CS perspective the language spoken by X may be analysed as composed of elements from English, Afrikaans and Tswana, whereas that of Y may be made up of Zulu, Afrikaans and English, but this may contradict the experiences of the speakers if we are interested in local language ideologies: how people understand their own language use locally.

In some cases, the so-called 'mixed languages' may be perceived as a 'fused lect' (Auer 1999) and not 'a mixture' (Meeuwis & Blommaert 1998). This suggests that the variety itself is a single language, a single code, and *not* a combination of different nameable languages. Because the speaker may not necessarily be able to articulate the same message in 'unmixed forms' (Kubhchandani 1997), each speaker's 'fused lect' is continuously varying and changing depending on each social encounter (Aycard 2008) and social biography, making it difficult to use a code-switching model which, to some extent, treats languages as a-historical reified categories. Owing to the variation between individuals' social biographies we are extremely careful when we group language practices into speech communities, or claim that particular features are peculiar to given contexts, urban or rural. We therefore prefer a model of analysis which captures singularity (uniqueness) while still indicative of plurality, i.e., a form of dynamic singular multilingualism or 'metrolingualism'.

From a philosophical standpoint, in the film *Tsotsi*, for instance, we cannot assume that if Boston uses what we as analysts view as multiple languages in one speech encounter, that he necessarily has full control of each of the different languages in their 'pure form' (i.e. unmixed). Indeed, it might be plausible that societal norms may militate against the use of these languages in their 'pure' form; after all, 'pure form' is, in any case, a linguistic myth (Harris 1998). Each speaker's 'fused lects' may vary in terms of degree, facility and complexity as these are based on the available resources associated with each language. The challenge for sociolinguistics is that 'there is no appropriate lexicon' with which to speak about such a phenomenon. The only way in which the phenomenon can be described is by referring to 'two' codes (languages) or at least two labels for the same code (Meeuwis & Blommaert 1998) or potentially contradictory terms such as 'multilingual Zulu' (Aycard 2008) which suggests both 'fluidity and'fixity'.

Nonetheless, notions such as fluid multilingualism and multilanguage may help in resolving the problem of describing language practices without referring to the idea of languages as codes, especially if we argue that speakers use 'features and not languages' (Jørgensen 2008: 166), and that participants may not necessarily orient to the juxtaposition of languages in terms of switching, but orient to a linguistic norm where all available linguistic and semiotic resources can be utilised to accomplish the goals of the speaker. From such a perspective it is not enough to categorise conversation as code switching or mixing or bilingual or multilingual because all the terms are based on the separability of language (Møller 2008: 218) and thus reinforce the idea of 'multiple solitudes' (Cummins 2008).

Studying sociolinguistic phenomena through film
The film *Tsotsi* allows us insights into the workings of such multilanguages for it is through the media of popular culture – film, popular music – that we can capture glimpses of this fleeting, changing world. There are of course good reasons for caution when using popular cultural texts as a source of sociolinguistic data. It might be argued, for example, that the language of film, music or novels is 'inauthentic, since these are artistic creations rather than linguistic descriptions and therefore represent something of a 'hyper-reality' (an exaggeration of speech variety for particular effect) rather than everyday speech. They do, however, reveal significant insight into people's actual understanding of their language use locally and the social indexicalities of particular types of language practices.

By and large, the central concern with the use of such data from film is 'authenticity'. Naturally gathered data are acceptable for sociolinguistics whereas 'constructed' data have only recently been used in sociolinguistic research. There are several reasons, however, why a rigid distinction between natural and constructed data cannot be sustained. The construction of artificial data builds upon perceived naturally occurring data. 'Naturally occurring data', even in the work of rigorous sociolinguists such as Rampton (2006), cannot escape elements of performance. We have always had to live with the paradox of observation, which is why, once we start to question sociolinguistic orthodoxies about what is natural, authentic and real, we ask '*Is* it in fact possible to define naturalness in speaking, and to determine when speaking is and is not natural?' (Coupland 2007: 25), and we may be better off thinking in terms of style rather than authenticity. Coupland points out that 'when we start to unpack the ideological politics of linguistic authenticity, we can't avoid seeing authenticity...as a discursive construction' (2007: 182). Once we therefore appreciate the commonality of performance and the importance of style, we can 'think of "authenticity in performance", or the construction of *second level authenticities*' (2007: 184; emphasis in original). This by no means reduces the need for good data and careful analysis, but it does suggest that the divisions between the 'real' and the 'non-real' (or, one might say, between the authentic and the real) need careful consideration. While remaining cautious and contextual about the claims being made, we can see that there are therefore good reasons to use film language as sociolinguistic data. We use film data because they do give insight into ground-level 'local' language practices and may therefore yield significant insight into multilingualism from below.

Background on language use in South African film: the role of Tsotsitaal

Very little English is used in South African-produced films and sitcoms. The absence of English might be construed as an indication of the extent to which African languages are dominant in film and in South Africa itself. The critical issue emerges when the converse is explored. The presence of English or other non-native languages in popular programmes reflects a much more complicated process than simply the domination of English because some programmes are popular even amongst an audience with limited proficiency in English. For example, *The Bold and the Beautiful* and *The Days of our Lives* (both America-based soaps) are popular amongst township and slum dwellers. The programmes are popular among working-class Africans because English acts as a linguistic indicator of affluence that transcends the class of speakers, without linguistic proficiency and intelligibility acting as barriers to engagement. Indeed the English programmes might be watched by those who lack proficiency precisely in order to enhance it. For such an audience sitcoms are modelled more along the framework of radio than private cinema (Nuttall & Michael 2000).

In South African films and TV dramas, however, there is a tradition of using multilanguages. Two notable examples are the pre-independence film *Mapantsula* (Beittel 1990) and the late-1990s series *Yizo Yizo*.[1] Although sitcoms and films such as *Hijack Stories, Drum, Yizo Yizo* and *Mapantsula* use an array of African languages, the predominant language is Tsotsitaal, a multilanguage, or in township parlance *de taal* ('the' language). In traditional sociolinguistic studies, which we are seeking to depart from and which are exemplified by the orthodox research of Mesthrie (2008), Tsotsitaal is described linguistically as a patois that is spoken in the African townships and draws heavily from Afrikaans, Xhosa, Zulu, Tswana and Sotho (Nxumalo 1989; Mfusi 1992; Slabbert 1994). The different varieties of Tsotsitaal are defined mainly on the basis of the source languages. Flytaal is quintessentially defined by its English and Afrikaans borrowings (Msimang 1987; Makhudu 1995; Ntshangase 1995) which differentiate it from Iscamtho that utilises Nguni languages as its source languages (Slabbert 1994; Childs 1997).

Thus, in earlier sociolinguistic research, *tsotsi* talk is named differently depending on the languages which it draws from and the geographical locales in which it is spoken. This recalls the fact not only that languages such as Tsotsitaal are

---

[1] The use of these multilanguages in popular culture can be found in countries in West Africa and East Africa as well.

oral languages but also that their very volatility defies their fixity in writing. Writing cannot capture multilingual fluidity. Despite the naming of these varieties of Tsotsitaal according to the different languages they draw on, they are better conceived as instances of multilingual fluidity or polylingualism. In the context of such linguistic fluidify, it is no longer feasible to view constituent parts of multilanguages as belonging to other languages. Once we acknowledge that 'all groups that come into contact with others, over time, develop their own unique "codes", "dialects", or "languages", that emerge through these interactions and shared knowledge, leading to the development of unique and collective identities' (Shohamy 2006:8), then it no longer makes sense to insist on the 'origins' or 'authenticity' of linguistic items.

Tsotsitaal has been associated with gangsters and has been described as 'a parlance of secrecy' (Molamu 2003: xiii). Describing the etymology of Tsotsitaal, Msimang (1987: 84) states that those who created Tsotsitaal 'were also motivated by participation in common activities, particularly crime'. Over time, however, the use of Tsoisitaal has diffused to other communities of practice, so that it is now used by speakers who define themselves, or are deflned by others, as urban-oriented or 'city slick'. Unsurprisingly, given its history, 'Tsotsitaal bears the unmistakable imprint of a quintessentially male language' (Molamu 2003: xiii), although it is now used increasingly by women, who may nevertheless as a result be seen as 'rough, tomboys and ill reputed' (Cook 2002: 12). The association of multilanguages with urbanity, males and a particular type of male moral behaviour is not limited to South Africa, but is found in other cities in Africa (Mclaughlin 2001; Dakubu 2009).

The growing incidence of multilanguages and their association with deviant behaviour is reported in a number of studies. Swigart (1994) points out that urban Wolof is associated with 'the young low lifes' (1994:7). Dakubu (2009) also describes Plashele (pleasure, a language for those into pleasure), an urban multilanguage associated with young thieves and drunkards. The connection between emergent urban multilanguages and forms of popular culture, such as hip-hop in African cities from Dar es Salaam to Libreville (Auzanneau 2002), also contributes to such negative connotations.

The widespread use and sociolinguistic significance of multilanguages have been accorded marked recognition through, in part, the use of *kwaito*[2] music (Aycard 2008). Most of the *kwaito* songs are sung in multilanguages, as if to provide them with a sense of credibility amongst their main consumers, the youth. Although it is certainly not the case that all *kwaito* songs use Tsotsitaal, it is the use of 'township lingo' (Magubane 2006) that gives the songs legitimacy. In as much as Tsotsitaal has a gendered manifestation, Stephens (2000: 276) argues that there is a gendered element in how *kwaito* is responded to. According to his study on the reception of *kwaito*, female respondents take offence at the sexist subject matter of *kwaito* inespective of the use of township lingo. In some ways, *kwaito* and Tsotsitaal share a mutually enriching, and gendered, relationship.[3]

The use of multilanguages in both *kwaito* and film suggests that linguistic hybridisation and multiple linguistic fusions are 'prevalent and heterogeneous in form and function' (Lee 2006: 429). These multilanguages, however, are not institutionally recognised in spite of their widespread use. Ironically, standard languages, although restricted in their usage, are disproportionately recognised institutionally. There is further irony that the film *Tsotsi* was awarded a Best Foreign Language Film Academy Award (with all the attendant problems of this categorisation) whereas the language of the film is not recognised amongst the eleven official languages of South Africa (it isn't 'a language'). The use of these multilanguages in popular culture has important sociolinguistic consequences in that it renders

---

[2] Kwaito is a post-apartheid form of rap which is an amalgam of rap, hip hop, reggae, and traditional music popular amongst the youth in South Africa.
[3] In song, Tsotsitaal is also used as the language of the lyrics in kwaito music.

them legitimate from the viewpoint of those outside the establishment, and may be part of a process of language standardisation from below. If multilanguage users do not treat their 'language' as consisting of separate languages, then code-switching, language mixing and language crossing may be theoretically inadequate sociolinguistic apparatus for explaining language practices in plurilingual contexts.

The film Tsotsi
The film consists of fourteen scenes (see Appendix 1) and revolves around two themes: the harsh teality of crime in post-apartheid South Africa and moral redemption for the perpetrators of crime. The film focuses on an individual living on the outskirts of Joharuresburg and uses Tsotsi as a *nom de guerre*. His name is revealed towards the end of the film as David. Tsotsi is a leader of a small gang of three; namely Die Aap played by Kenneth Nkosi), Butcher (the cold-blooded killer played by Zenzo Nqobe) and Boston (the failed teacher with a feigned sense of decency played by Mothusi Magano). Their favourite hangout is a *speakeasy* (a *shebeen* in township parlance) owned by Soekie (played by Thembi Nyandeni).

Although the film begins by presenting the main character Tsotsi as a heartless and illiterate thug, the audience gradually comes to understand how his character has been shaped. Tsotsi is a product of his environment, an environment characterised by intransigent poverty and with very little respect for human life. This message is communicated strongly through song, especially the use of *kwaito*. *Kwaito* is used to reinforce a sense of violence and replace language in talk. This association is consolidated because when the *tsotsis* are moving to commit violence it is always *kwaito* music which is played. The *kwaito* tracks are gut-wrenching, gritty, and conjure up the harsh reality which defines the lives of South African *tsotsis* (Mhlambi 2004).

Although the issue of race is kept at bay in the film, there is reference to the racial divisions in South Africa that have created the *tsotsi*. For instance, tracks such as *'umnt'omnyama'* (Black person) by Mafikizolo, and *'Vanhu Vatema'* (Black person) by Bongo Maffin are a constant and powerful reminder of the struggle of Blacks. Although Vusi Mahlasela's tracks are used in a number of scenes, these do not exploit the gangster theme nor do they carry heavy racial undertones, but rather draw on the sense of hope and redemption which is one of the film's underlying themes. By so doing, Vusi Mahlasela's songs bring out a redemptive and spirituál component of the film. The central theme of the film is the difficult social realities (Dovey 2007) of contemporary South Africa. The film is an 'updating and re-historicization, of Athol Fugard's 1950s' novel of the same name. The film 'offers a critique of contemporary violence in South Africa' (Dovey 2007: 151) although it does not address 'violence against women and children particularly baby rape' (151) which is endemic in contemporary in South Africa. Nor does the film in any way address the extent to which the spread of AIDS might be facilitated by patriarchal violence.

It seems as if the portrayal of violence in the post-apartheid era is a consequence of an integration of violence from the apartheid era and its metamorphosis in independent South Africa. This is also indicative of the difficulties of breaking away from an apartheid era in spite of the vocal interest and commitment to a 'new South Africa'. Although some have suggested that various portrayals of language, action and dress in the film are not convincing, social and class differences are clearly addressed. The film may also be seen as part of an emerging international genre that has been called 'slumploitation' (Machado 2008), the exploitation of slum-dwellers' lives, an accusation levelled at the more recent *Slumdog Millionaire* (2008). To the extent that slumdwellers are often depicted as lazy, drunk, violent, and illiterate, such films may actually alienate the very people who may want to align with the slumdwellers in their struggles to address their social problems. The linguistic dimensions of such films, however, await adequate description.

Language use in Tsotsi the film
Whereas many African states have settled for English, French or Portuguese as official languages, South Africa has taken a pluri-monolingual ('multilingual') approach underwritten by constructing eleven discrete boxes as official, which is a typical approach in top-down accounts of multilingualism. Within this pluri-monolingual layer of official languages, there are a multitude of other languages that do not enjoy official status and this includes a wide range of multilanguages such as Tsotsitaal which in and of themselves are multilingual in each rendition within the same geographical locale (Aycard 2008). In this discourse, language is an essentialised and highly abstract artefact. Since most of these languages are colonial constructs, contemporary South Africa is, ironically, challenging the effects of apartheid, but at the same time using some of the very same instruments which formed its basis (Makoni 1993). Such essentialisation and abstraction need to be understood as part of the colonial project (Mignolo & Escobar 2009). Viewed from this perspective, multilingualism understood in terms of pluri-monolingual practice and code-switching research runs the risk of serving as a continuation of empire. Both concepts, i.e. multilingualism and code-switching, suggest a form of 'linguistic differentiation through ... [a] border-making design in which each language is separated and segregated in its own discrete space' (Hadi-Tabassum 2006: 5). In contrast, the use of terms such as polylingualism, metrolingualism or multilanguages captures both the fixity and fluidity and reflects 'more dynamic ways of describing and understanding processes that move across, while becoming embedded in, the materiality of localities and social relations' (Connell & Gibson 2003: 17).

In *Tsotsi*, like the rest of South African films and sitcoms, the predominant language used in song and dialogue is Tsotsitaal. There is very little English in the film and when English is used by the characters, it is often interspersed with other indigenous African languages and Tsotsitaal both in song and dialogue. Languages used in the film include English, Afrikaans, Zulu, Xhosa, Tswana, Sotho and all the varieties of Tsotsitaal, though none of the official minority languages are used. Interestingly, there are scenes where individual characters use a number of multiple languages in parallel, i.e. without shifting to each other's language/s as might be expected in code-switching research. Multiple languages are used at times within the same song, and some of the songs are sung in languages which are not recognised as 'official languages' in South Africa. The gendered relations between languages discussed above also emerge: all female characters use standard varieties of African languages, and none of the female characters use Tsotsitaal or languages that are not recognised as 'South African'.

In song, the use of multiple languages in parallel is evident in the lyrics of '*Vanhu Vatema*' (Black person) by Bongo Maffin and '*Umnt'omnyama*' (Black person) by Mafikizolo. The song lyrics by Bongo Maffin are in chiShona (a language that is not officially seen as South African), Zulu and Tswana whereas those by Mafikizolo are sung in Zulu and Xhosa, both of which hold official status. In the song '*O Sale Noka*' Zulu and Sotho are used in the lyrics and the song appears to be an interactive discussion about a river in two different languages. The film *Tsotsi* therefore reflects a type of multilingualism different from the one framed in the language provisions of the 1996 South African Constitution. The South African Constitution is predicated upon a spatial diffusion of language and did not envisage a concentration of diverse language use in one site.

A type of multilingualism characterised by what appears to be mixes from multiple languages is evident in the film, though again the types of mixing here render such determinations difficult. For example, John's use of '*difinger*' in'*difinger prints*' (Extract 1) may be either the Sotho plural inflection '*di*' to pluralise fingers or a rendering of the English definite article 'the', the Afrikaans article 'de' or, of course, both.

Extract 1
1 John: Lerile kunale *difinger* prints?
(You said there are *the finger* prints?)
(You said there are finger prints?)

Difinger is an example of elements which may simultaneously belong to more than one language, what Woolard refers to as 'bivalency' (Woolard 1999:6). If we want to determine whether we are dealing with a Sotho affix or an African phonological rendering of an English/Afrikaans article or a simultaneous production of both Sotho and an African phonological rendition, the decision is ultimately an ideological rather than a linguistic one. A second example of bivalency is apparent in Extract 2.

Extract 2
Ya bafowethu, nihleli kanl'ani, *nayi vari*
(Yeah brothers, you stay how, *here truth*)

Sometimes **wenz' izinto** *ezigrand* **abantu bayakuncoma**
abanye *abancanywa*
(Sometimes you do things *that-be-good* people they-you-praise others *they-no-happy*)

Niyang'thola? *Niyaqondastanda!*
(***Do-you-me-find?*** *Do you understand!*)

The bottom line is *wawuyi* one **esiswini sikanyoko** for nine months
(The bottom line is *you were* one **in-womb of-your-mother** for nine months)

Akekh' umunu ongaku destroya.
(No person that-can-you destroy)

(*Yeah, brothers how do you stay/live? here is the truth. Sometimes you do good things and some people praise you, others do not. Do you get it? Do you understand? The bottom line is you were alone in your mother's womb for nine months and no one can destroy you.*)

(**Bold**: Zulu, *Italics*: Tsotsitaal (Iscamtho), Underline: English)

In terms of the above extract in 'traditional' sociolinguistics we could argue that the lyrics, sung towards the end of the film, are in a number of 'languages' ranging from Zulu to English and there is a pronounced use of Zulu inflections on English words and Sotho or Tswana inflections on Afrikaans and English words alike. In the above song examples such as *ezigrand wawuyi one, qondastanda*[4] and *destroya* are all examples of the use of inflections which are drawn from Zulu and used on English words whereas *frustani* and *screva* (Extract 6) may have their origins in Afrikaans. Similarly to *difinger, nowu, tseserious* (Extract 2) and, *imenang* (Extract 6) these are all examples of bivalency. Bivalency's linguistics has ideological functions: it provides resources which can be strategically utilised to express 'double consciousness, (Bakhtin 1981).

In the extracts below we try to illustrate the complexities of determining whether we are dealing with a single language or multiple languages. For example, in scene two Boston taunts Tsotsi for his lack of understanding of the meaning of 'decency' as shown in Extract 3.

---

[4] In formal linguistics, one could analyse *qondastanda* as constructed from the Zulu word *qonda*, which means 'understand', suffixed with the English 'stand', which presumably is taken from 'understand' . This kind of analysis is what a polylingual flamework tries to avoid, however, as everything becomes conjecture. In a polylingual account qondastanda reflects multiple linguistic resources that the user has encountered.

Extract 3
1 Boston: <u>Decency</u> Tsotsi, **oaetseba**? <u>Decency</u>. **Kibe kenao,** <u>so</u>
   keakula.
   (<u>Decency</u> Tsotsi, **you it know**? <u>Decency</u>. **I be it have,** <u>so</u>
   I be sick)

   De groot <u>man</u> **owatai, oanaleyona** <u>and nowu,</u> *udakile.*
   (*The good* <u>man</u> **of the tie, he-it-have** <u>and now,</u> *he be gone*)

   (*Decency, Tsotsi, do you know it? I had it, so I felt sick. The good man with a tie, he had it but now, he is dead*)

2 Butcher: **Soekie**

3 Boston: Jeses Butcher, **ke bua dintho tse**<u>serious</u>
   (Jesus Butcher, **I talk things** <u>they-serious</u>)
   (*Jesus, Butcher, this is serious*)

(**Bold**: Tswana, <u>Underline</u>: English, *Italics*: Afrikaans)

From a CS perspective in Extract 3, Boston may be construed as moving from English to Tswana, then to Afrikaans. The presumed movement across different languages can be further illustrated in an encounter between Morris and Tsotsi in scene five, as shown in Extracts 4 and 5 below:

Extract 4
1 Morris: <u>Aai</u> **man**, *djy moet fokken lyk waar djy loep* **man**
   (*Hey man! Fucking look where you going!*)

2 Tsotsi: (Looks at him and takes one step towards him)

3 Morris: *En toe?* **Obatla keri** *ekskuus met jou!*
   (*And now?* **You want I say** *excuse me to you?*)
   (And now, you want me to say I am sorry)

4 Morris: **Uthute kuri obeakai mawoto ako ka utsamaya. Tshepang**!
(You learn that you put where feet yours when you walk. Move)
(You must look where you put your feet. Move)

Extract 5
1 Morris: **Obatlang sana**? *Soek djy my geld*?
(**You-want-what kid**? *Want is my money*?)
(What do you want? Do you want my money?)

2 Tsotsi: *Staan op*!
(*Stand up!*)

3 Morris: *Wat*?
(*What?*)

4 Tsotsi: *Staan op* **utsamaye**
(*Stand up* **you-walk**)

5 Morris: *En wie es djy...***Jesus Christ***... ha*?
(*And who is you.* **Jesus Christ**, *hha*?)
(And who are you? Jesus Christ, hha?)

*Ek **is** 'n krippel* **man**
I is a cripple man)
(I am a cripple man)

6 Tsotsi: <u>Aai waiiya</u>. *Staan op*!
(<u>No you lie</u>. *Stand up*)
(You lie. Stand up)

7 Morris: *Voetsak djy*
(*Go to hell you*!)

8 Morris: <u>Sharp</u>! *Hiers al die geld wat ek het*
(Fine! *Here's all the money that I have!*)

9 Morris: **But why**! **Why** ong'lateletse? **Why**?
(**But why! Why** you-me follow? **Why**?)

(*Italics*: Afrikaans, **Bold**: Sotho, <u>Underline</u>: Tsotsitaal, **Bold & <u>Underline</u>**: English)

In Extract 4 Boston moves seamlessly between what appears to be three languages and in Extract 5 Morris carries out his conversation predominantly in Afrikaans and Sotho interspersed with English. Even if we concede that the characters are moving across languages, the movements by both Tsotsi and Morris are not easily predictable. For instance, it is unclear why Tsotsi uses Tsotsitaal in line 6. This unpredictability in the choice of language is also evident in the exchange between Fela and Boston in Extract 6 below.

Extract 6
Fela: **Nina fana ngabe** <u>ni</u>**spanela mina. Niyeke lobuhlanya enibenzayo.**
(You must be <u>you-working-for</u> me. you-stop this-mad that-you-be-doing)

Nawe teacher boy **wakhona. Ilokh'kukhabile le**<u>bhare</u>
(And-you teacher boy of-them. It-keep-you-kicking <u>this-bum</u>)
lokubuyela <u>njengesmakunyana</u> sebhandi s omfazi
(keep-returning <u>like-vulnerable</u> of-belt of woman)

(*You should be working for me. Stop this madness. That includes you, teacher boy. This idiot beats you regularly and you keep going back like an abused woman*)

Boston: Aai Tsotsi <u>ayasgela</u>. <u>Afrustani</u> decency.
(<u>No</u> Tsotsi <u>not-go-school. No-understand</u> decency)

Oatseba Fela, decency. *Oatsibe* **leku**<u>yriscreva</u> nne?
(You-it-know Fela, decency. you-it-know-not <u>to-it-write, he</u>)

(*No, Tsotsi never went to school. He does not understand decency. Do you know it Fela? Do you even know how to spell the word?*)

Fela: Decency, **awuthi ng'bone**. DECENCY, decency. <u>Ugrand</u>?
 oakuthlwa.
(Decency, let-me I ' see. DECENCY, decency. <u>You-ok</u>? You-I-understand.)

(*Decency. Let me see D.E.C.E.N.C.Y. Are you OK? Do you understand?*)

Boston: <u>Imenang</u>? Respect man, for yourself?
(<u>It-mean-what</u>? Respect man, for yourself?)
(*What does it mean? It means respect for yourself*)

Fela: **Awumame shane? usukhuluma nge**respect **manje**?
 Sthotho.
(Oh mom, shame? you-speak of-respect now? *Idiot.*)
(*Decency means making a fuckin' good living, sonny.*)

Ukuz'kwazi ukuthenga <u>imbomboshe</u>
(You-so-can-know how-to-buy <u>beer</u>)

(*Oh my, now you are talking about respect. Idiot. Decency means making money to afford a good living so that you can buy a bottle of beer*).

(*Italics*: Sotho, **Bold**: Zulu, <u>Underline</u>: Tsotsitaal)

It is not clear why Fela, for example, keeps adding linguistic features. Fela begins his conversation with Boston using Zulu and Iscamtho and unpredictably adds Tswana. This addition of languages is difficult to fathom since the interlocutor is the same person, Fela, and there has not been a change in the proposition. If Butcher's language is unpredictable, it means his speech is something new, which may put stress on fellow interlocutors. It is possible for fellow gang members to interpret what he is saying because the speech is deeply contextualised and there are adequate metapragmatic cues which militate against possible incomprehension of intended meanings, as Fela's language also demonstrates. More importantly, the different speakers may, in fact, be using the same language, a multilanguage, and its other 'regional varieties'. Fela's use of features, styles or resources foregrounds that users of such languages do not necessarily have multiple discrete languages.

The multiple varieties of Tsotsitaal used by *tsotsis* in the film create a further multilingual layer (also evident in song) when the individuals move with facility across different varieties. They are producing a complex landscape that has rarely been dealt with in studies on multilingualism. For example in Extract 4 above, Morris moves from Afrikaans to English to Sotho whereas Tsotsi moves from Iscamtho to Sotho. Although there is a temptation to describe this as code-switching, it is not clear what constitutes a 'code' and whether the speakers are indeed 'crossing' different language boundaries (Shohamy 2006). Since it is unlikely thata single individual will have full competence in all the different languages, the language practices in the film seem to imply that the underbelly of multilingualism does not mean they have comprehensive command of the different languages because 'urban residents often use different languages for different purposes with varying degrees of competence in the languages they speak' (Adejunmobi 2004a: 166).

The same phenomenon is evident in Extract 7 when Tsotsi visits the cement pipes where he used to stay, and the street children address him in a number of languages which may be perceived as Zulu and Sotho before changing to Tsotsitaal as if they are moving along a style continuum, which indeed might be a more useful way to understand this use of linguistic resources. Within their repertoires the street children have fragments of speech which might be interpreted as movement across different languages.

Extract 7
Street kid: **Obatlang? Kgonaring mobeking?**
   (**You-want-what? Is-what in-bag?**)
   (*What do you want? What is in the bag?*)
Tsotsi: <u>Sheba</u>
   (Look)
Street kid: *Utshunang kancosi?*
   (*You-do-what with baby*)
   (*What are you doing with a baby?*)
Tsotsi: **Oambatla?**
   (**You-it-want?**)
   (*Do you want it?*)
Street kid: *Fokof man, mina nevera kumgayel' igawu.*
   (*Fuck of man, me never I-it-fend food*)
   (*Fuck off, I will never be able to fend for it*).

(**Bold**: Sotho; *Italics*: Tsotsitaal, <u>Underline</u>: Tswana).

The street kid opens the conversation in what appears to be Sotho, and Tsotsi responds to him in what appears to be Tswana but it is unclear why the street kid changes to Tsotsitaal in lines 3 and 5. Rather than looking at this in terms of code-mixing or code-switching, which might imply certain levels of competence in separable codes, we must accept that speakers here appear to move seamlessly across codes, to draw from a repertoire of languages. This seems to be yet another case of 'fluid multilingualism because they rarely speak any of the languages in their unmixed forms' (Kubhchandani 1997: 241). The linguistic resources which constitute the basis of polylingualism or fluid multilingualism can be construed as a set of resources in which form-meaning connections are made, and idiolects are in discourse and then generalised by linguistics and 'ethno-linguistic entrepreneurs' (Brubacker et al. 2008) by calling them 'dialects, registers, styles and languages' (Johnstone 2009, personal communication).

Another way of framing the analysis is to argue that the elements are fused. Thus, it is not a seamless movement across different languages, as one might be inclined initially to think, in a discourse framed around the notion of a 'code, or a 'stand alone' language, but exemplifies 'fused lects' (Auer 1999). The notion of 'fused lects' reflects the problematic nature of distinctions between monolingualism and bilingualism when analysed from a speaker's perspective when the same linguistic resources may be interpreted as simultaneously monolingual and bilingual. The fusion can be construed as a single language or an ensemble of multiple languages and thus as multilingual. This means that it may not always be necessary conceptually to make a priori distinctions between monolingualism and bilingualism unless they are grounded in an individual's experiences and take speakers' linguistic resources into account. Whether the ensemble is viewed as monolingual or multilingual may therefore be strongly influenced by an individual speaker's experiences because language is inscribed on our individual experiences.

On the other hand, because *kwaito* adopts a conversational mode that mirrors (and conversely impacts on) the speech patterns of townships, multilanguages are central in the *kwaito* song lyrics. As Adejunmobi (2004b: 162) states, 'the mixing of languages is perhaps at its most pervasive in locally produced Hip Hop', that is, *kwaito*, in South African township parlance. Yet the notion of language mixtures or hybrid forms might be misleading for two reasons. First, the term presupposes the separability of languages which research in plurilingual contexts has shown might not be the case. Second, it creates the impression that the speaker can speak an unmixed speech – something whose validity might not be empirically sound (Makoni &

Meinhoff 2004). Perhaps instead of talking about mixed varieties it might be more prudent to talk about 'expressive inventories, that not only enable people to communicate with each other but about each other' (Cook 2002:111) or what Milroy refers to as 'pools of linguistic resources' (Milroy 2001: 540).

In light of the perspective above, instead of talking about mixtures, we argue that what the speakers are experiencing is discourse in context. It is illogical to argue that the mixtures are so prevalent and that the speakers rarely use 'unmixed' forms, because it is classifying the *widely occurring* on the basis of the one *rarely occurring*, the exceptional as if it is the unmarked. The metalanguage ought to be turned upside down. A way round the potential contradiction is simply to refer to what the speakers are experiencing as discourses in context and thus no a priori objective determination needs to be made whether the discourses are mixed or not prior to the analysis. If what the speakers are experiencing are discourses in context, and not languages, then the speakers cannot speak that which does not exist; this accounts for the opposing nature of Mesthrie's 'I didn't know that I spoke Tsotsitaal'. Since people cannot speak that which does not exist we can only conclude that Tswana, Zulu, etc. are 'myths' (Harris 1998). 'Myths' have, however, been extremely powerful in scholarly discourses about language, particularly when textualised in grammars and dictionaries, and have social effects as well (Makoni & Pennycook 2005).

If communication is carried out using 'pools of linguistic resources,' then the phenomenon evidenced in the language practices in the film is best described as polylingualism rather than multilingualism. The epistemological basis of multilingualism is the separability and numerability of languages, yet language practices in the film suggest that the characters exploit resources, a process defined as polylingualism (Jørgensen 2008) or metrolingualism (Otsuji & Pennycook, 2010). A polylinguistic framework draws attention to the use of multiple and interconnected linguistic resources rather than assuming mixing, borrowing or switching between separate, discrete and independent languages.

Conclusion
There is a tension in trying to describe the language use we are looking at here. On the one hand, we have argued that the multifarious nature and fluxity of language use by chatacters in the film are a reflection of polylingualism reminiscent of the simultaneous use of linguistic features drawn from multiple linguistic resources in plurilingual societies. A polylinguistic framework draws attention to the use of multiple and interconnected linguistic resources rather than assuming mixing, borrowing or switching between separate, discrete and independent languages. On the other hand, in many of the examples above, we have still marked language items as somehow 'belonging' to one language or another. In describing the multilanguaging practices of Tsotsitaal speakers, we have been drawn , partly against our will, to show that the different language resources 'come from' Sotho, Afrikaans, or Tswana, even at times from Tsotsitaal, as if this were a separate code itself that can be included in the mix. It is one thing to argue that such multilanguaging does not imply competence in these separate codes, but it is a much harder task to break away from their naming altogether. In trying to show how Tsotsitaal users fluidly draw on multiple resources, we have felt obliged to fall back on their linguistic naming. In doing se, we are still keeping one foot in the camp of colonial knowledge construction, still needing to use some of those tools to make our point.

In arguing against the assumptions about codes in accounts of code-mixing, or the ways in which hybridity still implies the mixing of elements, our goal has been to move away from views that depend on pre-existing elements waiting to be mixed. Ideally, in the next iteration of this sort of sociolinguistics, we can mobilise terms such as polylingualism, metrolingualism or multilanguaging without feeling the need to show what the elements of such language practices are. They need in fact to be understood as local language practices (Pennycook, 2010), not as hybrid mixes, abnormal assortments, unlikely fusions, but as the language practices of the everyday, which do not require the pre-existence of languages for their operation but rather get on with their work with whatever resources may do the job. They do not do so randomly, or as tokenistic acts, but rather as part of multilanguage style.

References
Adejunmobi, M. (2004a). "Polyglots, vernaculars and global markets: variable trends in West Africa" *Language and Intercultural Communication*, 4(3): 159-174.
Adejunmobi, M. (2004b). *Vernacular Palaver: Imaginations of the Local and Non-Native Languages in West Africa*. Clevedon: Multilingual Matters.
Auer, P. (1999). "From code-switching via language mixing to fused lects. Toward a dynamic typology of bilingual speech" International *Journal of Bilingualism*, 3(4): 309-332.
Auzanneau, M. (2002). "Rap in Libreville, Gabon: an urban sociolinguistic space" In Durand, A. (Ed.), *Black, Blanc, Beur: Rap Music and Hiphop Culture in the Francophone World*. Lanham, MD: The Scarecrow Press, 106-123.
Aycard, P. (2008). Speak as you want to speak: Just be free. Available at: http://vids.myspace.com/index.cfm?fuseaction=vids.individual&videoid=41252733 (accessed on 27 November 2009).
Bakhtin, M. M. (1981). *The Dialogic Imagination. Four Essays*. Edited by Michael Holquist. Translated by Caryl Emerson and Michael Holquist. Austin, TX: University of Texas press.
Beittel, M. (1990). "Mapantsula: cinema, crime and politics on

the Witwatersrand" *Journal of Southern African Studies*, 16(4): 751-760.

Brubacker, R. S., Fox, J., Feischmidt, M. & Liana, G. (2008). *Nationalistic politics, Everyday Ethnicity in a Transylvanian Town*. Princeton, NJ: Princeton University Press.

Bullock, B. E. & Toribio, J. (2009). "Themes in the study of code-switching" In Bullock, B. & Toribio, J. (Eds), *The Cambridge Handbook of Linguistic Code-Switching*. New York, NY: Cambridge University Press, 1-18.

Childs, G. T. (1997). "The status of Isicamtho, an Nguni-based variety of Soweto" In Spears, A. K. & Winford, D. (Eds), *The Structure of Pidgins and Creoles*. Amsterdam: John Benjamins, 341-367.

Connell, J. & Gibson, C. (2003). *Sound Tracks: Popular Music, Identity and Place*. London: Routledge.

Cook, S. E. (2002). "Urban language in a rural setting: the case of Phokeng, South Africa" In Gmelch, G. & Zenner, W.P. (Eds), *Urban Life: Readings in the Anthropology of the City*, 4th ed. Prospect Heights, IL: Waveland Press, 106-113.

Cook, S. E. (2009). "Street Setswana vs. school Setswana: Language policies and the forging of identities in South African classrooms" In Kleifgen, J.A. & Bond, G.C. (Eds), *Languages of Africa and the Diaspora: Educating for Language Awareness*. Clevedon: Multilingual Matters, 96-118.

Coupland, N. (2007). *Style: Language Variation and Identity*. Cambridge: Cambridge University Press.

Cummins, J. (2008). "Teaching for transfer: challenging the two solitudes assumption in bilingual education" In Cummins, J. & Hornberger, N. (Eds), *Encyclopedia of Language and Education, Vol.5 Bilingual Education*, 65-75.

Dakubu, K. M. E. (2009). "The historical dynamics of multilingualism in Accra. In Mclaghlin, F. (Ed.), *The Languages of Urban Africa*. London: Continuum Publishing, 19-31.

Dovey, L. (2007). "Redeeming features: from Tsotsi 1980 to Tsotsi 2006" *Journal of African Cultural Studies*, 19(2): 143-164.

Ferguson. G. (2003). "Classroom codeswitching in postcolonial contexts: functions, attitudes and polities" *AILA Review*, 16(1): 38-51.

Ferguson, G. (2009). "What next? Towards an agenda for classroom codeswitching research" *International Journal of Bilingual Education and Bilingualism*, 12(2): 231-241.

García, O. (2008). *Bilingual Education in the 21st Century: A global Perspective*. Malden, MA & Oxford : Wiley-Blackwell Publishers.

Hadi-Tabassum, S. (2006). *Language, Space and Power: A Critical Look at Bilingual Education*. Clevedon: Multilingual Matters.

Harris, R. (1998). *Introduction to Integrational Linguistics*. Oxford: Pergamon.

Jørgensen, J. N. (2008). "Polylingual languaging around and among children and adolescents" *International Journal of Multilingualism*, 5(3): 161-176.

Kubhchandani, L. M. (1997). "Defining mother tongue education in plurilingual contexts" *Language Policy*, 2(3): 239-254.

Lee, J. S. (2006). "Crossing and crossers in East Asian pop music: Korea and Japan" *World Englishes* 25(2): 223-250.

Machado, S. (2008). "Excrutiatingly bad "Slumsploitation" film: Tsotsi" Available at: http://unhoused.livejournal.com/25409.html (accessed on 21 November 2009).

Magubane, Z. (2006). "Globalization and gangster rap: Hip Hop in the post apartheid City" In Basu, D. & Lemelle, S. J. (Eds), *The Vinyl Ain't Final: Hip Hop and the Globalization of Black Popular Culture*. Ann Arbor, Ml: Pluto Press, 208-229.

Makhudu, K. D. P. (1995). "An lntroduction to Flaaital" In Mesthrie, R. (Ed.), *Language and Social History: Studies in South African Sociolinguistics.* Cape Town: David Philip, 298-305.

Makoni, S. (1993). "The futility of being held captive by language policy debates in South African Applied Linguistics" *Per Linguam*, 9: 12-21.

Makoni, S. & Pennycook, A. (2005). "Disinventing and reconstituting languages" *Critical Inquiry in Language Studies*, 2(3): 137-156.

Mclaughlin, F. (2001). "Dakar Wolof and the configuration of an Urban identity" *Journal of African Cultural Studies*, 14(2): 153-172.

Meeuwis, M. & Blommaert, J. (1998). "A monolectal view of code-switching: layered code-switching among Zaireans in Belgium" In Auer, P. (Ed.), *Codeswitching in Conversation: Language, Interaction, and Identity.* New York: Routledge, 76-98.

Mesthrie, R. (2008). "l've been speaking Tsotsitaal all my life without knowing it: towards a unified account of Tsotsitaals in South Africa" In Meyerhoof, M. & Ngy, N. (Eds), *Social Lives in Language: Sociolinguistics and Multilingual Development.* Amsterdam: John Benjamins, 95-100.

Mignolo, W. & Arturo, E. (Eds). (2009). *Globalization and the Decolonial Option.* New York: Routledge.

Mfusi, M. J. H. (1992). "Soweto Zulu Slang: A sociolinguistic study of an urban vernacular in Soweto" *English Usage in Southern Africa*, 23: 39-83.

Mhlambi, T. (2004). "Kwaitofabulous: the study of a South

African urban genre" *Journal of the Musical Arts in Africa*, 1: 116-127.

Milroy, L. (2001). "Language ideologies and the consequences of standardization" *Journal of Sociolinguistics*, 5(4): 530-555.

Molamu, L. (2003). *Tsotsitaal- a Dictionary of the Language of Sophiatown*. Pretoria; UNISA Press.

Msimang, C. T. (1987). "Impact of Zulu on Tsotsi-taal" *South African Journal of African Languages*, 7(3): 82-86.

Myers-Scotton, C. (Ed.). (1998). *Codes and Consequences*. New York: Oxford University Press.

Ntshangase, D. K. (1995). "Indaba Yami i-straight: language and language practices in Soweto" In Mesthrie, R (Ed.), *Language and Social History: Studies in South African Sociolinguistics*. Cape Town: David Philip, 291-307.

Nuttall, S. & Michael. C. (Eds). (2000). *Senses of Culture*. Oxford/New York: Oxford University Press.

Nxumalo, H. (1989). "The birth of a tsotsi" In Chapman, M. (Ed.), *The "Drum" Decade: Stories from the 1950s*. Pietermaritzburg: University of Natal Press, 18-23.

Otsuji, E & Pennycook, A. (2010). "Metrolingualism: fixity, fluidity and language in flux" *International Journal of Multilingualism* 7(3): 240-254.

Pennycook, A. (2010). *Language as a Local Practice*. London: Routledge.

Rampton, B. (2006). *Language in Late Modernity: Interaction in an Urban School*. Cambridge: Cambridge University Press.

Shohamy, E. (2006). *Language Policy: Hidden Agendas and New Approaches*. London/ New York: Routledge.

Slabbert, S. (1994). "A re-evaluation of the sociology of Tsotsitaal" *South African Journal of Linguistics*, 12(1): 31-41.

Spitulnik, D. (1998). "The language of the city: Town Bemba as urban hybridity" *Journal of Linguistic Anthropology*, 8(2): 30-59.

Stephens, S. (2000). "Kwaito" In Nuttall, S. & Michael C. (Eds), *Senses of Culture*. Oxford/New York: Oxford University Press, 256-278.

Swigart, L.(1994). "Cultural creolisation and language use in post-colonial Africa: the case of Senegal" *Africa*, 64(2): 1-14.

Woolard, K. (1999). "Simultaneity and bivalency as strategies in bilingualism" *Journal of Linguistic Anthropology*, 8(1): 3-29.

Films

Slumdog Millionaire. 2008. Written by Simon Beaufoy, directed by Danny Boyle and codirected in India by Loveleen Tandan. It is an adaptation of the novel *Q & A* (2005) by Indian author and diplomat Vikas Swarup.

Tsotsi. 2006. Written by Gavin Wood as an adaptation of Athol Fugard's novel Tsotsi, directed by Gavin Wood.

Mapantsula. 1988. Written by Olive Schmitz & Thomas Mogotlane, directed by Oliver Schmitz.

Yizo Yizo.2000. Written by Tebogo Mahlatsi and directed by Barry Berk and Andrew Dosunmu.

SUMMARY OF TSOTSI
Scenes / Major activity in each scene / Brief Summary

Scenes 1-4
1. Gang members
2. Decency
3. Car-jacking
4. Discovery of baby.

Tsotsi and his gang stab a man to death in order to rob him of his wallet. They then head to their usual hangout, Soekie's speakeasy. A drunken Boston has a guilty conscience and asks Tsotsi about what decency means to him and questions him about his real identity and family background. Tsotsi snaps and beats Boston to a pulp and quickly leaves into the darkness of the night on his own. As he wanders aimlessly in an affluent neighborhood he sees a woman trying to get into her driveway. He shoots the woman and escapes with the car. An infant child has been left in the back of the car. When the baby coos at the back, he crashes the car; tries to leave the baby behind but its incessant cries stop him. He takes the baby and decides to care for it.

Scenes 5-8
5. Morris
6. Miriam
7. Fela and the Gang
8. Tsotsi's past

Morris, a wheelchair-bound station beggar, was injured in a mining accident. Morris faces Tsotsi's murderous rage after Tsotsi trips and collides with Morris's wheelchair. Unable to feed the baby, Tsotsi holds a young widow with a small child, Miriam (Terry Pheto) at gunpoint. At first Miriam obeys because she is afraid of Tsotsi and his gun. A story she tells later makes it clear that another hoodlum like Tsotsi robbed her of her husband. But later, she breastfeeds the child because she cares for the baby. By being kind, gentle and willing to care for Tsotsi's young charge, she is able to convince Tsotsi to take back the baby to its mother. While Tsotsi is trying to take care of the baby, Fela, a leader of a competing gang encroaches on Tsotsi's gang and tries to recruit them. Tsotsi's past is also revealed in a series of flashbacks where young David, (Tsotsi), watches his mother slowly dying of AIDS and his violent father drinks himself into a stupor.

Scenes 9-12
9. Leaving the baby with Miriam
10. Helping Boston
11. Going back to the baby's house
12. Leaving Aap

Tsotsi decides to take care of Boston whom he had beaten up. Although he has difficulty convincing Boston to come and live with him, Boston finally relents and Tsotsi and the other gang members decide to go and do one last job so that they can raise money for Boston to sit for his exam and become a teacher. Tsotsi decides to return to the baby's family from whom he stole the car. At the house, Tsotsi shoots Butcher to death when he tries to kill John, the father of the infant. He collects the baby's belongings to take to Miriam and steals John's car and sells it to Fela. Tsotsi and Aap part ways as Aap wonders when Tsotsi will kill him too.

Scenes 13-14
13. Road to redemption
14. Surrender

As Tsotsi returns the child he listens to a song about purification from sins which is obtained through repentance. Tsotsi, for the first time in the film, wearing white, is surrounded on the street in front of the house by police officers, their weapons drawn on him as he weeps and returns the child to the mother. Vusi Mahlasela's 'O sale Noka' plays softly in the background as if to propel Tsotsi towards the river for his purification.

XIII

The use of heritage language: an African perspective
(with Janina Brutt-Griffler)

Jim Cummins's paper provides an excellent base for exploring the notion of heritage languages and the educational implications in what is becoming a vibrant area of inquiry. In this essay, we first analyze the notion of heritage language and subsequently explore to what extent the notion of heritage language can be generalized to other contexts.

From the perspective of the North American context to which it is most commonly applied, the idea of heritage language seems relatively straightforward. But it is not immediately obvious that it applies universally. Consider the definition provided by the Alliance for the Advancement of Heritage Languages: "Heritage language speakers are those whose home or ancestral language is other than English" (www.cal.org/heritage)

Although the notion of home language is clear enough, what is an ancestral language? For someone to qualify as a heritage speaker, must he or she have some proficiency in the language—or is it enough to have parents or grandparents who speak/spoke the language? If the latter, as appears implicit from this definition, how can one be said to have any linguistic relation to a language one does not speak, simply because a parent or grandparent may speak or have spoken it? From a linguistic standpoint, then, that definition describes not the speaker's language competence but rather emphasizes the functional identification of the speaker.

Of course, there cannot, perforce, be a linguistic category that combines a language that one speaks (home language) with a language in which one may not know a single word. There may or may not be a conceptual problem inherent in the term *heritage language,* but multiple definitions potentially limit its usefulness. Valdés (2005) offered a cogent analysis that provides an underlying linguistic basis for its construction. She described the range of competencies that characterize heritage language speaking bilinguals, noting that their language use often differs from that of monolinguals. Taking a broader understanding of language, Valdés suggested modifications of standard models of second language acquisition (SLA) to account for the linguistic first language (L1)/second language (L2) continua. One of the key issues for Valdes is the "actually developed functional proficiencies in the heritage languages" (p. 412).

Pedagogically, she stressed the importance of LI instruction for students who have already acquired some knowledge of the language. She underscored the importance of designing instruction "that is not only appropriate for their current and future needs but that is also based on coherent theories of instructed language acquisition for these particular groups of learners" (p. 416). She suggested that language learning must of necessity view

> L1 instruction in its many manifestations and involving several types of language acquisition and development (i.e., acquisition of D2s, acquisition of a standard language, acquisition and development of specialized language registers and styles, acquisition of written language) as well as L2 instruction. (p. 422)

Her exploration fits the African context, in which proficiencies are not always so separable. Canut (1998) made a critical observation of language continua among African multilinguals. He wrote that in a "city situated near the only Dakar-Bamako train line, differentiation between varieties is impossible. The fact that villagers (Sagabari) can frequently pass as city-dwellers (Bamako) accentuates the mixture among varieties" (p. 35). Writing on languages in the Mandingo region of Mali, Canut (2002) argued that

> The objective is no longer to describe abstract entities (language), so-called fixed and rooted systems situated one next to another, but rather to show that communicative practice is composed of an ensemble of varying subsystems in contact and in a process of permanent transformation and evolution. (p. 39)

Valdés's perspective on language and a view from the African context suggest a broader understanding of language learning that takes place in multilingual communities and the concomitant functional proficiencies that emerge.

If we further consider the definition cited above from the Alliance for the Advancement of Heritage Languages, we must consider the basis for excluding English—clearly not a linguistic but a sociolinguistic consideration. In the United States, in particular, English is represented as the dominant language in a nation often perceived, quite wrongly, as monolingual. The latter is a point that Cummins makes quite strongly, while failing to see that this very consideration renders the notion of heritage language problematic.

These limitations inherent in the term *heritage language* become significant when we attempt to generalize such ideas beyond the North American context and a few others similarly sociolinguistically constructed. In non-English-speaking nations, the set of speakers for whom home or ancestral languages are "other than English" would frequently—and meaninglessly—include the set of all speakers. If we take out the phrase "other than English," we are left with the set of all speakers who have either a home or an ancestral language—or both—which again leaves us with all speakers. To make this term more meaningful, we need to substitute a language for English. Which language do we choose? Implicitly, the term—at least as defined by the Alliance for the Advancement of Heritage Languages—is predicated on the assumption that most nations are monolingual, and so we can easily replace English with some other language.

If we cannot, we are left with the imperative to teach students their home or ancestral language. In collapsing these two very different cases into one term, *heritage language education*, we do little to achieve clarity. In some cases, it may work for the good of speakers denied mother-tongue medium education. In Ghana, particularly Accra, the largest ethnic group speaks Ga. Even though over the years there has been a steady influx of people from different ethnic backgrounds, instruction is in Ga even for students coming from other ethnic backgrounds. For example, a student from a Hausa background may still be assigned to a Ga mother tongue classroom even though Hausa is his or her mother tongue. In situations in which the mother tongue assigned administratively does not take into account the heritage languages of the students, the notion of a heritage language may serve as a corrective measure (see Adejunmobi, 2005). Suppose, however, that the home and ancestral languages coincide, as they may in a relatively homogenous ethnolinguistic community. In such cases, the notion of heritage language does absolutely nothing to promote bilingualism. Moreover, many contexts raise problems that the term *heritage language* is very ill-suited to address. Take a case where the home language is not recognized but the ancestral language is, a frequent occurrence in Africa. Assigning students to classrooms on the basis of a heritage language becomes problematic when the children use a language with their peers for everyday interaction that is different from their ancestral language. For example, the family may have Hausa as a heritage language but the children may not be able to speak it; so assigning students to a heritage medium may in actual fact disadvantage them. In such circumstances, the notion of *heritage language* might be used as a pretext to assigning a student to a non-mother-tongue educational medium—and such cases have occurred and occur with alarming regularity in fluid linguistic settings.

It is also important to keep in mind that the term *heritage* is in places tied to an exclusionary—and even anti-immigration—discourse that completely subverts the intention of its use in the United States. If we take the case of Zimbabwe, for example, the notion of heritage is strongly tied to discussions about land. The notion of *Zimbabwean heritage*—and the rights that should accompany it—excludes not only those people of purely European descent, but Coloureds, African "immigrants" from Malawi or Zambia (whose "ancestors" may have settled generations ago), and more recently Zimbabweans in the diaspora. Although in some cases *heritage* and *indigenous* can be distinguished from each other, at times they merge into one and the notion of *heritage* becomes a means of defining the ethnic other.

Within the South African constitution the term *heritage language* refers to the languages such as Hindi, Urdu, and others spoken by South Africans of Indian descent—not only excluding English (and Afrikaans) but the indigenous African languages as well. Here, in contrast to Zimbabwe, *heritage* is not only not coincident with the notion of indigeneity but actually directly opposite to it, because it describes only those persons who "came from elsewhere"—though again, often many generations ago. As such, the idea of heritage languages is therefore clearly racialized. Because of such connotations it is doubtful whether speakers of South Asian descent within South Africa, Zimbabwe, and Uganda, would refer to themselves as heritage speakers.

Migration in the African context challenges the link between a place and a language or what Canut (1998) called territorialization. In the African context, an emphasis on heritage languages can be said to be reinforcing the notion of an intrinsic connection between language and place. However, the connection between place and language is rendered difficult even in rural areas because of the constant movement between cities and non-urban places.

The notion of heritage languages—in the present world so necessarily tied to migrations—seems to impact differently inside and outside Africa. If the construct of heritage languages were to be widely used within African sociolinguistics and applied linguistics, it might have unintended negative consequences. Though the notion of heritage languages is largely foreign to Africa, the cases of its usage in Zimbabwe and South Africa demonstrate potential disadvantages of such use in contexts in which large-scale migrations have given rise to significant manifestations of anti-immigration sentiment. The notion of heritage descriptively draws attention to the speakers' history, either individually or collectively, and implies that they come from somewhere (and therefore labels them as indigenous or exogenous)—that is, it assigns them roots either real or imagined. Whatever its intent, it is easily co-opted for political purposes antithetical to the people defined either into or out of a particular sociopolitical identity in ways that may make groups given the label (as in South Africa) or excluded from it (as in Zimbabwe) uncomfortable. The discourse of heritage can fuel xenophobic tendencies as some people are defined as permanent outsiders and others as insiders.

If the notion of heritage languages is potentially problematic if it were widely used within Africa, its use within the diaspora might be more productive. It could encourage the teaching of African languages in schools that serve the ever-growing numbers of migrants from Africa. It is possible to argue that for African Americans, African languages are heritage languages to them in so far as some of them are willing to trace their roots to Africa. The notion of heritage languages thus provides opportunities to justify the allocation of resources to languages that might not necessarily be spoken widely within the diaspora.

Cummins's paper goes beyond notions of heritage languages and raises issues that are generally relevant to language policy. He argues, quite cogently, with respect to the importance of focusing on local communities and individuals. In short, Cummins is arguing for a bottom-up approach towards language policy. Cummins's argument is most welcome and consistent with an earlier trend in sociolinguistics (cf. Hornberger, 1997). The crucial issue here is not so much that the policies are implemented from a bottom-up perspective, but that we seriously take into account the question of language proficiency. This question of proficiency has gained recognition among academics, businesses, and some governments inasmuch as understanding and being able to communicate in other languages is increasingly important in our societies and in the global economy. Byrnes (2002) noted that around the world "a multilingual citizenry" will not only require the knowledge of foreign languages but that this citizenry will need "to be able to use an L2 competently in a wide variety of public and professional contexts and not only in private settings among family and friends" (pp. 34-35).

The practical consideration that the notion that bilingualism can be encouraged both by means of linguistic competence as well as by notions of imagined community provides a compelling justification for the heritage language approach. Still, there are reasons to be cautious. The term suffers from significant flaws. It saddles the field of applied linguistics—which still tends to revolve around a few, mainly Western, contexts—with a terminology that ill suits the majority of contexts in the world. It increases the tendency to isolate the North American setting from others in the world, which, if anything, only reinforces the monolingualist assumptions in a decidedly multilingual world.

A global perspective offers, in the long run (and particularly in this age of globalization), a better alternative conceptual basis.

References

Adejunmobi, M. (2005). *Vernacular Power: Imaginations Of The Local And Non-Native Languages In West Africa.* Clevedon, UK: Multilingual Matters.

Byrnes, H. (2002). "Toward academic-level foreign language abilities: Reconsidering foundational assumptions, expanding pedagogical options" In B. L. Leaver & B. Shekhtman (Eds.), *Developing Professional-level Language Proficiency* (pp. 34-76). Cambridge: Cambridge University Press.

Canut, C. (1998). "Perception des espaces plurilingues ou polylectaux et activité épilinguistique" In P. Zima & V. Tax (Eds.), *Language and Location in Space and Time* (pp. 155- 172). Munich, Germany: Lincom Europa.

Canut, C. (2002). "Perceptions of languages in the Mandingo Region of Mali" In D. Long & D. Preston (Eds.), *Handbook of Perceptual Dialectology* (pp. 33-39). Amsterdam: John Benjamins.

Hornberger, N. H. (Ed). (1997). *Indigenous Literacies In The Americas: Language Planning From The Bottom Up.* New York: Mouton de Gruyter.

University of California Los Angeles. (2001). *Heritage Language Research Priorities Conference Report.* Los Angeles, CA: Author. Available: www.cal.org/heritage

Valdés, G. (2005). "Bilingualism, heritage language learners, and SLA research: Opportunities lost or seized?" *Modern Language Journal*, 89, 410- 426.

XIV

The discursive construction of the female body in family planning pamphlets
(with Busi Makoni)

> *The contraceptive pill and injection are unique among technologies for their ability to stir up trouble: trouble between men and women, trouble between the old and the young, trouble between social conservatives and radicals, trouble of all sorts.*
> *(Kaler 2003: 1)*

1. Preamble

The aim of this chapter is to report on an analysis of family planning pamphlets distributed in Zimbabwe (from 1970 to 1982) as part of a campaign to promote deliberate forms of birth control through the concept of family planning. The focus is on the content and language used in the pamphlets, as this may provide significant insight into "the view of sexuality, contraception and the roles assigned by society to men and women" (Byrman 2001: 81). Contraceptives provide significant insight into the social construction and control of the body because even though the use of contraceptives is an individual and private exercise, its effects and consequences are an issue of public concern. This chapter is therefore an exploration of the discursive construction of the body in family planning pamphlets used to educate and promote the use of various kinds of contraceptives. Even though there is growing literature on the body in applied linguistics (Ramanathan 2010) and the effects of diseases such as HIV/AIDS (Higgins and Norton 2010; Jones and Norton 2010) and other conditions such as diabetes and epilepsy (Ramanathan and Makoni 2008) and Alzheimer's disease (de Bot and Makoni 2005; Ramanathan 1997), there is relatively little research in sociolinguistics "on the discursive construction of the female body generally, and the female reproductive system specifically" (Hayter 2005: 46).

Using a framework based on Fairclough's (1989) Critical Discourse Analysis (CDA) analysis, we explore how the female body is discursively constructed in family planning pamphlets. Two multilingual pamphlets were analyzed to determine how language and images are semantically integrated to form multi-semiotic texts in discussion of contraceptives and control of the female body. The analysis revealed three discursive elements related to contraceptive education and promotion. First is reproductive anatomy, which is described mainly in a very archaic language characterized by the use of metaphors of various kinds. The second discursive element relates to reproductive physiology that is described using a form of language in Shona used for expressing respect. An instructive description of the anatomy and physiology of the sex organs is conducted using a repertoire of descriptive terms drawn from the Shona language (a language spoken largely in southern Africa), all of which suggest the vulnerability of the female reproductive system. Third is education on the functioning of contraceptives, and the language used portrays the female body as highly vulnerable and at risk and therefore in need of protection. This aspect was described by the use of rhetorical strategies such as metaphors and imagery drawn from African languages. This approach seems linked to ensuring women's future contraceptive use. The discourse employed in the pamphlets suggests that the female body, especially its reproductive system, is highly vulnerable and therefore in need of protection at all times. The discursive construction of the female body as vulnerable is also reflected through the pictorial imagery of a road where caution and restraint have to be exercised at all times (Hunt 1999; Thomas 2003).

The use of western modes of contraception has been a "hot potato" since its introduction during the colonial period in Africa. Western modes of contraception, however, were introduced in a context where other forms of contraception were already in use, as Africans did practise deliberate forms of birth control which differed significantly from western modes of birth control. In this chapter contraceptives are used as prisms through which to analyze the social construction of the body, in particular the female body, and the intersection of socio-cultural history and dynamics of the body with colonial and political life, and colonial and nationalistic discourses in Zimbabwe. The "pill" provides significant insights into how biomedicine and colonialism have co-evolved (Bala 2009). In fact, regulating sexuality was one of the principal objectives of colonial institutions (Foucault 1980). The effects of "bio-power" have been a source of controversy (Thomas 2007), with some Africanists arguing that bio-power did not have as much penetration power as may have been imagined. In this chapter, however, the argument is that bio-power has deep penetration power because its effects could be felt in African bedrooms during debates about the desirability of the use of contraceptives between couples.

Over the years there has been much research into family planning and dissemination of information related to family planning (Byrman 2001). In this chapter an attempt is made at establishing a connection between family planning and linguistic practices related to the dissemination of information on family planning to different ethnic groups. These different ethnic groups have their own culturally defined repertoire of linguistic resources used for talking about issues pertinent to birth control. Birth control is central to the body and the language used in disseminating such information gives insight into the discursive construction of the body. Also, issues about fertility and reproduction are some of the defining features of the body which, when embedded in a social context, become a site of contestation.

This chapter is an analysis of the extent to which language practices in contraceptives may provide insight into language use, especially the discourse used for social reconstruction of the body. The reproductive system has been central to feminist research with regard to the body, power, and discourse (Howson 2001). Research in this area has argued that the descriptive terminology used for the female reproductive system portrays it as weak and fragile (Barrett and Harper 2001). Despite the interest shown in the female reproductive system, research on language used in the promotion of the use of contraceptives is lacking. Yet the use of contraceptives is closely related to the reproductive system in terms of pregnancy, fertility, and the female body, all of which are central to the female reproductive system. This chapter fills the gap by contributing to an understanding of contraceptive discourse within a family planning promotion and education perspective. In so doing, the chapter explores the points of intersection between gender and discourses of contraception. Using CDA as an analytic and interpretative framework, this chapter analyses pamphlets from the Family Planning Association of Rhodesia (FPAR)[1] to establish discourses about the body and how these intersect with issues of culture and body politics. Conceptually, the chapter adopts a three-pronged perspective which analyzes the complementary and sometimes highly conflicting perspectives on the body from African studies, sociolinguistics, and the politics of

---

[1] Note that the country now named Zimbabwe used to be called Rhodesia and the period under analysis falls under the phase when the country was still called Rhodesia.

body in gender studies. To a limited extent, the chapter reflects the relationship between the body and political ideology in Africa.

In the analysis of the family planning pamphlets the focus is on the discourses on reproduction and the body. The focus in the analysis is on how language is deployed in promoting the use of contraceptives and reinforced by visuals and what this reflects about how the body is discursively constructed.

In the light of the above this chapter seeks to address the following questions:

(i) What can we learn through an analysis of discourses about contraceptives in relation to the social, linguistic and political construction of the body?
(ii) What does the analysis of the pamphlets used by family planning campaigns show about the discursive construction of the body and representations of sexuality in Africa?

The chapter begins with a brief background about the origins and development of family planning and the use of contraceptives in Zimbabwe. This section establishes why the use of contraception is so controversial in Zimbabwe and possibly in other African countries. This section further provides a feasible explanation of what the conflict over contraceptives tells us about the various ways in which the body is discursively constructed and controlled. In other words, the background section focuses on the political tensions arising from the introduction of "modern" contraceptives as well as the politicisation of the female body. The chapter then proceeds to a description of the methodology used in analysing the pamphlets. The last part deals with a discussion of the findings and what these reflect in terms of the discursive construction of the body.

2. Background: Origins and development of family planning

The FPAR was a non-governmental organization (NGO) originally set up to address the reproductive concerns of white women but later changed its name to the Zimbabwean Family Planning Association after Zimbabwe got its independence from the government of Ian Smith. Relatively early in its career, however, it was expanded to include Africans, particularly African women. The genesis of the FPAR is, by and large, a product of a series of visits by a representative of the US-funded Pathfinder Fund, Edith Gates. Her main commitment was "to spread the gospel of birth control to all who would listen, black and white" (West 1994: 452). The role of the Pathfinder Fund in Rhodesia reflected the complex interconnectedness between globalisation, Rhodesian local politics, reproduction and fertility (Thomas 2007; Hunt 1999). Local Rhodesian politics was highly racialized and divisive whereas the Pathfinder Fund was focused on birth control methods irrespective of race. At an international level, the Pathfinder Fund was one of the major sources of funding for the FPAR. The impact of the Pathfinder Fund and the FPAR occurred in a context in which issues about sexuality had been one of the major concerns of British colonialism. This concern is reflected in the domesticity ideology espoused in courses such as hygiene, sewing, etc. (Summers 2002), which were taught to all African females of school age.

  The Rhodesian government was a major "local" source of funding for the FPAR although, for various reasons, it preferred to keep its participation in family planning matters at "arm's length." The Rhodesian government distanced itself from family planning activities because its philosophy of population control in order to avert a "national catastrophe" was contested by a lot of other stakeholders, especially African men and African nationalists. All these different stakeholders had ideas about how fertility and the female body in particular had to be controlled and protected either from excessive procreation or from interference with procreation. Fears of an impending national catastrophe by the Rhodesian government were at times articulated in highly apocalyptic discourses, as the following remark by Esther Sapire reflects:

> For many years there has been an ostrich-like attitude and an ominous silence about the population problem, but recently demographers, economists, world organizations and responsible governments have been uttering dire warnings about its consequences . . . the problems are vast and urgent and to quote Dr Roger Bernard of the Pathfinder Boston, who visited us recently after going to India "In India the time has run out, but in Rhodesia you have five minutes more!" (Sapire 1971: 105)

These discourses were sharpened towards the end of the 1970s and coincided with the military confrontation between African nationalists and the white regime. Discourses reflecting fear of an impending national catastrophe were expressed by Peter Dodds, the third director of the FPAR, when he went to the extent of proposing that hormonal contraceptives should be available to African women without prescription or medical supervision because of the urgent need to control African population growth (Dodds 1978: 160). In fact, the FPAR annual report states that "sterilization be freely and conveniently available as a method of contraception to competent adults" as a recommendation to curb a possible population explosion (*FPAR Annual Report and Accounts 1977–1978*, no pagination). The political fears of an impending population explosion and its challenges to African hegemony were justified through a series of local and regional scientific journals such as the *Rhodesian Journal of Economics*, the *Rhodesian Science News*, and the *South African Medical Journal*. Scientific knowledge about the female body and its relationship with economic issues was therefore mobilized to serve family planning objectives.

Until late into the 1970s, family planning only targeted African women and thus portrayed it as an exclusively female enterprise. African men were antagonistic to the use of modern contraceptives because from a male perspective family planning was feminized; after all a majority of the distributors of contraceptives were women. Most of the distributors came from the communities they served, and sometimes contraceptives were sold by women going from door to door. It is conceivable that the feminization of family planning and men's exclusion from most of its operations intensified their antagonism. In a highly patriarchal society, such antagonism was based on fear of being marginalized. Resistance to "modern" contraceptives is also evident in the negative portrayal of the distributors of contraceptives. In nationalist discourses the distributors were referred to pejoratively as "saboteurs" or "baby killers." Politically, the distributors were perceived to be complicit with white rule. The relationship between the distributors and white rule was more complicated than that, however, because there were "ambiguous lines that divided engagement from appropriation, deflection from denial, and desire from discipline, [which] confounded the colonial encounter" (Cooper and Stoler 1997: 6).

The question that arises, however, is to what extent the FPAR was successful in its mission. If the FPAR is assessed against the number of "contraceptive acceptors," then it succeeded in its enterprise, but if its objective was to propose methods of contraception which superseded traditional methods, then it was only partially successful. In the period from 1970 to 1980, the FPAR reported an increase in women who visited clinics for family planning in August from 9,000 in 1972 to 46,000 in 1978. By 1979, 14 percent of married women between the ages of 15 and 44 were reported to be using "modern contraceptives," a proportion extremely high compared with most sub-Saharan African countries (Kaler 2000). Interestingly enough, the 1977–1978 FPAR annual report also records a substantial increase in the use of condoms as contraceptives. Condoms were also made available to "virtually all urban beer halls in the country" (FPAR 1977–1978, no pagination). Since most Africans socialized at beer halls, farm stores, and European owned stores it was therefore strategic to make the condoms readily accessible in such places. Because about 10 percent of the African population worked in European farms, farm stores and beer halls became important sites for the distribution of condoms. There is no evidence, however, that an increase in the number of sites necessarily resulted in an increase in the use of condoms by African men. Even though it has been shown that men do have knowledge of contraception they do not necessarily utilize that knowledge (Tularog, Deressa, Ali and Daven 2006).

The FPAR disseminated its message through a number of different but closely related avenues such as films, radio programmes, distributed pamphlets, and direct contact between the FPAR nurses and educators and the communities which they served. Important FPAR films that were shown were entitled: *Family talks about sex*, *His Responsibility*, and *Life before birth*. The films were shown in mobile vans to maximize their distribution and extend their reach in "big" and "small" cities alike. The campaigns of the FPAR were part of colonial coercive strategies consolidated through films and included a wide distribution of pamphlets celebrating the use of contraceptives and warning against the disadvantages of "big" families. Politically, family planning was an important enterprise because controlling sexuality and reproduction was an integral part of institutional regulation of "African sexuality," (Thomas 2003: 8). It was argued that the "moral perversion" (Jeater 1993) of Africans was apparent in the presence of polygamy, child marriage, and domesticity (Comaroff and Roberts 1977). Family planning projects, particularly, the easy availability of condoms, reflected white men's fears of black men's sexuality. White men feared the development of sexual relations between white women and African men or the so-called "black Peril" (Kennedy 1987; van Onselen 1982). White women sought to retain control over their own reproductive systems while, at the same time, in their sexual encounters with African male houseboys, sought to control the sexuality of the houseboys by encouraging them to use condoms. Euro-American anxiety was obviously not restricted to

Rhodesia as similar experiences have been reported in countries such as Kenya (Thomas 2003) and Uganda.

Even though one of the recurring concerns in most African colonies was the desire to control the African body, the project was motivated by different reasons. For example, in Uganda, the family planning objective was to increase the number of African births so as to meet anticipated increased demands for labor. In order to increase population growth and fertility, Ugandan family planning launched vigorous anti-syphilis campaigns because it decreased chances of female fertility which, in turn, reduced labour. In Rhodesia the strategy was exactly the opposite. The objective was to facilitate population control. On commercial farms, white farmers were strongly in favor of the use of contraceptives by African women in order to maximize their profits and increase the utility of their labor. White farmers were averse to pregnancies because repeated births limited the time female workers would spend working on the farms. White farms were a "total institution" (Goffman 1961) which controlled both male and female bodies. The coercive power of white farmers was intensified by the fact that most farm workers were not indigenous Zimbabweans. They were part of migrant labour from neighbouring countries such as Zambia, Malawi and Mozambique. This created space which rendered them vulnerable to exploitation and easy manipulation.

Nonetheless, Zimbabwean nationalists, like all other male-dominated nationalist movements, were strongly patriarchal and therefore felt the need to control female bodies on grounds of cultural practices. They vehemently objected to the use of contraceptives, and some of the family planning facilities became targets of military attacks. Nationalists treated family planning as part of "a conspiracy to control the black population," "a form of genocide, uncalled for population control" (West 1994: 447). The objection to family planning was framed in discourses such as "de-stocking." De-stocking was a strategy used to limit the number of cattle for each household in order to prevent overgrazing. Africans viewed de-stocking as a ploy to control their accumulation of wealth since cattle were an important index of wealth and social status. De-stocking was extremely unpopular in African communities and was used as a prism through which to frame the activities of the FPAR.

Although African nationalists were opposed to family planning, there was tension between family planning announcements and practice, topdown and ground level. Whereas African nationalists strongly opposed any form of population control, young women who became pregnant were confined to isolated camps as a form of punishment, called Osibisa (Lyons 2004; Nhongo-Simbanegavi 2000). During the liberation war pregnant female guerrillas were referred to as "prostitutes." This was a surprisingly negative characterization of femininity among nationalists who strongly supported female fertility and were strong advocates for African cultural practices. African cultural practices view pregnancy as a celebration of femininity. Yet the treatment women combatants received was incompatible with the rhetoric of a return to African cultural practices. It was also incompatible with the "newly" developed mantra of gender equality. What it shows, however, is that male nationalist leaders were able to take sexual liberties, and yet they made different rules for women. During the liberation war, "in sexual matters one moral law . . . applied to men and another to women" (Byrman 2001: 93).

Discourses on family planning and the use of contraceptives suggest that African liberation fighters, on the one hand, constructed a socialist politics from the material experience of the female body in sex and motherhood. This politics was rooted in concerns about the plight of working-class women and shaped by contemporary ideas of modernity, sexuality, and feminism. The interest in the female body, sexuality, and politics led nationalists into controlling and pursuing what appear to be conflicting discourses suggesting a tension between the materiality of the body and its discursive meaning. It is therefore not surprising that the use of contraceptives meant different things to different people of different genders. As already established, some men and, in particular, African nationalists, regarded the use of contraceptives as a form of "genocide." In spite of the different objectives of Rhodesian whites and Zimbabwean nationalists, both camps seem to have had similar approaches towards the body, especially the female body. They regarded the female body not as a physical entity but as a social entity which they aimed to regulate. African female voices were excluded and silenced in official discourses even though issues pertinent to family planning directly affected them.

Prior to the introduction of western forms of contraceptives, African women used other birth control methods such as *coitus interruptus* and in order to space their children effectively they practised abstinence for two years after childbirth. This was made possible because most of the males (i.e., husbands) were working in urban areas or had been taken to neighboring South Africa to work in the mines as migrant labour. The birth control procedures were variously referred to as *Kuronga mhuri kwechiShona kwekarekare* ('old Shona methods of arranging the family') or *kuzvibata* ('holding oneself '). There were birth control methods which were primarily dependent on men such as *kurasira panze* ('throwing outside'), which in western terminology would be equivalent to the withdrawal method. Others were female in orientation such as the practice of jumping over some shrubs to seal or open the womb. The new contraceptives did not replace traditional methods, but were integrated into the pre-existing contraceptive frameworks, producing a type of hybridization. What this shows is that there was a repertoire of terms used to describe the reproductive system as well as an established lexicon to describe traditional forms of contraception, which were then transposed and used in describing "new" forms of contraception. Discourses of family planning drew upon pre-existing discourses and subsequently redeployed them in new contexts.

The use of traditional methods of birth control was partially dependent upon the advice of older female members of the community. Knowledge about these birth control methods is imparted to the males and females alike during rites of passage ceremonies such as "virginity testing" or circumcision for males. Nevertheless, understanding the use of both traditional and modern forms of birth control has to be viewed through the lens of the social networks in which the individuals were embedded. For instance, the collection of the "pill" might be made by friends, acquaintances, and other associates so as to evade the attention of husbands who were often against the use of western forms of birth control. The myth was that western forms of birth control, including the pill, affected male virility.

There was, however, one major difference between the "traditional" and "modern" forms of birth control, a difference based on the political dynamics of the body and who had control over it. The "pill" as a form of modern "contraceptive technology" (Wilder 2004: 822) was infused with multiple and variable and sometimes conflicting meanings. As Kaler (2003) notes, the plasticity of the meaning of the pill created acute social division and tension between the old and the young, wives and husbands, daughters-in-law and mothers-in-law, nationalists and colonial governments, depending on the social role which they performed (Kaler 2009; West 1994). Although at face value acrimony occurred over whether women should use contraceptives, at a more philosophical level the discord was part of a complex power struggle over who controlled the female body, the nature of femininity and the social and political significance of that control between men and women, the white regime and African nationalists, men and women, and indeed amongst women themselves.

Even though both African women and the colonial regime supported the use of contraceptives they were motivated by different reasons. For the colonial regime the objective was to control the increase of African population as a group, whereas

African women were using contraceptives to consolidate control over their own bodies. The orientation of women towards contraceptives varied, however, depending upon the social roles that they played. In some situations the same women may have been willing to use contraceptives when they were spouses, whereas they may have strongly objected to the use of contraceptives when they were socially identified as sisters-in-law or mothers-in-law, a category of powerful women who wielded considerable power and influenced decisions in the clan. As sisters-in-law or mothers-in-law, women focused on the interest of the clan rather than individual interests. Since the clan has to "grow," contraceptive use was anathema and therefore had to be discouraged at all costs. Women were therefore not a homogeneous group. Similarly, men were not a monolithic category in their reactions to the use of modern contraceptives.

Notably, the cooperation between whites and African women over the use of the "pill" destabilized the balance of reproductive power in their families. Men faced a challenge to their authority not only from women but from a white colonial apparatus; the "pill." The clinic, and all that it embodied, represented the degree to which colonialism now had an impact on the privacy of Africans even in their most intimate lives (Kaler 2000). White colonial infiltration of the bedroom should be read as part of a wider project of shaping African domesticity, the fact that women were, on the one hand, subverting patriarchal hierarchy, while, on the other hand, reinforcing patriarchy reflects deep seated contradictions within each social body. After all, social construction has long established that the body is not just a biological entity but rather that perceptions about the body are socially constructed (Hancock et al. 2000). In this regard, "discourse socially constructs the body" (Hayter 2005: 47) in specific ways "that reflect the dominant discourse of the time" (Hayter ibid.). The discourse is value-laden, and it reflects power and influence (Armstrong 1993, 1998; Williams and Bendelow 1998).

Although Zimbabwean nationalists were initially vehemently opposed to the African "baby boom," they subsequently shifted to control population growth. The population control policy of the Zimbabwean government was expressed in terms of child spacing and not through the "foreign" discourses of family planning. The discourse of child spacing was not intended to limit the growth of the African population but to encourage the spacing of children. The Zimbabwean government preferred the rhetoric of "child spacing" because the discourses of family planning had negative connotations, so there has been a change in the rhetoric from that of the Rhodesian government:

> There is, however, one respect in which the policy has shown remarkable consistency: namely, in the role expected of women in family planning. African women, though having little say in the male dominated circles where such decisions have been made, albeit they were expected dutifully and unquestionably to accept the prevailing nationalist position on family planning. (West 1994: 470)

Although the Zimbabwean government reversed its position from anti- to pro-natal and the frame was written largely by men, there is significant awareness that it is an illusion to conceive decisions about family planning as individualistic, *homo economicus*, and that the idea of "economic planning and indeed political planning are independent and separate sets of processes and problems" (Freireman undated: 1).

Nonetheless, Zimbabwe was not the only African country that had family planning policies. For instance, countries such as Ghana, Tunisia and Kenya have very explicit family planning policies. In fact, more recently, attempts in Rwanda to limit family size to three have been resisted as families seek to become bigger to compensate for lives lost during the genocide.

Another important aspect related to the challenges of family planning is its failure to take cognisance of the different types of sexual intercourse and their cultural meanings. Given the paucity of written records, however, an understanding of traditional beliefs and practices related to deliberate birth control might be complicated. The cultural meanings can be established through a combination of both oral and written records. Family planning is therefore a socio-historical exercise, and a framing of body terms has to be sensitive to such socio-historical traditions.

3. Methodology

The methodology used in analyzing the family planning pamphlets is drawn largely from the work by Fairclough (1989) and multimodality. The pamphlets are analyzed as multimodal texts using the meaningmaking features specific to the relevant semiotic system, the text and the accompanying graphics (i.e., the visuals) that complement the text-image as part of meaning-making. Analyzing the text without taking into consideration the accompanying images would be inadequate: as Kress points out, it "is now impossible to make sense of texts, even of their linguistic parts alone without having a clear idea of what these features might be contributing to the meaning of the text" (2000: 337). This approach is particularly suited for the analysis of such promotional material as pamphlets because these are multi-semiotic. They integrate language and images into a semantic unit. The analysis makes it possible to investigate the "linguistic and visual forms of semiosis in order to determine how metaphorical constructions of meaning (i.e., semiotic metaphors or ideational meanings) are deployed across the linguistic and visual modes of communication" (O'Halloran 2008: 444).

4. Findings

The content of pamphlets on contraceptives emphasizes the vulnerable state of the female body and the need for it to be protected. In figure 1, the upside-down triangle is a visual metaphor in which an implied comparison is made between a road sign and the reproductive system.

The upside-down triangle is reminiscent of a "give way" road sign in Zimbabwe. The sign is a signal to drivers that caution should be the watchword on that part of the road. Pictures of different forms of contraceptives are included inside the "yield" sign and the implied meaning between text and image seems to be that the reproductive system is at risk and contraceptives are precautionary measures. The imagery invoked is that of a road and the metaphorical message of safety and protection, control and caution, with reference to the reproductive system is conveyed through the image in its totality. The upside-down triangle with pictures of various types of contraceptives creates a composite image (Smith, Moriarty, Barbatsis and Kenney 2005), suggesting that because of the risk and vulnerability of the female reproductive system, caution has to be exercised in the use of the products inside the upside-down triangle. The analogical juxtaposition of graphics provides pictorial metaphors, all of which revolve around a discourse of restraint, control and vulnerability.

In figure 2, which is the second page of the same pamphlet, the focus is on education about the functioning of the "pill".

The graphics show three packets of different types of pills. To put the graphics into context the text (extract [1]) above the graphics states that the pill is a female-oriented type of contraceptive which can be used by women for a long period of time without any side-effects:

Extract (1)
Mapirisi inzira yemadzimai yokuronga mhuri yokushandisa kwenguiva pfupi. ('Pills are a way for women to arrange the family and they are used over a period of time.')

[Figure 1 and Figure 2 are on the following pages]

NZIRA DZOKURONGA MHURI

NZIRA DZINOSHANDA KWENGUVA PFUPI

Mapiritsi · Hwidibiro · Zvinopupuma · Makondomu · Makondomu

NZIRA DZINOSHANDA KWENGUVA REFU

Rupu · Jekiseni · MaImplant

NZIRA DZOKUSUNGA MBEREKO

- Kusungwa mbereko yemurume
- Kusungwa mbereko yemukadzi

MAPIRITSI

Mapiritsi inzira yemadzimai yokuronga mhuri yokushandisa kwenguva pfupi. Anemushonga unodzivirira zai raamai kuti risaita mwana.

Pakiti rimwechete rine mapiritsi makumi maviri nemasere.

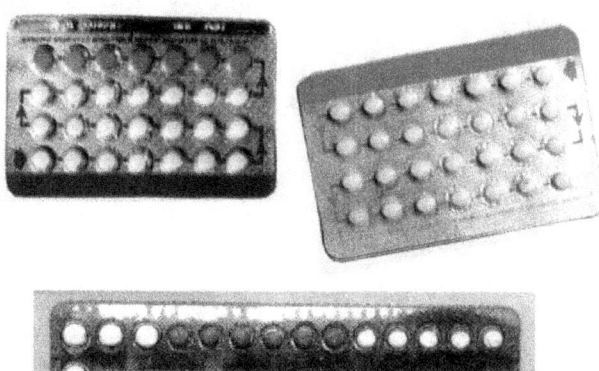

Mapiritsi anonwiwa zuva roga-roga, panguva imwecheteyo kuti ashande zvakanaka.

Kana akanwiwa nemazvo mazuva ose, mapiritsi inzira inoshanda zvikuru pakudzivirira pamuviri. Kana baba naamai vavakuda kuita mwana, mai ngavapedzise pakiti ravarikunwa vorega zvavo. Mapiritsi anobatsira madzimai kuti vazorore vasati vaita pamwe pamuviri kuitira kuti vave nehutano hwakakwana. Anobatsirawo mhuri kuti ive neupenyu hurinani. **Mapiritsi haadziviriri kubata STD kana AIDS.**

The road metaphor, i.e., *nzira*, runs through all the pamphlets in order to continue the discourse of vulnerability, caution, and restraint. The efficacy of the pill is explained by the repeated use of the word *dzivirira* ('close, stop, restrain,' etc.). The word is used in a metaphorical sense. In this context it is used to underscore the notion of maintaining protection and the implied emphasis is on "the role of contraception in protecting the body" (Hayter 2005: 49). The body is therefore discursively constructed as highly vulnerable, and the language used in the text seems to suggest that women have no control over their bodies but that contraceptives do have the power to control the female body. For example, in extract (2) the pill provides women with periods of rest and good health:

Extract (2)
Mapirisi anobatsira madzimai kutivazorore vasati vaita pamwe pamuviri kuitira kutivave nehutano hwakakwana. ('Pills help women so that they rest before making another baby so that they can have good health.')

Implicit in the above extract is the claim that the woman is no longer in control of her body as she needs the pill to allow her to rest; and failure to maintain the pill regimen places the female body in a vulnerable state. The terms discursively construct the reproductive system as vulnerable to pregnancy and therefore in need of protection for reasons related to women's health and the couple's economic well-being, hence:

Extract (3)
Anobatsira mhuri kuti ive neupenyu hurinani. ('They help the family to have a better quality of life.')

There are discernible protocols in explaining how contraceptives work. The first relates to body education in which a specific discursive technique is adopted in discussing the functioning, and efficacy (or lack thereof) in contraceptive use. In this technique both anatomical and physiological discourse are used in combination with a discourse reflective of "control, restraint, vulnerability and protection" (Hayter 2005: 49). In extract (4), for instance, in the description of the function of the pill, the discourse of restraint is evident in the explanation regarding the importance of keeping to a contraceptive regimen:

Extract (4)
Mapiritsi inzira yokuronga mhuri inoshandiswa nemadzimai mazhinji. Anemushonga unodzivirira zai raamai kuti risaita mwana. ('Pills are a way to arrange the family used by most women. They have medicine that protects the woman's egg from making a baby.')

In extract (5) below, a discourse of restraint and extreme caution is used in describing the need to adhere to a specific contraceptive regimen. If the strict regimen is not followed, then the body is placed at risk, which underscores the vulnerability of the female reproductive system to pregnancy. The role of the pill is to *dzivirira* ('stop, restrain') the release of an egg, which again is an emphasis on the discourse of protecting the female body:

Extract (5)
Anonwiwa zuva roga roga panguuva imwecheteyo kuti ashande zvakanaka. Kana akanwiwa zvakanaka mazuva ose, mapirisi inzira inoshanda zvikuru kudzivirira pamuviri. ('They are taken every day at the same time for them to work well. If taken properly daily, pills are a way (i.e., method) that works very well to prevent pregnancy.')

In the above extract the description of the adherence to a contraceptive regimen suggests that the female reproductive system needs a regulatory mechanism and the contraceptive provides

Mapiritsi

Mapiritsi inzira yokuronga mhuri inoshandiswa nemadzimai mazhinji. Anemushonga unodzivirira zai raamai kuti risaita mwana.

Pakiti rimwechete rine mapiritsi makumi maviri namasere.

Anonwiwa zuva roga roga panguva imwecheteyo kuti ashande zvakanaka.

Kana akanwiwa zvakanaka mazuva ose, mapiritsi inzira inoshanda zvikuru kudzivirira pamuviri.

Kana baba naamai vavakuda kuita mumwe mwana, ngavadzokere kukiriniki kana kuona mbuya vezvekuronga mhuri (CBD) mudunhu ravo.

Mapiritsi anobatsira amai kuti vazorore vasati vaita pamwe pamuviri.

Anobatsira mhuri kuti ive neupenyu hurinani.

Figure 3

such a mechanism. Failure to follow this regimen leads to a breakdown; hence the emphasis on the metaphor of caution because of the vulnerability of the female reproductive system and, ipso facto, the female body.

In figure 3, the first picture in the pamphlet is a woman taking a pill from a cup. She is also wearing a head turban, which is traditional headgear for married women.

The drawing is reinforced by a text made up of three paragraphs. The text explains that the pill prevents pregnancy by "restraining" the woman's egg. Notably, the woman who takes the pill is referred to as *amai* ('mother', even if there is no biological relationship between the individuals) with the accompanying turban underscoring her marital status. In Shona this is a formal and respectful way of addressing a married woman or a senior woman in the community who also happens to be married. By using terms such as *amai*, the FPAR was appropriating traditional status terms and using them in a new format for a different type of discourse in which the status of *amai* is enhanced whereas that of *baba* ('father') is not. This means the family planning campaigns have a strong impact on gender relations within Shona communities because *amai* unlike *baba* is not treated as a source of knowledge. Through the use of terms such as *amai* as the source of advice "interpersonal relationships" of respect are fostered.

The text and the graphic suggest, however, that the FPAR focused on married women at the exclusion of unmarried women who might have been divorced or widowed and yet sexually active as well. In figure 4 the graphic shows a nurse pointing to the different types of contraceptives.

Figure 4.

The graphic showing a man and a woman suggests a changed outlook on contraception. As has been pointed out, initially African men did not want their wives to use contraceptives. The inclusion of an African man in the graphic perhaps reflects a shift in ideology in that birth control now included men and was no longer restricted to African women only, which, essentially, is a contrast in that in the early phases of family planning men were excluded from direct engagement and were treated as antagonists who at times had to be deceived. Since family planning had in the early phases of its inception been feminized, the presence of a male figure in the drawings marks a shift in family planning to include both genders (Kim, Marangwanda and Kols 1996; Byrman 2001). It appears that this particular pamphlet and the accompanying text are directed towards couples for purposes of birth control. As Byrman (2001: 92) states, it is conceivable that owing to "the condemnatory attitude of society to premarital and extramarital relationships" unmarried individuals engaged in sexual relationships are left out. In this regard, family planning, especially the use of contraceptives, is used as a means to shape reproductive behavior, sexuality, and what constitutes an ideal family life.

Terminology of protection and risk is used repeatedly in the pamphlets. The notion of "cover" is also used repeatedly in explaining the function of the diaphragm. The cervix needs to be "covered" and hence the diaphragm is described as *inodzivirira muromo wechibereko* ('closing the mouth of the womb'). The socially and culturally constructed ideology of masculinity and femininity emerges, however, in the language used to describe the male and female reproductive anatomy. Sperm is referred to as *mbeu yababa* ('father's seeds') although *mbeu yemurume* ('male seeds') would also have been appropriate. The expression carries connotations of respect. If this expression is juxtaposed with *zai ramai* ('mother's egg'), however, it is possible that the intended meaning is that procreation occurs within marriage and therefore the terms used are for couples rather than women or men in general. Nonetheless, there is also a possibility that the use of *mbeu yababa* is contrasted with the female reproductive organs to indicate a differentiation between the sexes. A woman's ovaries are termed *basikiti* ('basket'), suggesting permeability or porosity. The text also utilizes differences in the status or position of men and women in society. All the vital male reproductive organs are described as belonging to the father; for example, *mbeu yababa* ('father's sperm'), *nhengo yababa* ('father's penis'), *mabhora ababa* ('father's balls'), etc. whereas the female organs are described using a container metaphor.

Terminology used in the discourse related to the discursive construction of women's bodies is value-laden. This is something that has also been observed by other researchers in this area (Laquer 1987; Weeks 1989; Hawkes 1996; Shorter 1997). The prevailing metaphors used in constructing the female body discursively revolve around vulnerability and unpredictability.

5. Discussion and concluding comments

The main focus of this chapter is the discursive construction of the female body through contraceptive education contained in pamphlets from the Zimbabwe Family Planning Association. The pamphlets were produced during the period 1970 to 1982. In the pamphlets, the female reproductive system is discursively constructed "as vulnerable to pregnancy and requiring contraceptive protection" (Hayter 2005: 46). This chapter sought to explore the discursive strategies used in disseminating information and the manner in which the body is discursively constructed. The findings suggest that discourses used in the pamphlets are similar to discourses that have been used in medical discourse to describe the female reproductive system. The template of depiction of the usage of contraceptives is similar to that used in other parts of the world, notably the UK (Hayter 2005). This creates the impression that the Zimbabwean pamphlets are a localization of a British, perhaps even western, template. In the pamphlets the female reproductive system is discursively constructed as weak and vulnerable. This discourse is part of an awareness-raising strategy so that women are knowledgeable about the health risks of frequent pregnancy and the economic benefits of having fewer children. This strategy is commonly used in other medical discourse educating individuals about health practices.

Martin (1989) and Laws (1990) point out that in medical discourse the female body is discursively constructed as breaking down and degenerating. The terminology and discourse used to describe the reproductive organs do not underscore a degenerating body or failing system but rather a "fully functioning machine liable to produce if not kept in check" (Hayter 2005: 51). The purpose of the pamphlet is to provide women with knowledge about family planning, but also to motivate them to "self-care" and to continue the use of contraceptives; hence the language used emphasizes the requirement for protection. In the pamphlets, risk discourse is used to underscore the notion of the susceptibility to illness of the female body if it is subjected to frequent pregnancies. The notion of risk, however, has been used in medical discourse and plays a key role in encouraging individuals to care for themselves (Lupton 1997; Nettleton 1997). The rationale in using risk discourse is that "risk and its reduction or management" (Hayter 2005: 52) are central to self-care, and in the case of contraception this would be in the form of continued and effective use of contraceptives. In the pamphlets the concept of reproductive vulnerability is discursively constructed in order to educate women about their bodies and in the use of contraceptives. Central to body education is a process of "facilitating effective contraceptive use" (Hayter 2005: 52).

Another discourse that emerges from the pamphlets relates to differences in describing the male and female reproductive organs. For instance, whereas the female reproductive system is described in commonly used stereotypical terms associated with females being weak and in need of protection, the male reproductive system is described by metaphors associated with strength and virility (Martin 1991).

Family planning pamphlets are likely to be effective because they are distributed in tandem with those which address issues about women's rights, HIV/AIDS, and other contagious disease. The pamphlets are distributed both publicly and in schools as part of health education in the school curriculum in both elementary and high schools. The co-depiction of contraception with chronic conditions depicts the former (contraception) as a risky enterprise, rather than an integral aspect of women. The co-presence of text and visuals in the pamphlets enhances its reader friendliness even to women with relatively limited formal literacy and who are likely to concentrate on the visuals more than the text. In spite of the effectiveness of the co-depiction of text and visuals, the philosophy in family planning and women's rights is that the individual has ultimate control over their individual body. This, however, runs contrary to an Afrocentric philosophy in which the community has ultimate responsibility over the female body, as exemplified in the case of the Shone, the Ngwa-Igbo, and the Ubang in Nigeria. The differences in the status and role of the individual in family planning and African discourses militate against the effectiveness of family planning campaigns. Family planning may have to propose new types of discourses which establish a dialogical relationship between individual and community responsibilities towards contraception and health upkeep rather than the individuated discourses underpinning the family planning pamphlets and other health campaigns (Airhihenbuwa 2000) currently constructed in Africa.

The tension between the individual and the community in family planning reflects the degree to which modern health campaigns have to be sensitive to cultural practices. This is not to suggest that all types of cultural practices should be retained irrespective of their potential adverse effects. In other words, family planning campaigns can be used to challenge some aspects of Zimbabwean cultural practices. The extent to which family planning campaigns can be used to challenge some cultural practices has to be subject to extreme caution because the campaigns may be construed as covert political campaigns, opposing the government via the female body, so to speak. In order for the family planning campaigns to be more readily accessible to the young and have a sense of credibility, it may be necessary to write them in urban vernaculars rather than standardized African languages which are rarely used by the young.

6. Recommended reading
(1) Thomas, L. 2003. *Politics of the Womb: Women, Reproduction and the State in Kenya.* Berkeley, CA: University of California Press.

The main theme of the book is women's bodies, particularly female genital cutting, pre-marital pregnancy, abortion, and other practices. The book demonstrates the various ways in which the body and reproductive health shaped and shifted owing to the impact of colonialism.

(2) Hunt, R. 1999. *A Colonial Lexicon: of Birth Ritual, Medicalization, and Mobility in the Congo.* Durham, NC: Duke University Press.

This book is an important contribution to the development of an understanding of the historiography of medical practice, missionary activities, gender and social class in Congo. The book traces the history of childbirth medicalization and movement from pro-natalism to post-colonialism. Medical knowledge constituted a site of conflict between colonisers and colonized.

References

Airhihenbuwa, C. (2000). "A critical assessment of theories/ models used in Health Communication for HIV/AIDS" *Journal of Health Communication* 5. 5–15.

Armstrong, D. (1993). "Public health spaces and the fabrication of identity" *Sociology* 27. 340–393.

Armstrong, D. (1998). "Bodies of knowledge/knowledge of bodies" In C. Jones and R. Porter (eds.), *Reassessing Foucault*, 17–27. London: Routledge.

Bala, P. (2009). *Biomedicine as a Contested Site: Some Revelations In Imperial Contexts*. Lanham, MD, Boulder, CO, New York: Rowan & Littlefield.

Barrett, G. and R. Harper (2001). "Health professionals' attitudes to the deregulation of emergency contraception (or the problem of female sexuality)" *Journal of Sociology of Health and Illness* 22(2). 197–216.

Byrman, G. (2001). "From marital precautions to love power: Gender construction in Swedish contraceptive brochures" *Nordic Journal of Women's Studies* 9(2). 89–97.

Comaroff, J. L. and S. Roberts (1977). "Marriage and extra-marital sexuality: the dialectics of legal change among the Kgatla" *Journal of African Law* 21(1), 97–123.

Cooper, F. and A. L. Stoler (1997). "Between metropole and colony: Rethinking a research agenda" In F. Cooper and A. L. Stoler (eds.), *Tensions Of Empire: Colonial Cultures in a Bourgeois World*, 1–58. Berkeley, CA et al.: University of California Press.

Cooper, F. and A. L. Stoler (eds.) (1997) *Tensions of Empire: Colonial Cultures in a Bourgeois World*. Berkeley, CA, Los Angeles & London: University of California Press.

de Bot, K. and S. Makoni (2005). *Language and Aging in Multilingual Contexts*. Multilingual Matters: Clevedon.

Dodds, P. (1978). "The community and family planning" *Rhodesia Science News* 12(3) 160–162.

Fairclough, N. (1989). *Language and Power*. London:

Longman.

Foucault, M. (1980). *The History of Sexuality. Vol. 1: An Introduction* (transl. by R. Hurley). New York: Vintage Books.

Gallagher, C. and T. Laquer (eds.) (1987). *The Making of the Modern Body Sexuality and Society in the Nineteenth Century*. Berkeley, CA: University of California Press.

Goffman, E. (1961). *Asylums: Essays on the Social Situation of Mental Patients and Other Inmates*. Doubleday: New York.

Hancock, P., B. Hughes, E. Jagger, K. Patterson, R. Russell, E. Tulle-Winton and M. Tyler (2000). *The Body, Culture and Society: An Introduction*. Open University Press: Buckingham.

Hawkes, G. (1996). *A Sociology of Sex and Sexuality*. Open University Press: Buckingham.

Hayter, M. (2005). "The social construction of "reproductive vulnerability" in family planning clinics" *Journal of Advanced Nursing* 51(1) 46–54.

Higgins, C. and B. Norton (eds.) (2010). *Language and HIV/AIDS*. Clevedon: Multilingual Matters.

Howson, A. (2001). "Embodied obligation: the female body and health surveillance. In S. Nettleton and J. Watson (eds.), *The Body in Everyday Life*, 218–240. London: Routledge.

Hunt, N. (1999). *A Colonial Lexicon: Of Birth Ritual, Medicalization, and Mobility in the Congo (Body, Commodity, Text)*. Durham, NC & London: Duke University Press.

Jeater, D. (1993). *Moral Perversion And Power: The Construction Of Moral Discourse In Southern Rhodesia*. Clarendon: Oxford University Press.

Jones, S. and B. Norton (2010). "Uganda's ABC program on HIV/AIDS prevention: A discursive site of struggle" In C. Higgins and B. Norton (eds.), *Language and HIV/AIDS*, 155–177. Clevedon: Multilingual Matters.

Jones, C. and R. Porter (eds.) (1998). *Reassessing Foucault*. London: Routledge.

Kaler, A. (2000). " 'Who has told you to do this thing?' Toward a feminist interpretation of contraceptive diffusion in Rhodesia, 1970–1980" *Journal of Women in Culture and Society* 25(3) 678–708.

Kaler, A. (2003). *Running After Pills: Politics, Gender, and Contraception in Colonial Zimbabwe*. Portsmouth, NH: Heinemann.

Kennedy, D. (1987). *Islands of White: Settler Society and Culture in Kenya and Southern Rhodesia, 1890–1939*. Durham, NC: Duke University Press.

Kim Y. M., C. Marangwanda and A. Kols (1996). *Involving Men In Family Planning: The Zimbabwe Male Motivation And Family Method Expansion Project, 1993–1994* (IEC Field Report Series, No. 3). Baltimore, MD: John Hopkins Centre for Communication.

Kress, G. (2000). "Multimodality: Challenges to thinking about language" *TESOL Quarterly* 34, 337–340.

Laquer, T. (1987). "Orgasm, generation, and the politics of reproductive biology" In C. Gallagher and T. Laquer (eds.), *The Making of the Modern Body: Sexuality and Society in the Nineteenth Century*, 1–41. Berkeley, CA: University of California Press.

Laws, S. (1990). *Issues of Blood: The Politics of Menstruation*. London: Macmillan.

Lupton, D. (1997). "Foucault and the medicalization critique" In A. Petersen and R. Bunton (eds.), *Foucault, Health and Medicine*, 94–112. Milton Keynes: Routledge.

Lyons, T. (2004). *Guns and Guerilla Girls: Women in the Zimbabwean Liberation Struggle*. Trenton: World Press.

Martin, E. (1989). *The Woman in the Body*. Milton Keynes: Open University Press.

Martin, E. (1991). "The egg and the sperm: How science has

constructed a romance based upon stereotypical male-female roles" *Journal of Women in Culture and Society* 16(3), 485–501.
Nettleton, S. (1997). "Governing the risky self: how to become healthy, wealthy and wise" In A. Petersen and R. Bunton (eds.), *Foucault, Health and Medicine*, 207–222. Milton Keynes: Routledge.
Nettleton, S. and J. Watson (eds.) (2001). *The Body in Everyday Life*. London: Routledge.
Nhongo-Simbanegavi, J. (2000). *For Better or Worse: Women and ZANLA in Zimbabwe's Liberation Struggle*. Harare: Weaver Press.
O'Halloran, K. L. (2008). "Systemic functional-multimodal discourse analysis (SF-MDA): Constructing ideational meaning using language and visual imagery" *Visual Communication* 7(4). 443–475.
Petersen, A. and R. Bunton (eds.) (1997). *Foucault, Health and Medicine*. Milton Keynes: Routledge.
Ramanathan, V. (1997). *Alzheimer Discourse: Some Sociolinguistic Dimensions*. Mahwah, NJ: Lawrence Erlbaum.
Ramanathan, V. (2010). *Bodies and Language: Ailments, Health, Disabilities.* New York: Multilingual Matters.
Ramanathan, V. and S. Makoni (2008). "Bringing the body back in body narratives: The mislanguaging of bodies in biomedical, societal, and poststructuralist discourses on diabetes and epilepsy. *Critical Inquiry in Language Studies* 4(4). 283–306.
Sapire, K. E. (1971). "Family planning" *Rhodesia Science News* 5(4). 104–108.
Shorter, E. (1997). *Women's Bodies: A Social History of Women's Encounter With Health, Ill-health and Medicine.* New Brunswick, NJ: Transaction Publishers.
Smith, K. L., S. Moriarty, G. Barbatsis and K. Kenney (eds.)

(2005). *Handbook of Visual Communication: Theory Method and Media*. New Jersey: Lawrence Erlbaum Associates.

Summers, C. (2002). *Colonial Lessons: Africans' Education in Southern Rhodesia, 1918–1940*. Portsmouth, NH: Heinemann.

Thomas, L. (2003). *Politics of the Womb: Women, Reproduction, and the State in Kenya*. Berkeley, CA: University of California Press.

Tularog, T., W. Deressa, A. Ali and G. Daven (2006). "The role of men in contraceptives use and fertility preference in Hossana Town" *Ethiopian Journal of Health Development* 20(3) 152–159.

Van Onselen, C. (1982). *The Witches of Suburbia: Domestic Service on the Witwatersrand, 1890–1914* (vol. 2). London: Longman.

Weeks, J. (1989). *Sex, Politics and Society: The Regulation of Sexuality Since 1800*. London: Longman.

West, M. (1994). "Nationalism, race, and Gender: the politics of family planning" *The Society of the Social History of Medicine* 7(3) 447–471.

Wilder, E. I. (2004). Review of the book *Running after pills: Politics, gender, and contraception in Colonial Zimbabwe. American Journal of Sociology* 110(3), 822–823.

Williams, S. J. and G. A. Bendelow (1998). *The Lived Body: Sociological Themes, Embodied Issues*. London: Routledge.

XV

The wordy worlds of popular music in Eastern and Southern Africa: possible implications for language-in-education policy
(With Busi Makoni and Aaron Rosenberg)

Abstract
Language-in-education policy in Africa is replete with debate regarding the use of standard African languages as part of mother-tongue education. An issue inadequately addressed within this debate is the role and function of urban vernaculars which have become "the" mother tongue of the greater part of Africa's population. Using data from the lyrics of popular music from eastern and southern African songwriters as an instance of ground-level language practices, this article argues that, to the extent that urban vernaculars and standard African languages act as international languages in popular music, there is justification for using urban vernaculars as languages of instruction. The extensive use of urban vernaculars in popular music has led to its popularity, and if these urban vernaculars are used as part of mother tongue education, socio-cultural relations between the school and society may improve. Despite

the fact that educational strategies based on language practices in popular songs subvert social hierarchy, the use of urban vernaculars reshapes and blurs linguistic boundaries and, thus, constructs plurilingual identities. Using urban vernaculars not only provides access to education for a large portion of the population but also consolidates "glocal" identities while affirming cultural roots.

The most well-known language policy debate in non-Western postcolonial contexts relates to the status and function of indigenous/local languages vis-à-vis that of European languages (Cook, 2006, 2009; Meeuwis, 1999). In terms of language-in-education policy, this debate translates to discussions about the use of local languages as languages of instruction in mother-tongue education programs. In African contexts, this has meant the introduction of indigenous African or minority languages as languages of instruction in schools.

While there is a tendency to dwell inordinately on the merits and demerits of mother-tongue instruction and at what stage it should be introduced, reduced, and replaced by the former colonial languages, "the value of mother tongue instruction is literally incontestable" (Prah, 2002, p. 3). Yet what constitutes the mother tongue for the greater part of the population in plurilingual contexts such as Africa is highly contestable. In sub-Saharan Africa, for instance, there are strong suggestions that the majority of the population use urban vernaculars or hybrid varieties and that these varieties are indeed "the" mother tongue of most school-going children (Calteaux, 1996; Cook, 2009; Makoni, Brutt-Griffler, & Mashiri, 2007; Mungai, 2008). The first challenge that African children face in the classroom is the use of and identification with standard varieties of African languages.

Focusing on the status of African languages vis-à-vis former colonial languages is "a language ideological debate"

(Meeuwis, 1999, p. 401) that has "erased" from view a long-standing and more pertinent debate about the role and status of varieties of African languages, including the different dialects and urban hybrid forms. This article focuses on "this less visible debate" (Cook, 2009, p. 96). In addition, this article "starts from the premise that language and in particular the distinction between standard African languages and urban vernaculars provides a critical lens into the process of identity formation, ideological tensions" (p. 96) and, most importantly, considers how different varieties of African languages can be utilized in education for effective learning.

In Africa's educational milieu, discussions of the role and functionality of urban vernaculars show "a contradictory impulse of simultaneously denigrating and celebrating the vernacular" (Nero, 2006, p. 503). While the worlds of advertising and book publishing have seen the value of urban hybrid varieties for promoting brand products, education seems stuck in a standard-language ideology that associates urban vernaculars with low socioeconomic status and lack of education. Yet some researchers have argued for the use of urban vernaculars as languages of instruction (Calteaux, 1996; Cook, 2009), noting that the characterization of urban vernaculars mirrors a similar debate of the 1930s in which standard African languages were rejected (Adejunmobi, 2004).

Nonetheless, others have called for the promotion of urban vernaculars as national languages because they reflect commonality and a shared identity, which is, at times, cross-national in nature. After all, urban vernaculars cut across national and ethnic boundaries and, therefore, do not reflect a rigid ethnic or linguistic-based identity (Leischa, 2005) that standard varieties enhance. Thus, urban vernaculars "invoke a collective identity," thereby avoiding "ethnic othering" (Wa Mutonya, 2007, p. 163).

A more paradoxically polemical issue is that prior to most African communities' colonial encounters, African identities were not founded on rigid ethnic and linguistic lines. Thus, if one of the major objectives of national language policies founded on standard languages is to facilitate the consolidation of postcolonial Africa, then the use of standard languages is essentially a return to colonial practices, while such policies seek to advance postcolonial interests by mitigating the effects of colonialism.

This article focuses on analyzing popular music, primarily the language used in the lyrics. As Alim and Pennycook (2007) point out, "putting language at the centre of the analysis opens up levels of significance in terms of language choice, style and discrimination" (p. 90). By analyzing language use in the lyrics of popular music, the aim of this article is to establish the potential implications for and use of urban vernaculars in education. Drawing on songwriters from eastern and southern Africa, the article uses ground-level evidence to evaluate critically the descriptive adequacy of current language-in-education policy by focusing on language use in popular music and the politics it implies.

The choice of popular music as a site for ground-level language practices is based on the premise that music as a form of social practice has complex transnational links and deep historical and social roots in Africa, permeating many aspects of African social life. After all, Africans experience music from the "cradle to the grave" (Mbambi-Katana, 1977, p. 26). Popular music is also "an important site of educational practice" (Alim & Pennycook, 2007, p. 90), and as a "significant pedagogical site," it "is inevitably part of school culture and becomes either formally or informally part of the school curriculum" (Alim & Pennycook, p. 90). The analysis of popular music, therefore, "brings together issues of language, identity, and education" (Alim & Pennycook, p. 89).

Popular culture as an area of social and linguistic experience has rarely featured prominently in language-in-education debates in Africa. This article seeks to argue that while issues of mother-tongue education in Africa have revolved around the role of English vis-à-vis that of African languages, few have sought to confront the grassroots debate among African language communities about which variety is appropriate for use as a language of instruction. Yet research has shown that standard African languages lack popularity and that most students find these standard varieties incomprehensible. Herbert (1992), for example, cites evidence that students who have Zulu attributed to them as a mother tongue based on their ethnicity liken learning in Zulu to learning in a foreign language, to an extent that teachers have to shift to urban vernaculars. In light of the problematic nature of using standard African languages as languages of instruction, we ask whether urban varieties can provide a viable alternative. In this case, the language practices in music represent an interesting area to study, not only in terms of the interpretable meanings of the lyrics, but also in the symbolic significance of the varieties of language used and the possible reasons for using such varieties. Instead of framing standard versus nonstandard languages as "other," this article proposes a radical shift in language in education for speakers of African languages that has a potential to validate different varieties of African languages in the classroom and perhaps to render the African medium of instruction more comprehensible (Jeater, 2001).

Setting the scene
The centrality of popular music in Africa is evident from the large number of studies conducted from a cultural studies tradition (Njogu & Maupeu, 2007). Most of these studies emphasize how urbanization, globalization, and commercialization have influenced traditional African music. Although the language of the lyrics has not been the central focus, some studies have remarked that different musicians use various languages in a single song, including local vernaculars (Mphande, 2007; Nyoni, 2007; Wa Mutonya, 2007).

In this article, we use the term *popular music*, which is sometimes used interchangeably with the term *world music*. However, the use of the term *popular music* "reflects, cultural, social and economic categories, particularly those found in North America and the UK" (Tagg, 2005, p. 135), while *world music* is an umbrella category used for music variously referred to as "Afro-pop," "Afro-music," "African jazz," and "Afro-beat" (Guilbault, 1993; Rasolofondrasolo & Meinhof, 2003). These terms refer to different types of music that originate in non-English-speaking countries. Because of these conflicting definitions, it may be more appropriate to conceptualize popular music as a form of practice, a field of activity produced primarily in controlled environments with a variety of acoustic and electrified instruments.

The controlled nature of the environments has a bearing on the forms of language used. Auzanneau (2002), for instance, notes that "the choices are generally conscious" (p. 120) or "intentional" (Billiez, 1998) since they take place during the compositional phase and constitute "a deferred speech act" (Auzanneau, p. 120). The choices are not "acts of identity" (Le Page & Tabouret-Keller, 1985) but "intentional identity acts" (Auzanneau, p. 120) because the language used closely approximates carefully crafted and stylized language (Rampton, 1995) in order to project the artificial or rehearsed as "authentic." The concern for authenticity is "linked to broader notions of authenticity and Afrocentricity" (Mitchell, 2000, p. 41).

The choices of language in most popular music reflect particular ideologies held by the musicians or songwriters. Thus, the discourses used in the lyrics are usually a reflection of popular beliefs in the communities where the musicians or songwriters come from. However, this is not to suggest that popular music is a mimetic commentary. As Negus (1997) posits, "No music can be a mirror to capture events or activities in its melodies, rhythms and voices" (p. 4) as the artists are also contributing toward creating alternative futures and, hence, affecting the present and not simply passively reflecting it.

The ability of musicians to either directly reflect or create these possible futures may be constrained by recording companies who have some influence in shaping and determining what gets edited in and edited out in the lyrics. This is evident in situations such as those in immediate post-independence Tanzania, where the government controlled both the production and distribution of music. In spite of the influence of recording companies, the varieties of languages used in the lyrics speak more directly than standard varieties and create feelings of being part of "imagined local communities" (Anderson, 1983) oftentimes with translocal affiliations. Such translocal affiliations are captured using urban vernaculars because these reflect a melting pot of languages, identities, or fluid ethnicities of the communities where these varieties are used. The use of urban vernacular or multiple languages and varieties in popular music is strategic. It reflects and emphasizes plurilingual dexterity; after all, the use of multiple codes corresponds to the way people talk in plurilingual contexts (Mitchell, 2000).

While language use in the lyrics of popular music from Africa has not received significant attention in applied linguistics and sociolinguistics, Kwaramba's (1997) study of the language of protest in *Chimurenga* (colonial struggle) songs by Thomas Mapfumo is seminal. Kwaramba undertook a narrative analysis of Chimurenga songs using critical discourse analysis. Kwaramba's findings suggest that the discursive use of pronouns from varieties of African languages and urban mixtures has the effect of excluding some and including others and, thus, sharpening the "them" and "us" dichotomy, which serves to conscientize the audience on the power of the collective force toward a shared goal. Similarly, in Palmberg and Kirkegaard's (2002) *Playing with Identities in Contemporary Music in Africa*, chapters by Akindes, Palmberg, and Nannyonga-Tamusuza on Cote d' Ivoire, Cape Verde, and Uganda, have substantial sections on language issues relating to music. Akindes, for example, shows how musicians have used "Ivorian French," an urban vernacular developed as a medium of communication by "illiterate laborers, house servants, shop attendants, and other low-rank workers with little or no formal schooling" (p. 98), to reach a wider audience. In addition, Palmberg points out that the use of "Kriolu language" in Cape Verde music had a substantial impact in corpus planning. It facilitated its codification and "reduction" into a written language, thereby changing its status.

The studies cited above reflect the degree to which non-standard varieties or urban vernaculars are widely used and the extent to which a wide range of African communities identify with them. Perhaps when these varieties are used as a medium of instruction, students might identify with them more easily than with standard varieties, rendering it possible for students to construct more meanings for the school content. Thus, use of urban vernaculars in the classroom may erase "the putative home/school language divide" (Rampton, 1985, p. 188).

Methodology and objectives
The songs used in the analysis were from the "Top Ten Africa's lifetime favorites" played on DTSV Africa-to-Africa channel. These songs were initially in the top 50, then made it to the top 20 in all of Africa's African languages radio stations. The compilation of the songs was through Africa-to-Africa channel's phone-in, write-in, e-mail, and fax message requests made by community members through the community radio stations. The songs that were in the top ten led us to specific songwriters and the specific albums on which each song was released.

Data collection occurred in early 2007. That the songwriters who made it to the top 10 were from southern and eastern Africa was a coincidence. Nevertheless, one of the authors, a DJ who had worked in eastern Africa, provided the transcriptions of all the songs that formed the basis of our analysis.

The methodology used in analyzing the language of the lyrics in popular music is discourse analysis with particular focus on language choice. In analyzing the language of the lyrics of popular music, we explored the nature and type of language varieties the musicians used and how they fashioned and constructed the identities of their audiences or "taste publics" (Scannell, 2001, p. 22; Weber, 1975, p. 10). Specifically, the questions asked were as follows:

1. What are the role and status of African languages in popular music?
2. What are the role and status of European languages in popular music?
3. What types of multilingualism are exhibited in popular music?
4. What is the relevance of the responses to the above questions for language in education?

Findings: status and role of the different languages in popular music

In order to investigate the role and status of different languages (i.e., African languages, English, and French) in popular music, this study analyzed the languages used in the lyrics and explored the implications for language in education in African contexts. Examining language use in the lyrics of popular music shifts the focus away from state-level language policy pronouncements toward more "authentic" ground-level linguistic practices, not imposed linguistic boundaries (Cook, 2009).

Extracts of song texts from the music of the following popular musicians from southern and eastern Africa were analyzed: Oliver Mutukudzi, Yvonne Chaka Chaka, Paul Ngozi, Chris Chali, Samba Mapangala, Hukwe Zawose, Shalawambe, Eric Wainaina, Abou Chihabi, and Chebli.

Most popular musicians in eastern and southern Africa use a wide range of African languages and linguistic mixtures or urban vernaculars in their music. In addition, there is a predominant use of indigenous minority languages. For instance, Comorian songwriters such as Abou Chihabi have adopted Swahili as a linguistic identity marker. However, some of the titles and lyrics of the songs on Chihabi's album *Folkmor Ocean* (1997) are in languages other than Swahili. One such language used in this album is Shingazidja. For example, "Sote Ndugu" is a close approximation of standard Swahili, while "Vura Nkasiya na Pondro" is in Shingazidja. The use of various other African languages reflects the multilingual character of the Comoros in which Swahili is but one of the languages spoken. In some cases, the spelling of the words in Chihabi's titles differs significantly from the textbook version of standard Swahili, a tendency that also shows up in the work of the Congolese performing artist Samba Mapangala. In standard spelling, song titles such as "Lewo! Lewo!," "Maesha," "Tsi Haki," or "Masiwa" would be rendered as "Leo! Leo!," "Maisha," "Si Haki," and "Maziwa," respectively.

While Chihabi's songs are in Swahili and Shingazidja, the songs of the late Hukwe Zawose, the most famous traditional singer and musician in Tanzania and possibly in the whole of east Africa, are sung in both Swahili and Kigogo. The title track from his album *Mateso/Suffering* (1989) deals with the situation in South Africa during the apartheid era. The song "Sisi Vijana (We who are young)" mirrors the camaraderie in Chihabi's "Sote Ndugu." However, other songs such as "Nhongolo," "Kononze," "Mbiji," and "Chosanga" are all exclusively in Kigogo. As a counterpoint to Chihabi, the language strategies employed by Chebli, another Comorian singer, suggest that he has moved away from "traditional" forms of musical composition, such as the accordion-driven *twarab*. However, Chebli still composes his lyrics in Shingazidja.

The analysis of the language of popular-music lyrics indicated that African languages, including their hybrid forms, play a prominent role (Njogu & Maupeu, 2007; Nyoni, 2007). A number of scholars working in Africa have raised serious questions about the "language-killing potential" (Edwards, 1994, p. 8) of languages such as English, French, and Portuguese. From the viewpoint of popular music, African languages are not likely to be endangered in the near future. However, the language of the lyrics suggests that the standard varieties are promoted at the government policy level. It is equally true that ground-level language practices in the music industry fly in the face of such policy orientations. In popular music, the linguistic hybrids are more frequently used than English, French, or Portuguese.

Developing countries justify the elevation of exogenous languages such as English, French, and Portuguese by claiming that these languages allow their citizens to participate in the world economy. Popular songwriters and their audiences, however, are receptive to alternative visions of the global community and the sort of interactions and transactions most relevant to their own lives. Many of the ways in which their songs express these concepts can be ascertained through attention to the linguistic strategies that they employ and systems of deployment which frequently countermand the official policies. A case in point is the song "Sote Ndugu" by Abou Chihabi.

Extract 1: Abou Chihabi, "Sote Ndugu" (We are brothers)

Afrika Kusini ina ubaguzi.	South Africa is rotten with racism.
Kwa nini ndugu?	Why brethren?
Ni aibu.	It's shameful.
Yo yo yo yo yo yo yo yo!	Oh oh oh oh oh oh oh oh!
Unasikia kama huko kwetu,	[Here] you feel as if you are at home,
Sote vijana tunapendana sana.	All us youngsters really love one another.
East Africa—sote ni ndugu.	East Africa—we are all brethren.
West Africa—vile vile ndugu.	West Africa the same we are brothers.
South Africa—eyahh!	South Africa—eyahh!

North Africa . . .	North Africa . . .
Dunia nzima sote ni ndugu—kweli!	Through the world we're brethren truly!
Kweli ndugu—kweli!	Truly brethren—truly!
India, Arabia, China, Japan, Russia	India, Arabia, China, Japan, Russia
Amerika,	America,
Europa—ropa ropa Comorock.	Europa—ropa ropa Comorian rock
Afrika—Freedom	Africa—Freedom
Afrika—Music.	Africa—Music
Chantons tous	Let's all sing
Dansons tous	Let's all dance
We will get it someday	We will get it someday
We will get it someday	We will get it someday

In a linguistic analysis of Chihabi's "Sote Ndugu," the first element that is immediately obvious is the minor role of French in the song. The entire song contains only two lines in French (lines 18 and 19), which do not convey any serious propositional content. Reducing the role of French to a few lines is striking when one considers that the album was released in France and was composed by a former French colonial subject. This seems to suggest that there is a complementary relation between French and African languages in France. In the universe of popular music, African languages and their hybrid varieties are dominant. Conversely, English and French are dominant in a different linguistic universe. Although there is a single physical world, each language is dominant in a different social world.

Not only do French and, indeed, English have minor roles to play in the lyrics, but more significantly, the use of African varieties of French and English also shows that there are "several French languages today, and allows us to conceive of their unicity according to a new mode, in which French (and indeed English) can no longer be monolingual" (Glissant, 1997, p. 119). This raises an interesting point about social identity and language learning. If, as part of their social identity, African children already feel that they speak English and all the other African languages, they may not see the need to learn the standard varieties of the same languages in school. Pierce (as cited in Nero, 2006), states that "a person's investment in learning a language is an investment in his or her own evolving social identity" (p. 508). To the extent that African students already identify with varieties of English, French, Portuguese, and African languages and their linguistic bricolage, "they are less likely to make a deliberate investment in learning" (Nero, p. 508) them as separate languages.

Nonetheless, the practice of singing the same songs in different languages is also evident in the music of southern African musicians such as Oliver Mutukudzi in his songs "Todii (What Shall We Do?)" and "Magumo (The End)." As shown in Extract 2, in "Todii" he sings first in Shona, then Ndebele, and lastly in English (Sibanda, 2004).

Extract 2: Oliver Mutukudzi, "Todii" (What Shall We Do?)
Chorus:
Hooo todii; senzeni what shall we do
What shall we do, tingadii
Senzenjani, what shall we do
Senzeni
Tingadii; senzenjani, what shall we do

The same line is repeated in three different languages. What is significant is the implied hierarchy in the sequencing of the languages. Mutukudzi sings first in Shona, then sings in Ndebele, and concludes with English, suggesting a hierarchy that runs counter to the Zimbabwean language policy of English as an official language and Shona and Ndebele as the two national languages. This seems to suggest that within Mutukudzi's singing universe English is not a "dominant" language, lessening the language's power in the same way that French is reduced to insignificant lines in Chihabi's song. However, the implied hierarchy changes in "Magumo" in that Mutukudzi sings in Ndebele before Shona. The suggested hierarchy in "Magumo" is interesting because it runs counter to sociolinguistic literature from Zimbabwe that has argued that Shona is the only dominant African language. For instance, Hachipola (1998) states the following:

> One could be misled by politics to think that the government sees Shona and Ndebele on par. The truth is that Shona has a much higher status than Ndebele. In the media, for example, on television, radio, news is read in Shona first (p. xxi).

This state of affairs, Ndhlovu (2006) suggests, has rendered Shona the only dominant African language in Zimbabwe. Yet in "Magumo," Mutukudzi seems to challenge this position. The song lyrics in Magumo are initially in Ndebele and then Shona, as shown in Extract 3.

Extract 3: Oliver Mutukudzi, "Magumo" (The End)
Ndebele: Ma ulemali eningi besuhlupha abantu uzotholani
      ngalokho, (*If you have a lot of money, then you mistreat others*)
      Uzophelelaphi *(Where will all this end?)*

Shona: Kuzvirova dundundu (*You beat your chest*)
      Tozvinzwa kuti ndisu tiri pano (*Feeling all your importance*)
      Magumo acho chii (*How will it all end?*)

As shown in "Magumo," some of the musicians sing in languages that are not their first language/s, suggesting that we need to be skeptical of the tendency to assume a one-to-one relationship between language and ethnicity encouraged by the ethnonyms in common use (Blommaert, 1999). For example, the South African singer Yvonne Chaka Chaka sings in Shona in one of her songs: "Kana uch chma" (which rendered in native form would be "Kana uchichema").

Popular songs in Zambia likewise bear witness to the variety of language choices among the creative artists who compose them. Artists such as the Amayenge band have developed a fusion of "traditional" musical performance with modern instrumentation, reflecting hybridity not only at the level of language but also at the level of music, style, and instrumentation, indicating the extent to which mixing at both linguistic and musical levels is mutually reinforcing. The lyrics of these songs are sung almost exclusively in "indigenous" Zambian languages. In a recent album, *Dailesi* (Amayenge, 2004), one finds that the songs are in Nsenga, Chewa, Bemba, Tumbuka, Lunda, Lenje, Luvale, Soli, and Lamba; this list indicates the extent of linguistic diversity in Zambia and the degree to which these indigenous languages are utilized as a resource rather than a constraint in the universe of music (Ruiz, 1984).

Just as common as these songs with lyrics composed in languages native to Zambia are those that contain linguistic mixtures within a single song. This ability to carry out fluid and seemingly instantaneous movement from one language or lect to another within the course of an oral performative work may serve any number of purposes, depending on the intentions of the artist. A case in point is the song "Samora Machel" by the group Shalawambe (1989).

Extract 4: Shalawambe, "Samora Machel"
Chinshi Chalenga	What has caused this? (6 times)
Samora Machel Aya	Samora Machel is gone
Zambia balelila	Zambia is in mourning
Samora Machel Aya	Samora Machel is gone
Zimbabwe balelila	Zimbabwe is mourning

Samora Machel Aya	Samora Machel is gone
Mozambique	Mozambique
Samora Machel Aya	Samora Machel is gone
Afrika Mama	Africa mother
Samora Machel Aya	Samora Machel is gone
Africa Mama Iye!	Africa mother iye!
Samora Machel Aya	Samora Machel is gone
Oh! Shalawambe iko matata	Oh! Shalawambe the problems are overwhelming
Oh! Shalawambe iko matata	Oh! Shalawambe the problems are overwhelming
Oh! Shalawambe iko matata	Oh! Shalawambe the problems are overwhelming
I fell very sad mama here we go	
Yalila yalila Shalawambe	Shalawambe is in tears
Nalelo Ilelila Shalawambe	Today Shalawambe is crying
Samora Machel Aya	Samora Machel has disappeared
Africa Mama	Africa mother
Samora Machel—o	Samora Machel is gone[1]

Between lines 14 and 18, the song diverges from its main text in Bemba into both Swahili and English, possibly in order to impress upon the listener the true weight of Samora Machel's death, which had and continues to have serious political repercussions throughout the region.[2] Politically, Shalawambe's strategy of employing lingua francas used throughout the region literally "gives voice" to those communities impacted by Machel's assassination.

The use of these mixed languages is also evident in the work of artists such as Paul Ngozi, who is credited with creating some of the most memorable Zambian songs. "Half Mwenye Half Muntu" (re-released 2003) is one of these songs and is feat-

---

[1] Transcription and translation by Maureen Mulenga.
[2] Samora Machel was the first Mozambican President and was allegedly assassinated by South Africans through a manufactured plane crash.

ured on the recently released *Greatest Hits* album. The song deals with sexual relations between Zambians of Indian origin and "indigenous Zambians." Most of the song is sung in Nyanja. There is a chorus sung in English by women singers, but there is no Hindi, Panjabi, or Gujarati anywhere in the song. Yet Ngozi claims at one point to be paraphrasing the words of such men, as shown in Extract 5:

Extract 5: Paul Ngozi, "Half Mwenye: Half Muntu"

Manja a mwenye	Now these Indians
Kuti akwatile	When told to marry
Akuti iyayi	They say no
Ise isiti kwatila banthu	We, we don't marry Africans
Chifukwa kwathu	Because where we come from
Chechi chikana	Our church doesn't allow us
Kuti iyayi osakwatila munthu	To marry Africans

In the first chorus, Ngozi appeals to the sentimental feelings of his listeners by assuming the voice of a half-Indian, half-African child (singing in Nyanja).

Ife tabana muti sausa	We the children are mistreated
Atate athu siti baziba	We don't even know our fathers
Kufunsa mai a waya waya	When we ask our mother she doesn't answer
Kusukulu batiseka	At school they laugh at us
Akuti patelo uyo shame-shame	Saying there is Patel, shame-shame

The above is an example of a song sung using linguistic mixtures. Words such as *chechi* (church), *Kusukulu* (at school), *waya waya* (way lay), and *shame* (shame) are not drawn from standard Nyanja.[3] One recent work that appears to quintessentially encapsulate many of the issues of language use touched

---

[3] Note the similarity with examples from Street Setswana in Cook (2009).

upon in this article is the title track from the album *Twende Twende* (*Let's Get a Move On,* 2006), recorded by the Kenyan artist Eric Wainaina in collaboration with the Zimbabwean recording artist Oliver Mutukudzi (mentioned elsewhere in this article). The title song moves faultlessly between Swahili, Shona, and English in its attempt to promote a pan-regional if not pan-African message of self-motivation and love.

Extract 6: Eric Wainaina [singing in Swahili] and Oliver Mutukudzi [singing in Shona], "Twende Twende"
VERSE 1
Eric: Kuja nami tuungane tuache kuzozana
(*Come with me let's join hands and stop being divided*)
Oliver: Ngatiende tiende mberi
(*Let's move moving forward*)
Eric: Wajua Upendo hauna mfano hauna adui kaka
(*Love has no equal or enemies*)
Oliver: Takabatana savatema
(*United as Blacks*)

Chorus
It's pole pole going slow
But still we're keeping time moving on
We're facing forward looking up
Forgetting what's behind
E: Twende Afrika heyo!
(*Let's go Africa heyo!*)

Extract 7: Oliver Mutukudzi [singing in Swahili] and Eric Wainaina [singing in Shona]
Oliver: Ukiumizwa hata mimi ninasikia uchungu
(*When you are wounded I feel your pain*)
'kiangaishwa ninalia ukilia dada
(*I cry when you cry*)

Eric: Chikakubada misodzi yangu inobuda
(I will cry when something happens to you)
Paunosuwa moyo wangu unorwadza
(When you are sad, my heart aches)

Chorus
I wish we had a fighting chance
To show you who we are
We'd stand up proud for Africa
Nkosi Sikelela

  Both singers sing various sections of the song in English. Interestingly enough, while it might be expected that a Kenyan singer such as Wainaina would limit himself to singing the sections in Swahili and English, leaving the Shona passages for a native speaker such as Mutukudzi, that is not the case, and the song contains numerous points at which we find Mutukudzi singing in Swahili and Wainaina in Shona. The singing in Shona by Wainaina and Swahili by Mutukudzi is a type of language "crossing" (Rampton, 1995) because the singers are appropriating forms of identity which, conventionally, do not belong to them.
  However, this form of crossing is an expansion of the term *crossing* as defined by Rampton(1995) in that *both* interlocutors appropriate each other's languages, unlike in Rampton's research in which only one interactant appropriates the other individual's language. This type of crossing can be referred to as "double crossing," which has significant implications for language in education. In plurilingual contexts, appropriating each other's language is the norm. In contrast, the use of a single standard language in a classroom setting is an aberration.
  Wainaina's entire album, in fact, speaks (or rather sings) profoundly to the issues of language hybridity and multiplicity (Njogu & Maupeu, 2007). While perhaps two of the songs on the album are exclusively in one language, the remaining songs

reveal a concentrated effort to incorporate a variety of languages spoken throughout Kenya and, as mentioned earlier, as far away as Zimbabwe. Wainaina's utilization of Luo and Panjabi in his songs is especially important, given the historical animosity between these groups and the Gikuyu, Wainaina's ethnic group. The incorporation of these languages into his songs, as he himself stated in a recent interview, is a political move intended to provide a space to interrogate and undermine such hostile relationships through sociocultural interaction.

In sum, the analysis of the language of the lyrics of popular music has demonstrated the following:

1. The use of indigenous African languages is predominant in the recording and performance of popular music in local and international markets. The corollary to this is that English, French, Portuguese, and so on, as international languages, play a very limited role in African popular music.
2. In the lyrics of popular music, the varieties of African languages used are often nonstandardized urban vernaculars.
3. Language practices in popular music reflect a language hierarchy wherein urban multilingual varieties come first, followed by standard African languages, with English, French, and so on, in third place.

Discussion

This article set out to analyze the language of the lyrics of popular music and to establish the role and status of African languages, English, and French in popular music from eastern and southern Africa. Furthermore, the article sought to establish the potential implications of the language of the lyrics in popular music for language, identity, and education in African contexts. Music as performance draws attention to communicative processes, which foreground speech as social action. The language of the lyrics of popular music is important insofar as it provides insight into the language practices of the music industry and the consumers of the music, which essentially is a reflection of the language practices of the subaltern.

Language use in African contexts is not a simple matter. Notwithstanding the multitude of African languages, colonial languages such as English, French, Dutch, and Portuguese were official languages as well as media of instruction in schools. After independence, the status of African languages changed to either official or national languages. In post-colonial Africa, English and French are "link languages" to the international world. Yet the language of the lyrics of popular music suggests that access to the international world is achievable through using indigenous African languages in either their standard form or using urban mixtures supported by the use of English in marketing.

In the previous section, we suggested that Chebli's songs are in Swahili and Shingazidja. The fact that Chebli's song titles, which circulate in international contexts, are not translated from their original Swahili in such titles as "Mwana" (Child), "Haki" (Truth), or "Mapinduzi" (Revolution) is a reflection of an increasing confidence in the social validity of Swahili as an "international" language. This suggests that Swahili has entered the same discursive space previously dominated by English and French. The issue is not whether Swahili is "factually" an international language or whether it can compete with English as an international language but that it is discursively imagined to be. To some extent, this suggests a dramatic revalorization of African languages possibly due to globalization and the proliferation of recording and broadcasting technology. The revalorization takes part largely based on the initiatives and choices made by the musicians themselves, perhaps as part of a complex realization of their individual identities.

In Western and North American contexts, the audiences may regard popular music sung in African languages and mixed varieties as more "African" than those sung in, for example, French or English. This critical observation raises a paradoxically polemical issue. In order for African musicians to penetrate Western markets, they need to sing in African languages and not in English. From such a perspective, English is the local language, and African languages are foreign. Put differently, African languages and urban vernaculars are local and "link languages."

This suggests that the same language may be "valued and evaluated" differently across contexts and, indeed, across historical space (Perullo & Fenn, 2003, p. 4); thus, the same language may have different associations (Dlamini, 2006). If the same language is valued and evaluated differently, then uniformity in policy produces divergent results, even within the same state or continent. This is crucial in light of numerous calls for national language policies for the African continent as shown, for instance, in the Language Plan of Action for Africa.[4]

Popular music constitutes a powerful site of socialization, perhaps more important than schools (Woolard, 1985). If language-in-education policy is to succeed in African contexts, it needs to follow ground-level language practices rather than running contrary to them, even if the practices subvert the notions of language and identity that underpin them.

Viewed from the perspective of popular music, the promotion of standard indigenous African languages in language education is not only a conduit through which African students are taught but also a powerful mechanism that alters the worldview of the students and contributes toward developing their folk metatheory of language and language practices (Kramsch, 2006). Notwithstanding the fact that most African students do not speak standard African languages, using standard African languages creates a conundrum for African students. Using indirect, obfuscated language in indigenous languages indicates depth or intellectual sophistication, whereas in a school setting, this shows confusion or lack of clarity in thinking.

---

[4] See http://www.bishrat.net/Documents/OAU-LPA-86htm.

Education requires a more direct relationship between form and meaning. In contrast to standard African languages, urban varieties use a very direct and explicit style that enables the songwriters to deal directly with what would be considered "taboo" or highly sensitive topics in standard languages (Mungai, 2008). Urban vernaculars are, therefore, more appropriate for use in education than the standard varieties. Perhaps it is for this reason that Calteaux (1996) states that standard African languages used in the classroom are "remote from the everyday life of the learners" (p. 14). If the primary purpose of language in education is to facilitate learning, utilizing urban vernaculars will support effective learning in schools and may consequently improve social lives (Busch & Schick, 2006).

The use of standard African languages is, not only teaching through a medium, but it is also teaching a very specific view of language (Harris, 2008), which might run counter to the students' experiences and perceptions of language. Students from plurilingual contexts may not be aware that they speak "different" languages, as the distinctions or boundaries between the languages may be insignificant. The idea of being taught in a medium called a "language" is a metalinguistic extrapolation that creates and imposes boundaries between the language of the students based on a particular language ideology. Standard African languages are a "languageteaching construct," an extrapolation reinforced by a school timetable in which they are languages called Shona, Zulu, and so forth.

Conclusion and reflections
The research reported in this article is consistent with interest in local perspectives on language planning, using a site that is rarely explored in language planning research: the wordy world of popular music. Analysis of the language of lyrics has shown that extensive use of African languages, especially urban vernaculars, runs counter to claims of the limited role that African languages play in domains such as education. Popular music as a site

of research provides evidence that policies that promote standard African languages have not been able to resolve and exploit the tensions between standardized African languages as "rigid, monolithic structures" (Haugen, 1972, p. 325), on the one hand, and flexibility, fluidity, and ambiguity, on the other.

The analysis of the language of lyrics in popular music suggests that ground-level language practices and language-in-education policies differ significantly. Language policies in education are founded on the notion of languages as discrete codes that belong to particular states and ethnicities with specific linguistic identities. Language practices in popular music are based on everyday language practices and their discursive perceptions and interpretations of lived linguistic realities. Musicians reflect, in part, how they appropriate and resist dominant-language ideologies associated with top down language policies.

The significance of research into music is that it provides empirical evidence of the descriptive inadequacy of language-in-education policy, which enhances "the putative home/school language divide" (Rampton, 1985, p. 188). However, utilization of such mixtures in curricular activities also raises potential problems. If the mixtures are not directed at a pre-given target, it means that proficiency in such contexts is always provisional. It depends, not so much on how close the individual is approximating an imagined target, but on how well individuals' language use meets their current requirements, the demands of the situation, and the ways in which they are able to exercise their agency.

An attempt to link popular music with language-in-education policy draws attention to the need to develop approaches to language planning firmly grounded in local perspectives. Clearly, popular music highlights the diversity of linguistic styles, while language-in-education policy is founded on assumed, predetermined groups sharing common linguistic features and focuses on a "linguistics of language." Popular music is oriented toward a radically different direction: emphasis on commonality. After all, use of urban vernaculars reflects that these varieties have "an international reach, a fluid capacity to cross borders" (Alim & Pennycook, 2007, p. 90). By using urban vernaculars in the classroom, one taps into both the local and global identities of the students.

References

Adejunmobi, M. (2004). *Vernacular Palaver: Imaginations Of The Local And Non-Native Languages in West Africa.* Clevedon, UK: Multilingual Matters.

Akindes, S. A. (2002). "Playing it "loud and straight": Reggae, Zouglou, Mapouka and youth insubordination in Côte d'Ivoire" In M. Palmberg & A. Kirkegaard (Eds.), *Playing With Identities in Contemporary Music in Africa* (pp. 86–103). Uppsala, Sweden: Nordiska Afrikainstitutet.

Alim, S. H., & Pennycook, A. (2007). "Glocal linguistic flows: Hip-hop culture(s), identities, and politics of language education" *Journal of Language, Identity, and Education,* 6, 89–100.

Amayenge Band. (2004). *Dailesi*. Zambia: Mondo Music.

Anderson, B. (1983). *Imagined Communities: Reflections On The Origin And Spread Of Nationalism.* London: Verso.

Auzanneau, M. (2002). "Rap in Libreville, Gabon: An urban sociolinguistics space" In A.-P. Durand (Ed.), *Black, Blanc, Beur: Rap Music And Hip Hop Culture In The Francophone World* (pp. 106–123). Lanham, MD: Scarecrow.

Billiez, J. (1998). *Alternance des langues: Enjeux socio culturels et identitaires.* Ellug: Argentina.

Blommaert, J. (1999). "Reconstructing the sociolinguistic image of Africa: Grassroots writing in Shaba (Congo)" *Text,* 19(2), 175–200.

Busch, B., & Schick, J. (2006). "Educational materials reflecting heteroglossia: Disinventing ethnolinguistic differences in

Bosnia-Herzegovina" In S. Makoni & A. Pennycook (Eds.), *Disinventing and Reconstituting Languages* (pp. 216–233). Clevedon: Multilingual Matters.

Calteaux, K. (1996). *Standard And Non-Standard African Language Varieties In The Urban Areas of South Africa: Preservation of the Standard Languages vs. Recognition of the Changing Nature of Language Use.* Pretoria: Human Sciences Research Council.

Chebli, M. (1999). *Swahili Songs.* Malvern, PA: Evasion Records.

Chihabi, A. (1997). *Folkomor Ocean.* France: Productions Sunset.

Cook, S. (2006). "Language policies and the erasure of multilingualism in South Africa" In M. L. Achino-Loeb (Ed.), *Silence: The Currency of Power* (pp. 52–69). New York: Berghahn.

Cook, S. (2009). "Street Setswana vs. school Setswana: Language policies and the forging of identities in South African classrooms" In J. A. Kleifgen & G. C. Bond (Eds.), *Languages of Africa and the Diaspora: Educating for Language Awareness* (pp. 96–118). Clevedon: Multilingual Matters.

Dlamini, S. N. (2006). *Youth and Identity Politics in South Africa, 1990–94.* Toronto: University of Toronto Press.

Edwards, J. (1994). *Multilingualism.* London: Routledge.

Glissant, E. (1997). *Poetics of Relation* (B. Wing, Trans.). Ann Arbor: University of Michigan Press.

Guilbault, J. (1993). "On redefining the local through world music" *The World of Music*, 35(2), 33–47.

Hachipola, S. J. (1998). *A Survey of the Minority Languages of Zimbabwe.* Harare: University of Zimbabwe Publishers.

Harris, R. (2008). "Implicit and explicit language teaching" In M. Toolan (Ed.), *Language Teaching: Integrational Linguistic Approaches* (pp. 24–46). London: Routledge.

Haugen, E. (1972). *The Ecology of Language.* Stanford:

Stanford University Press.

Herbert, R. K. (Ed.). (1992). *Language and Society in Africa. The Theory and Practice of Sociolinguistics*. Johannesburg, South Africa: Witwatersrand University Press.

Jeater, D. (2001). "Speaking like a native: Vernacular languages and the state in southern Rhodesia" *Journal of African History*, 42, 449–468.

Kramsch, C. (2006). "From communicative competence to symbolic competence" *The Modern Language Journal*, 90(2), 249–252.

Kwaramba, A. D. (1997). *Popular Music And Society. The Language Of Protest In Chimurenga Music In The Case of Thomas Mapfumo*. Report no. 24. Oslo, Norway: Department of Media and Communication, University of Oslo.

Leischa, C. (2005). Let's make Tsotsitaal the national language. *Red Star Coven*. Retrieved March 5, 2009, from http://redstarcoven.com/2005/01/31/lets-make-tsotsitaal-the-national-language/

Le Page, R. B., & Tabouret-Keller, A. (1985). *Acts of Identity*. Cambridge: Cambridge University Press.

Makoni, S., Brutt-Griffler, J., & Mashiri, P. (2007). "The use of "indigenous" and urban vernaculars in Zimbabwe" *Language in Society*, 36(1), 25–49.

Mbambi-Katana, S. (1977). "A song for every season: Music in African life from the cradle to the grave" *Courier*, 30(5), 26–32.

Meeuwis, M. (1999). "Flemish nationalism in Belgian Congo versus Zairian anti-imperialism: Continuity and discontinuity in language ideological debates" In J. Blommaert (Ed.), *Language Ideological Debates* (pp. 381–423). Berlin, Germany: Mouton de Gruyter.

Mitchell, T. (2000). "Doin' damage in my native language: The use of "resistance vernaculars" in hip hop in France,

Italy, and Aotearoa/New Zealand" *Popular Music and Society*, 24(3), 41–54.

Mphande, L. (2007). "If you're ugly, know how to sing: Aesthetics of resistance and subversion" In K. Njogu & H. Maupeu (Eds.), *Songs and Politics in Eastern Africa* (pp. 377–401). Dar es Salaam, Tanzania: Mkuki na Nyota.

Mungai, M. (2008). "Swahili advertising in Nairobi: Innovation and language shift" *Journal of African Cultural Studies*, 20(1), 3–14.

Nannyonga-Tamusuza, S. (2002). "Gender, ethnicity and politics in Kadongo-Kamu music of Uganda: Analysing the song Kayanda" In M. Palmberg & A. Kierkegaard (Eds.), *Playing with Identities in Contemporary Music in Africa* (pp. 134–148). Uppsala, Sweden: Nordiska Afrikainstitutet.

Ndhlovu, F. (2006). "Gramsci, Doke and the marginalisation of the Ndebele language in Zimbabwe" *Journal of Multilingual and Multicultural Development*, 27(4), 305–318.

Negus, K. (1997). *Popular Music in Theory: An Introduction*. Hanover, NH: Wesleyan University Press.

Nero, S. (2006). "Language, identity and education of Caribbean English speakers" *World Englishes*, 25(3/4), 501–511.

Njogu, K., & Maupeu, H. (Eds.). (2007). "Foreword" In K. Njogu & H. Maupeu (Eds.), *Songs and Politics in Eastern Africa* (pp. xi–xvii). Dar es Salaam, Tanzania: Mkuki na Nyota.

Nyoni, F. P. (2007). "Music and politics in Tanzania: A case study of Nyota-wa-Cigogo" In K. Njogu & H. Maupeu (Eds.), *Songs and Politics in Eastern Africa* (pp. 241–272). Dar es Salaam, Tanzania: Mkuki na Nyota.

Palmberg, M. (2002). "Expressing Cape Verde, Mourna, Funana and national identity" In M. Palmberg & A. Kierkegaard (Eds.), *Playing With Identities in Contemporary Music in Africa* (pp. 117–134). Uppsala, Sweden: Nordiska Afrikainstitutet.

Palmberg, M., & Kierkegaard, A. (Eds.). (2002). *Playing With Identities in Contemporary Music in Africa*. Uppsala, Sweden: Nordiska Afrikainstitutet.

Perullo, A., & Fenn, J. (2003). "Language ideologies, choices, and practices in eastern African hip hop" In H. Berger & M. T. Carroll (Eds.), *Global Popular Music: The Politics and Aesthetics of Language Choice* (pp. 19–51). Oxford: University Press of Mississippi.

Prah, K. K. (2002, April 22–24). *Going Native: Language Of Instruction For Education, Development And African Emancipation*. Keynote address to the Launch of Language of Instruction in Tanzania and South Africa (LOITASA), Morogoro, Tanzania.

Rampton, B. (1985). "A critique of some educational attitudes to the English of British Asian school children, and their implications" In C. Brumfit, R. Ellis, & J. Levin (Eds.), *English as a Second Language in the United Kingdom: Linguistic and Educational Contexts* (pp. 187–198). Oxford: Pergamon.

Rampton, B. (1995). *Crossing Language and Ethnicity Among Adolescents*. London: Longman.

Rasolofondraosolo, Z., & Meinhof, U. (2003) "Popular Malagasy music and the construction of identities" *AILA Review* 16:127–148.

Ruiz, R. (1984). "Orientations in language planning" *NABE Journal*, 8(2), 15–34.

Scannell, P. (2001). "Music, radio and the record business in Zimbabwe today" *Popular Music*, 20(1), 1–28.

Shalawambe. (1989). *Samora Machel*. Johannesburg, South Africa: Teal Record Company.

Sibanda, S. (2004). "'You don't get to sing when you have

nothing to say': Oliver Mutudzi music as a vehicle for social-political commentary" *Social Dynamics*, 30(2), 36–63.

Tagg, P. (2005). "Can we get rid of the 'popular' in popular music? A virtual symposium with contributions from the International Advisory Editors of *Popular Music*" *Popular Music,* 24(1), 133–145.

Wainaina, E. (2006). *Twende Twende!* Nairobi, Kenya: Christian Kaufman.

Wa Mutonya, M. (2007). "Ethnic identity and stereotypes in popular music: Mugiithi performance in Kenya" In K. Njogu & H. Maupeu (Eds.), *Songs and Politics in Eastern Africa* (pp. 157–175). Dar es Salaam, Tanzania: Mkuki na Nyota.

Weber, W. (1975). *Music and the Middle Class: The Social Structure Of Concert Life in London, Paris and Vienna*. London: Holmes & Meier.

Woolard, K. A. (1985). "Language variation and cultural hegemony. Toward an integration of society and social theory" *American Ethnologist*, 12, 738–749.

Zawose, H. (1989). *Mateso*. United Kingdom: Triple Earth Records.

XVI

Multilingual discourses on wheels and public English in Africa: a case for 'vague linguistique'
(with Busi Makoni)

Introduction

This chapter briefly reviews some dominant research traditions in the use of English in Africa, questioning some of their assumptions about languages, and then focuses on a new emerging analytical framework based on the concept of *'vague linguistique'* (Thomas 2007). *'Vague linguistique'* differs from traditional structuralist approaches to language research in Africa, which tend to focus on the linguistic system, even if the researcher acknowledges the social context of their data. In contrast, *'vague linguistique'* is a plurilanguaging approach whose goal is to capture the dynamic and evolving relationships between English, other indigenous African languages and multiple open semiotic systems, from the point of view of the language users themselves; i.e. an insider or emic perspective. We apply this approach to a discussion of multimodal data from taxi culture in Ghana in the mid-twentieth century and South Africa in the early twenty-first century.

The chapter is divided into:

- a brief review of research traditions in the use of English in Africa;
- an outline of the '*vague linguistique*' approach;
- an analysis of taxi-lingua cultures in mid-twentieth-century Accra and early twenty-first-century Johannesburg.

Researching the use of 'English' in Africa
In Africa, there are at least four main research traditions into the use of English and the role of African languages therein. The first tradition addresses the official status of English vis-à-vis that of African languages, as the media of instruction in post-colonial Africa. This approach focuses on the historical and contemporary status and functions of English and so-called indigenous African languages. English is the official language widely used for administrative and educational purposes whereas the use of African languages for educational purposes is often limited to the first four years of schooling. Thus African children initially experience mother-tongue education before switching to English. During this period, exposure to English is very limited as it is only experienced by the children as one subject among many, before it is introduced as a language of instruction from the fifth grade onwards. The switch to English is often abrupt and this

> inadequate linguistic preparation of the pupils in the [English] language prior to its use as the medium of learning and the pupil's lack of exposure to the [English language] outside the classroom generally result in high failure rates and dropouts. (Kamwangamalu 2000)

An extended use of mother-tongue education has also been seen as contentious. Some educational linguists have argued that the use of indigenous African languages has advantages whereas others argue that research in support of mother-tongue education is inconclusive as there are no lifespan studies that show the longevity and sustainability of the gains. In fact, 'for every research report that indicates that mother tongue education is effective there is another one that indicates that it is not' (Fasold 1984: 312). A subtext to this argument is a body of research which is critical of the validity of the construct of mother tongue itself. Irrespective of the efficacy of mother-tongue education, there are suggestions that promoting it results in the separation of ethnic groups within the educational system, thus accentuating the ethnic divisions that are largely an artefact of colonialism.

This yin and yang argument, so to speak, has led to the suggestion that English should be the sole language used in education and that other languages should be limited in their functions. But the increasingly dominant use of English as an official language of business and education in some parts of Africa has led to an assumption that English poses a threat to the survival of indigenous African languages. Although English is an official language in some African countries, we would argue that it does not necessarily constitute a threat to the viability of African languages, whose position may be more seriously challenged by the Urban African Vernaculars which dominate popular culture and circulate widely.

The second research tradition involves identifying and mapping the number of languages in Africa and their geographical distribution. The underlying assumption is the countability (or numerability) of languages and speakers of each language. The countability of language as autonomous 'things' is a prerequisite for the management of states and 'countability' is an important philosophical trope for this research strand (Joseph 2006). However, radical social constructionists have begun to challenge the assumptions which form the basis for the countability of languages and the rationale in the differentiation of language from other semiotic systems (Reagan 2005; Yngve 2004). They argue that languages are historically contingent and political from the top down (Joseph 2006). Their view that languages are created on-line, in the context of multimodal social practice, challenges the notion that languages are 'natural'. If languages cannot be readily separated from social context and other semiotic systems, they cannot be easily counted and counting them, although useful for 'governmentality' (Foucault 1991), is not otherwise very meaningful.

Radical social constructionism also questions the nineteenth-century notions in which languages are tied to specific geographical localities and speaker national identities (Mignolo 1996: 182) such as 'I live in France and speak French, therefore I am French'. The combined effects of migration in the nineteenth century from Europe to Africa and from Africa and Asia to Europe in the twentieth and twenty-first centuries have led to a 'disarticulation' in relations between language and territory (Shohamy 2006). This 'disarticulation' of language from geographical location has substantial epistemological consequences and researchers are beginning to develop conceptual frameworks which can accommodate subaltern knowledge practices and views about language (Mignolo 1996).

The third strand of research on English in Africa stresses how English is indigenized and localized in diverse African contexts, to produce 'New Englishes'. One of the main findings from research on New Englishes (or World Englishes, i.e. non-Anglo Englishes) is a cataloguing of linguistic features which are typical of each country (thus linking with the 'counting languages' approach above). Ghanaians speak Ghanaian English because they are Ghanaians and Zimbabweans speak Zimbabwean English because they are Zimbabweans. The nation state is one of the key units of analysis in spite of the fact that the validity of the construct '*state*' in contemporary African political philosophy is open to debate. Krishnaswamy and Burde (1998) state that this research tradition takes 'a nationalistic point of view' (1998: 30) to the extent that nations and their varieties of English are brought into being. Yet not only is there considerable diversity within states but also similarities between them, particularly along borders. Thus '[by] focusing centrally on the development of new national Englishes, the world Englishes approach reproduces the very linguistics it needs to escape from' (Pennycook 2007: 21).

The fourth and last research tradition is founded on notions of linguistic hybridity apparent from the characteristics of urban vernaculars in contemporary Africa. The examples used to support the so-called hybrid forms are words such as *smallinyana* (very tiny) which is a result of the English word 'small' inflected with the Nguni diminutive suffix-*nyana* (/small/tiny). *Smallinyana* is found in some varieties of language used in Southern Africa. Whilst this particular tradition is interesting as it touches on issues of creolization and languages in contact, it is also predicated on, and privileges, the notion of languages as discrete entities wherein one can determine where one language begins and the other ends.

In a bid to move away from the terminological trappings inherent in the use of the term 'hybridity', some researchers view this mélange of urban varieties (Githiora 2002) as 'vague linguistique', *courants/influences linguistiques* or '*linguistic current*'. It appears that '[t]erms such as *vagues* or flux waves [and] courants ... might be more appropriate and partially overcome the problems inherent in the notion of hybridity' (Thomas 2007: 3). In the '*courants*' research strand, varieties shown in the use of such lexical items as *smallinyana* or *huchest* (sweetest; drawn from *huchi* which means honey in Shona and -est which is the English superlative degree suffix) are viewed not from a formalist approach to hybridity which identifies segments from different languages, but as examples of linguistic fluidity that arise from exposure to multiple linguistic sources. The notion of *vague linguistique* focuses on the ongoing social process which involves a mobilization of diverse linguistic resources (plurilanguaging) in semantically open ways. It captures the unpredictability of the source of the *courants* situated in everyday life and the speaker's 'agency', both of which are overlooked in linguistic theories in which languages seem to operate independently of their speakers (Joseph 2006).

A *vague linguistique* approach accepts that speakers may have 'bits and pieces' of languages and partial semiotics, and uneven proficiencies in these languages. In the context of this approach it becomes difficult to sustain notions about the validity of English as a 'killer' language, because English, just like any other language, provides a linguistic resource amongst the other multiple resources (i.e. indigenous African languages) available to the speaker. *Vague linguistique* also challenges a dictionary perspective in which the relationships between form and meaning are fixed and predetermined in advance and not open-ended design systems. In an open-ended system, meanings are not wholly inherent in specific forms but their resonances vary depending on the speaker's agency. Recognition of open-ended meanings and of the disarticulation between the speaking self and geographical location (Mignolo 1996) challenge conceptualizations founded on an assumption of the existence of an autonomous, agentive, truth-telling self (Robbins 2000).

Taxi culture in Accra and Johannesburg

In this section we extend *vague linguistique* research by focusing on the combination of 'plurilanguaging' and multimodality within the lingua culture of taxis or what Wa Mungai in Kenya calls *'matatu culture'*. Wa Mungai (2007: 28) defines *matatu culture* as

> a combined range of activities and symbolic acts, verbal or written, either deployed upon the vehicle or embodied by *matatu* workers and passengers, in interactions with each other upon and in reference to the site of the material culture object known as *matatu* taxi culture.

Wa Mungai's study of matatu culture differs from our own study in that, whilst he focuses on popular media and the analysis of 'matatu discourse as a narrative of identity-making' (Ogude and Nyairo 2007), our focus is on language use and multimodality.

The empirical data presented in this chapter comes from the culture of *trotros* (lorry-taxis named after three-pence of Ghanaian currency) in 1950s and 1960s Accra and minibus taxis in Johannesburg in South Africa in the early twenty-first century. One of the defining features of public transport in African urban centres is taxi culture. Because taxis are the main modes of public transport in Ghana and South Africa, a relatively large number of Africans experience language used in the inscriptions on and inside taxis. They also encounter the interrelated semiotic systems of music and paintings on, in and through inscriptions and this complex semiotic environment shapes their language ideologies. The ways in which English is embedded in the taxi-lingua culture merits serious consideration because unmetered taxis are used extensively in African cities, and form an important part of people's everyday experience of English.

The Ghanaian data discussed below were gathered from inscriptions written on the wooden sides, front and back of the tro-tros or '*mammy lorries*' which first appeared in Ghana in 1948 (Kyei and Schreckenbach 1976). In the early 1950s and late 1960s Kyei and Schreckenbach[1] collected photographs of *mammy lorries* on Ghanaian roads and in the lorry dumping compounds referred to as *mammy grave yards*. They also carried out a series of interviews with the drivers on their motivations for using particular inscriptions, and for their choices of colour and font size. We have reanalyzed the photographs and interviews, focusing on the semantically open-ended nature of the *mammy lorry* inscriptions. The South African data were collected by ourselves and associates in Johannesburg in 2007, from a variety of African townships. Although the inscriptions on the

---

[1] The data were collected as part of a photographic exhibition showing different constructions of self and social reality with the aim of establishing the role of culture and self in the construction of interdependence.

Ghanian *mammy lorries* do not exhibit the vast array of popular visual images which we found on South African taxis in 2007, some of the paintings from both the 1950s Ghana *tro-tros* and the South African minibus taxis reflect the 'profusion of grotesque detached human and non-human bodies – wide eyed monstrosities with flaring nostrils and cavernous mouths drawn on these vehicles' which Wa Mungai (2007: 26) documents in contemporary Kenya. Some of these monstrosities appear to be human skeletons immersed in fire (see Figure 17.2).

Inscriptions and discourses from Ghanaian *tro-tros*

The inscriptions on the 1950s *tro-tro*s were written mainly in standard English and forms of pidgin English used in and around Accra. They provide a social commentary on current affairs, reflecting engagement with prevailing political events, domestic issues and interpersonal relations with family members or neighbours. This social commentary, however, is often indeterminate: for example, in the inscription '*Blackman dei ibi trouble*' (A blackman is in trouble again) (Kyei and Schreckenbach 1976: 71) it is not clear whether the writer is admonishing the man, or praising his insurrection or commenting on a political state of affairs. In the category of inscriptions focusing on political issues, one *tro-tro* driver displayed the inscription *Congo* on his *tro-tro*, at a time when there was serious political upheaval in the newly independent Congo as a result of the assassination of the president Moise Tschombe in a military coup. The driver uses his inscription to point to a complex and intractable political reality, bringing it into the public domain. It is possible that the word *Congo* may have been used metaphorically, to capture the problematic nature of his taxi symbolically, drawing a mocking parallel with the disruption associated with the Congo. However, it is also possible that the use of the word *Congo* was unrelated to the political events taking place in the Congo and that the *tro-tro* river used the word because he had heard it on radio or seen it through the print media. The meaning of the words is therefore indeterminate and open to a number of different possible interpretations.

In some cases the political commentary was, according to the drivers interviewed in the 1950s, unambiguously celebratory. For example, the industriousness of the Americans was reflected in the popular inscriptions of 'USA' or its variant 'the US' which the *tro-tro* drivers described as an acronym for *Uncle Sam*. The 1950s *mammy lorry* drivers also claimed that *Uncle Sam* was the name of rice that was imported from the USA. (In fact, the name of the rice that was imported from the USA was *Uncle Ben's*.)

Another category of inscriptions relates to domestic issues: happy moments, or tension and conflict within the family. For example, an inscription such as *'home hard Grow lanka lanka'* referred to hardships in the domestic space. When asked to provide a context and meaning for his use of this particular inscription, the *tro-tro* driver explained:

> *This struggle I struggle I go on empty stomach sometimes at times my wife and children and we* **chop** *(eat) only kenkey and shito and tatare for a week, like that then we grow* **lanka lanka** *(thin) like bamboo stick chief home hard.* (Kyei and Schreckenbach 1976: 6)

This inscription reflects the linguistic expertise of the *tro-tro* drivers who stretch the meaning of words to express individual opinions. For example, *'lanka lanka'* is drawn from the English word *'lanky'* and yet the grammatical from of *'lanka lanka'* is a duplicative verb form for emphasis and it comes from Twi; one of the African languages of Ghana. It appears that *'home hard'* could either be a basilect feature of linguistic resources which, from a strictly linguistic perspective, might be described as Ghaaian English in which there is no copula (see, however, our earlier critique of categories such as Ghanaian English and

Nigerian English – our use of such categories reflects the problems of escaping the structuralist paradigm).

Part of the social commentary relates to interpersonal relations with other members of the community at large and the personal histories of individuals and their families are sometimes translated into taxi inscriptions. In fact, *mammy lorry* drivers not only transport people but also ideas and moral lessons. Hence, there are inscriptions that admonish others or talk back at society and share wisdom with the general populace, as in the following examples.

1. *Mind your own. In 99 out of 100 cases you find that you let sleeping dogs lie if you mind your own* (i.e. mind your own business);
2. *Stop poking your nyama nyama nose into other people's business* ('nyama nyama' means chunky, meaty);
3. *You pack your books and head for booze sessions instead of school sessions you pose a professor while actually a flop-ester* ('flop-ester' means a failure, a noun derived from the English verb to flop).

While inscriptions use fragments of English idiomatic expressions, most are written in a combination of English and African languages. For example, '*nyama nyama*' (nominal duplication for emphasis drawn from the local African languages) nose refers to a chunky nose. It seems that English is used as another local language, without any suggestion that it has a superior status. For example, in 1 above '*Mind your own*' would be incomplete as an idiomatic expression in standard English and yet, in this local version, it is an acceptable 'English expression' and used to humorous effect.

Inscriptions on the *tro-tros* also included the portrayal of foreign characters or situations, for example the inscriptions '*Big Boy*' and '*De Great*' seem to invoke the voice of the Black American boxer Muhammad Ali. The driver explained:

> I suppose you know me now de great it's not within accepted norms of modesty, but if you are the greatest, you are the greatest, you are the greatest, and you don't need actually need to wait for others to blow it for you.
> (Kyei and Schreckenbach 1976: 71)

The driver reproduces a version of what appear to be Muhammad Ali's phrases to acknowledge that he is bragging but justifies this by stating that if he does not indulge in self-praise, then it is highly unlikely that other people will blow his trumpet about his achievements. The inscription on his *tro-tro* could be either a parody or a straight reproduction of Muhammad Ali's familiar boasts.

In summary, the inscriptions by *mammy lorry* drivers are interesting examples of language use in the public space. They provide a social commentary on personal experience, political conflicts and national current issues and reflect a certain level of creativity in the use of linguistic resources drawn from a number of different languages, including English. The drivers make choices between languages and opt for a localized version of English or any one of the urban varieties that they are exposed to. In *'vague linguistique'* inscriptions are closely tied to the experiences which shape them and which they, in turn, shape. Inscriptions are situated in specific contexts and they drag with them the contexts of their creation as well. The various possible meanings of inscriptions like *'Congo'* or *'De Great'*, the indeterminate reference of 'I' and 'you' and the combination of features from different languages indicate the open-ended and flexible nature of the cultural resources, which are not necessarily constrained by the norms of any one particular language. There is thus an unusual degree of ambivalence in the evaluative meanings and taxi drivers exercise considerable agency in manipulating the expressions in ways which suit them; depending on the 'voice' which they seek to project (Blommaert 2006).

The South African taxi inscriptions: multilingualism on wheels

The inscriptions on South African taxis reflect modern-day South African polyglossia. They are written in what, from a western-educated linguist's perspective, is a variety of different standard/official languages and non-standard 'languages'. When we say that the inscriptions are in English or localized varieties of English, we are therefore using an etic (outside) perspective, which is substantially different from the emic experience which forms the focus of a '*vague linguistique*' approach. The South African taxi inscriptions are embedded within a multitude of semiotic systems and some of the social commentary challenges both socially and linguistically prescribed norms.

The meaning or message in these inscriptions is also obfuscated and this is one of the critical features of taxi-lingua culture which makes it amenable to '*vague linguistique*' as a theoretical framework. It is not always clear who the inscriptions are directed to and what the referent is. For example, in Figure 17.1

Figure 17.1 'The Outsider' inscription

it is unclear who '*The outsider*' is or who is the 'me' in '*It's me against the world*'. However, the driver does provoke social commentary with his inscription '*Legalise marijuana*' found on the front of the taxi which enacts 'ideological insubordination' (Porter 1995: 101). This insubordination is also evident in the taxi drivers' well-known flagrant disregard of road regulations and in their use of unbridled obscenities in public. Their defiance is further expressed through a preference for Kwaito music, which emerged after the first democratic elections in 1994 and is usually construed as a South African version of American hip-hop. Kwaito is an aesthetic forum that taunts and defies social norms just like American hip-hop[2] and the language of the lyrics in Kwaito music is equally raw and colourful. In some instances the words are drawn from African-American Vernacular (AAV), suggesting that Kwaito musicians are avid devotees of American hip-hop. What is worth noting, is that both American hip-hop and Kwaito deal with ghetto life and brazenly challenge social norms. Thus, taxilingua culture is 'a space from which a subaltern category dabbling at subversion talks back at larger society' (Wa Mungai 2007: 30).

In fact, the expression '*It's me against the world*' is a song title of 2pac's[3] rap album whilst '*The outsider*' may be an album by American rap artist DJ Shadow, a film or a novel by the same name. Irrespective of what the source of the inscription is, it suggests an attempt at appropriating and glamorizing foreign material culture, possibly taking a celebratory stance like the USA inscription in the Ghanaian data. However, it is also

---

[2] The similarity between Kwaito and American hip-hop is that both types of music are 'an expression and a validation of a modern, urban way of life, sung in street slang'
(www.tsotsi.com/english/index.php?m1=pressandm2=Kwaito, accessed 19 April 2008). The South African street slang used in Kwaito is a mixture of South African languages.

[3] 2pac was a stage name for the American rap artist Tupac Amaru Shakur who gained recognition and endured a backlash for his controversial lyrics. He was killed in a drive-by shooting in 1996.

possible that the use of music such as hiphop has a linguistic impact on the inscriptions by the taxi drivers. Taxi drivers are able to 'pick' particular expressions from AAV which become part of their speech repertoire. One way in which language contact takes place between AAV and African languages is through hip-hop, which taps into the drivers' experiences of hardship in the townships and of growing up surrounded by violent conflict. The drivers thus, arguably, use music as an additional semiotic resource within taxi culture, alongside and related to their use of words and images.

The inscriptions written on the outside of the taxi in Figure 17.1 are in many colours and the words vary in terms of font size and type, reflecting the playful carnivalesque nature of taxi-lingua culture. The general trend, however, is to use very bright colors on the outside body of the vehicle as if to attract the attention of those who can read, while the more subversive inscriptions are written in places that will not immediately attract attention. For instance, in Figure 17.1, the inscription calling for legalizing marijuana is not emblazoned in bright red, orange or in as big a font as the inscription 'The Outsider', but more discretely placed below the front number plate of the vehicle.

The inscriptions on the outside of the taxi seem to be a commentary on the drivers themselves and an expression of their own views about their surroundings. For example, in the inscription from Figure 17.2 below the driver declares that he is *'Bad 2 Tha Bone'* and uses the saying *'IF YOU GOOD, YOU GOOD. BUT IF YOU BAD YOU BETTER'*. The meaning of *'bad'* in this inscription may be from AAV, in which case *'bad'* means 'good'. Because taxi drivers in South Africa are perceived as rude, uncouth and thuggish in their behaviour, it is therefore possible that when the taxi driver declares that he is *'Bad 2 Tha Bone'*, he is, with tongue in cheek, reiterating this public perception or underscoring his insurection by playing on the AAV meaning of *'bad'*. In emphasizing this message of how

Figure 17.2 'Bad 2 tha Bone'.

Figure 17.3 'If you good. . . .' inscription.

'*bad*' the driver is, there are also dark objects drawn on the body of the vehicle, for example a human skull or a dark demon vampire fleeing the fires of hell. Thus, the words on taxis are presented in combination with images which may reinforce or underscore the main message of the inscriptions.

In contrast to the inscriptions on the outside of the South African taxis, the discourses that emerge from the inscriptions inside the taxis (which are usually in a smaller font and handwritten) revolve around relationships between the drivers and the general public, or reflect drivers' attitudes to women. Some of these inscriptions read like instruction manuals, with instructions to the passengers expressed in a mixture of languages as if to suggest that they are engaged in a fictional dialogue with the driver:

1 *If you are late don't rush me, cos I'm on time.*
2 *Don't say dankie driver, say shot right or shot lef*
  (Don't say thank you driver, say turn right or turn left).
3 *Ungathi kealebokga driver, mina ngithi, kebatla tshelete yaka*
  (If you say thank you driver, me I will say I want my money).
4 *Don't say keatheokga driver, say shot lef, or shot right*
  (Don't say I am disembarking here driver, say turn left or turn right).

In these examples, the driver dialogically weaves together different South African languages. In example 3, he begins his instruction in Zulu then uses Tswana (*kealebokga* for thank you) to repeat what the imaginary passenger should not say, and then goes further to illustrate how he would respond to the passenger in Tswana. This 'template' for his instructional manual is also evident in examples 2 and 4 below. In example 2, the taxi driver uses English first and then Afrikaans in order to imitate the imaginary passenger. However, this time he goes further and instructs the 'passenger' in what has become popularly known as *'taxi lingua'* by saying *'shot lef*[4] *or shot right'* (i.e. take the road that turns to the left or the road that turns to the right).

The taxi industry in South Africa is predominantly male-dominated, rough and macho and this is evident in the sexually suggestive taunts directed at women in some inscriptions:

i. *Wamuhle G-string kodwa uyasidunusela* (Oh, what a nice g-string but you are showing me your bottom).
ii. *A beautiful woman is a multiplication of problems, an addition of enemies and subtraction of money.*
iii. *How is your wife and my children.*
iv. *Nice g-string but angiyifuni iZ3.* (You have a nice g-string but I do not want to catch the HI virus).

These sexual fantasy discourses are reinforced by the loud Kwaito music played in the taxis, whose lyrics are replete with obscenities and the portrayal of women as sexual objects. Thus, music provides a framework within which the male taxi drivers' language, their harassment of women drivers and their 'eve teasing' (Khosa 1997), can be interpreted (Hansen 2006). Inscriptions are also read in the context of transgressive taxi-lingua culture: drivers mock the police, both on the road through their reckless driving and in the paintings on their windows which reinforce their defiance, for example in drawings of traffic police watching taxi drivers violate traffic regulations. The anti-establishment positions adopted by the taxi drivers are also apparent in their non-conventional spelling of English words, which challenges the standard language ideology (Milroy and Milroy 1999), in examples such as *Symp-athy* and *2nd 2 none*. Interestingly, while the written inscriptions draw on English, the use of spoken English by passengers in the taxis is strongly opposed and construed as putting on white mannerisms or claiming superior social class. Such passengers are described in a disparaging manner as 'biting [their] tongue' (Dlamini 2005:

---

[4] In township parlance, 'lef' is equivalent to the English word 'left'.

127). The fact that written nonstandard English is more acceptable than spoken English in this context suggests that discourse practices legitimated in one semiotic system are not necessarily admissible in another.

Concluding reflections
The inscriptions from Ghana were written in the middle of the last century and indicate the degree and extent to which English/pidgin had, by that time, permeated public life. They provide evidence of the drivers' engagement in social affairs, often with ambivalent evaluative meanings, and contribute to a taxilingua culture which is continued half a century later in South Africa. There are also differences, such as the more oppositional quality of the South African taxi inscriptions, and the more intensely interrelated use in the contemporary data of words, font and colour, images, music and driving behaviours.

The inscriptions on the *tro-tro*s and South African minibus taxis show creativity in the construction of multimodal discourses which can involve the appropriation and subversion of publicly available expressions as in *'driver is instructed to run away from the police'*, or the culling of materials from different media sources, with expressions migrating from one medium to another. In contrast to research approaches referred to at the beginning of the chapter, a *vague linguistique* approach acknowledges the plurilanguaging, semantically open nature of the taxi inscriptions. We have extended this approach by focusing on the multi-semiotic nature of the inscriptions which have to be read against and at times in combination with other semiotic systems. These systems mutually reinforce one another, for instance in macho sexist discourses, and cannot be treated as discrete within the analysis. A multimodal analysis of the taxilingua culture enables us to move away from a structuralist orientation in the analysis of language practices in Africa, and is consistent with the more postcolonial and postmodern approach of *vague linguistique*.

References

Blommaert, J. (2006) *Discourse: A Critical Introduction*, Cambridge: Cambridge University Press.

Dlamini, S. (2005) *Youth and Identity Politics in South Africa*, Toronto: University of Toronto Press.

Fasold, R. (1984) *The Sociolinguistics of Society*, Oxford: Basil Blackwell Ltd.

Foucault, M. ([1978] 1991) 'Governmentality', trans. R. Braidotti, in *The Foucault Effect: Studies in Governmentality*, G. Burchell, C. Gordon and P. Miller (eds) London: Harvester Wheatsheaf, 87–104.

Githiora, C. (2002) 'Sheng peer language Swahili dialect or emerging Creole', *Journal of African Cultural Studies*, 15(2): 159–81.

Hansen, T.B. (2006) 'Sounds of freedom: Music, taxis, and racial imagination', *Public Culture*, 18: 1185–208.

Joseph, J.E. (2006) *Language and Politics*, Edinburgh: Edinburgh University Press.

Kamwangamalu, N.M. (2000) *Language Policy and Mother-tongue Education in South Africa: The Case for a Market-oriented Approach*, Georgetown University roundtable, accessed 12 April 2008 at: http://digital.georgetown.edu/gurt/2000

Khosa, M.K. (1997) 'Sisters on slippery wheels: gender relations in the taxi industry in South Africa', *Transformation*, No. 33: 18–33.

Krishnaswamy, N. and Burde, A. (1998) *The Politics of Indians' English: Linguistic Colonialism and the Expanding English Empire*, Delhi: Oxford University Press.

Kyei, G. and Schreckenbach, H. (1976) *No Time to Die*, Accra, Ghana: Catholic Press.

Mignolo, D. (1996) 'Linguistic maps, literary geographies, and cultural landscapes: languages, languaging and (trans)nationalism', *Modern Language Quarterly*, 57(2): 181–97.

Milroy, J. and Milroy, L. (1999) *Authority in Language: Investigating Standard English*, third edition, London: Routledge.

Ogude, J. and Nyairo, J. (eds) (2007) *Urban Legends, Colonial Myths Popular Culture and Literature*, Trenton: Africa World Press.

Pennycook, A. (2007) *Global Englishes and Transcultural Flows*, London: Routledge.

Porter, R.A. (1995) *Spectacular Vernaculars: Hip Hop and the Politics of Post-modernism*, Albany: State University of New York.

Reagan, T. (2005) *Critical Questions, Critical Perspectives: Language and the Second Language Educator*, Greenwich, CT: Information Age Publishing Inc.

Robbins, J. (2000) 'God is nothing but talk: modernity, language, and prayer in a Papua New Guinea society', *American Anthropologist*, 103(4): 901–12.

Shohamy, E. (2006) 'Reinterpreting Globalization in Multilingual Contexts', *International Multilingual Research Journal*, 1(2): 127–33.

Thomas, D. (2007) *Black France: Colonialism, Immigration and Transnationalism*, Indiana University Press.

Wa Mungai, M (2007) 'Kaa Masaa, Grapple with spiders: the myriad threads of Nairobi matatu discourse', in J. Ogude and J. Nyairo (eds) *Urban Legends, Colonial Myths Popular Culture and Literature*, Trenton: Africa World Press, 25–58.

Yngve, V.H. (2004) 'Issues in Hard Science Linguistics', in V.H. Yngve and Z. Wasik (eds) *Hard-Science Linguistics*, New York: Continuum. 14–27.

www.ingramcontent.com/pod-product-compliance
Lightning Source LLC
Chambersburg PA
CBHW071217080526
44587CB00013BA/1404